MW00616540

Demystifying the Vision Experience of Louis Farrakhan

Revised from "Who Do You Say I Am?
The Betrayal & Crucifixion of Louis Farrakhan"

Demystifying the Vision Experience of Louis Farrakhan

Revised from "Who Do You Say I Am?
The Betrayal & Crucifixion of
Louis Farrakhan"

Michael T. Muhammad

Michael T. Muhammad
PO Box 666 Levittown,
PA 19058

Revised from Who Do You Say I Am: The Betrayal and Crucifixion of Louis Farrakhan
Copyright © 2010, 2014, 2018 by Michael T. Muhammad
3rd Revised Edition

All rights reserved. No part of this book may be reproduced or transmitted in any form or by any means without written permission from the publisher except in the case of brief quotations, reviews and articles.

Table of Contents

PART ONE 9

Prophecy, Revelation, and the Reality of the Mother Plane......9

Introduction.. 11

1   Prophecy and Revelation..15

   1.1   Why Prophecy and Revelation?................... 15

   1.2   What Elijah Muhammad Teaches 17

   1.3   A Contemporary View................................. 22

2   Rules of Interpretation................................. 34

   2.1   Typology 35

   2.2   Laws and Rules of Interpretation 45

3   The Mother Plane, Prophets, and Visions from God....53

   3.1   Visions from God, the Wheel, and Its Power 53

   3.2   The Wheel and the Prophecies of the Bible............. 57

4   Close Encounters of Antiquity................................73

   4.1   Communication, Technology and History of Wheels 73

   4.2   Beneath our Planet: The Hollow Earth 83

PART TWO.. 91

A REAL ~~Vision~~ Experience: "Whether in the Body or Out of the Body"..91

5   Elijah Muhammad, Farrakhan, and the Unseen World.. 93

   5.1   The Announcement: Fact or Fiction?........................ 93

   5.2   The Testimony of Faithful Witnesses.................... 97

5.3   We Want Farrakhan! How Do You Want Him? Dead!...109

5.4   Testimony of the Vision Experience........................ 120

5.5   The Value of the Vision Experience: What is it? 125

6   **True Dreams, Visions and the Spirit of God** 137

6.1   Visions: Thought, Spirit and Mind 137

6.2   The exaltation of the Lamb of God........................... 143

6.3   Debunking the Mystery God 150

6.4   The Physiology of Spirit and Soul throughout History...157

7   **What Really Happened?**.................................... ...172

7.1   Farrakhan's Vision: How did it happen?.....................172

7.2   Prophet Muhammad, Paul, and Out of Body Experiences.. ...182

7.3   The Transfiguration on the Mount 190

PART THREE... 200

They Planned and God Planned.................................... 200

8   **Betrayal and Crucifixion**...................................... 201

8.1   And they said, "Kill Him!"..201

8.2   Judas: The Dissatisfied Laborer.............................. 216

8.3   Post-Betrayal 228

9   **Letters of Warning and Guidance to America and the World**...235

9.1   Open Letter to the President George W. Bush 235

9.2   Open Letter to the President George W. Bush (Second)..244

9.3   Open Letter to the Abraham Foxman 248

9.4   Open Letter to the Muammar Gadhafi 253

Bibliography... 258

Glossary.. 270

Index..275

This Page Intentionally Left Blank

PART ONE

Prophecy, Revelation, and the Reality of the Mother Plane

This Page Intentionally Left Blank

Introduction

It is not expedient for me doubtless to glory. I will come to visions and revelations of the Lord. I knew a man in Christ above fourteen years ago, whether in the body, I cannot tell; or *whether out of the body, I cannot tell* [emphasis mine]: God knoweth; such a one caught up to the third heaven. And I knew such a man, *whether in the body, or out of the body, I cannot tell* [emphasis mine]: God knoweth; How that he was caught up into paradise, and heard unspeakable words, which it is not lawful for a man to utter. 2 Corinthians 12: 1-4.

The above passage is the experience of the Apostle Paul in his message to the Corinthians. The announcement of this experience was also a defense of himself against his detractors or super-apostles[1]. These detractors presented themselves as legitimate apostles of Jesus. This is analogous to Minister Farrakhan's experience on the Wheel, and also his October 1989, and November 2017 press conferences to the President(s) of the United States. Something similar occurred with the prophet Ezekiel where the text says, *the spirit lifted me up between the earth and the heaven.*[2] **Demystifying the Vision Experience of Louis Farrakhan** is as revision of my book *Who Do You Say I Am? The Betrayal and Crucifixion of Louis Farrakhan*. This writing like the previous two editions focuses on the importance of Minister Farrakhan's *vision experience* as it relates to prophecy and revelation and the value of his vision as a testimony of the Honorable Elijah Muhammad, but as the arisen Christ and more. The Honorable Minister Louis Farrakhan's vision experience is really *more* than a vision. This particular reference *more than a vision* was introduced by Minister Jabril Muhammad; longtime friend and companion of Minister

---

[1] Super-apostles were false teachers in Paul's time, also called "false apostles". They were detractors of Paul, but appeared to be superior due their exaggerated teaching. Paul facetiously called them "super" or the "very chiefest" in the King James Version of the Bible.

[2] See footnote 182.

Farrakhan and student of the Honorable Elijah Muhammad. Jabril Muhammad's *More Than a Vision Part 1-19* series is probably the most informative writing on Minister Farrakhan's vision experience to date. Read them!

Minister Farrakhan's more than a vision experience doesn't require elaborate explanations beyond what Minister Farrakhan has already offered and explained. This includes the extensive writings of Jabril Muhammad and Mother Tynnetta Muhammad (wife of the Honorable Elijah Muhammad). Each of them have taught on this subject since 1985-86, not long after Minster Farrakhan's experience on the Wheel, and his public announcement in 1986 in Tripoli, and again in 1989 in Washington, DC. Demystifying his experience is only making reference to helping the reader understand better "how" his experience possibly happened.

Merriam-Webster Dictionary defines *demystify* as - to eliminate the mystifying features of, to make clear and easy to understand: to explain so that it no longer confuses or mystifies someone. Other words associated with *demystify*; clarify, clear (up), construe, demonstrate, explain, elucidate, explicate, expound, get across, illuminate, illustrate, interpret, simplify, spell out, unriddle, decipher, decode, analyze, break down, disentangle, undo, unravel, unscramble, untangle, resolve, solve, define, specify, annotate, commentate, gloss.

More Than. The word *more* is an adjective and means; greater; additional; or further. Synonyms associated with *more* are; added, another, else, farther, fresh, further, additional, and other. Webster's New World Dictionary defines *than* as; introducing the second element in a comparison. Synonyms associated with the word *than*; apart from, aside from, bar, barring, beside, besides, but, except for, excluding, exclusive of, except, outside, outside of, save, and saving.

How do we authenticate an experience like Minister Farrakhan's? More importantly, how do we know that it is from God and the Honorable Elijah Muhammad? Minister Farrakhan's impeccable character, integrity, and love for God, self and humanity should be considered when looking into how to authenticate his experience. Also, what he received from the wheel, has it help or benefited people? Yes. Minister Farrakhan's work since 1985 is proof. Since 1977 his work among the people to rebuild the Nation of Islam throughout the world is further proof. Every aspect of the work of Minister Farrakhan is evidence presented, and if studied will provide proof. The Bible and Holy Quran, the lives of the Prophets, and all the prophecies they present should be studied and considered when determining the authenticity of an experience like Minister Farrakhan's.

It is the hatred of his success among the original people, and humanity in general that keeps Minister Farrakhan in an ongoing battle, or confrontation with Satan. It is no secret to his detractors who the God of Elijah Muhammad is, and it is no secret to them that Minister Farrakhan represents him and the Honorable Elijah Muhammad. This revised edition will attempt to show (like its previous editions) the value of Minister Farrakhan's experience, how it happened, and the prophecies associated with it, including what he received on the Wheel and more. Why? Because the world needs to know that Minister Farrakhan did not lie about what he experienced on the Wheel in 1985. If this book can provide some insight to the reader or increase awareness, and the importance of this serious subject; then my intent and purpose would have been fulfilled.

This Page Intentionally Left Blank

1   Prophecy and Revelation

1.1   *Why Prophecy and Revelation?*

>   ...People claim to know prophecy, when writing books or articles, but
> do they really know The Supreme Being, Who is God, Himself? Can
> you leave The Supreme Being, Himself out of prophecy? If you do, for
> what purposes? What is the meaning of the word "prophecy?"[3]

Prophecy and Revelation are two important components to
understanding the Messianic mission of the Honorable Elijah
Muhammad. It is also important to understand the period of time in
which the prophecy and revelation takes place. Time is critical to
unlocking the hidden truth of scripture. Dwight Pentecost in his writing
Things to Come explains that,

>   Any individual who refers to the Scriptures as Old and New
> Testaments bears witness to the fact that God has divided His
> program into time segments. The history of revelation evidences the
> progress of divine revelation through successive ages.[4]

Pentecost's acknowledges the natural progression of prophecy and
its fulfillment. The Honorable Elijah Muhammad taught, that Allah (I
use "God" and "Allah" interchangeably, unless cited as Allah) in the
Person of Master Fard Muhammad, taught him of history and how the
Bible and Holy Quran are written.[5] What is written in the Bible and
Holy Quran have relevance today, specifically to the work of Minister
Farrakhan. To comprehend the scriptures beyond mere belief, there
must be an understanding of the writers of scripture and their intent.

---

[3] Jabril Muhammad, "Farrakhan the Traveler: The True Meaning of Prophecy", *FinalCall.Com*,
July 24, 2014. http://www.finalcall.com/artman/publish/Columns_4/article_101638.shtml
[4] Dwight. J. Pentecost, ***Things to Come: A Study in Biblical Eschatology*** (Grand Rapids, MI:
Zondervan Publishing House, 1965), 129.
[5] Elijah Muhammad, ***Message to the Blackman in America.*** (Chicago, IL: Muhammad's Temple
2.1965), 108-09.

This understanding lies with what was taught to the Honorable Elijah Muhammad by Master W. Fard Muhammad.[6]

How much do people know about the Bible and Holy Quran, beyond what they believe? Belief is not reality, whether it is a belief in right or wrong. To have belief, without proof, is just belief and cannot stand against knowledge.[7] To understand scripture there must be a study of history, prophecy, revelation, (among other things) and then belief slowly disappears and grows into faith when knowledge is applied. A person's lack of knowledge on a subject does not negate the truth. Popular view, orthodoxy, and dogma, does not qualify itself as truth, just because it is accepted.

The Honorable Elijah Muhammad took very complex mathematical formulas and made them simple to understand. He taught on the history of the moon sixty-six trillion years ago and the forming of mountains; the rebellion of a powerful man named Shabazz, 50,000 years ago, and the forming of kinky hair; the history of Yacub 6,000 years ago and the making of the Caucasian; and the coming of God as a man to perfect ex-slaves. Some believe that this history of Islam that he taught his followers is mythological and made-up to draw Blacks to a greater hidden truth. In terms of appearance, how much more mythological and how much more of a fairytale is the Big Bang Theory, dinosaurs, Neanderthals, or Darwin's Theory of Evolution? What about white Hebrew Jews who were enslaved by Blacks and even questionable Caucasians in Egypt? How much of a fairytale are Easter bunnies that lay eggs, a 400 pound Caucasian man sliding down chimneys, or little Caucasian baby angels with bows and arrows shooting people to make them fall in love? What about a Caucasian man name Jesus who was

---

[6] "Above all, you must understand that no prophecy of Scripture came about by the prophet's own interpretation. For prophecy never had its origin in the will of man, but men spoke from God as they were carried along by the Holy Spirit." (NIV 2Peter 1:20-21).
[7] Muhammad, *Theology of Time*, 186.

killed for man's sins, rose from the dead, only to hide for 2000 years, and then afterwards, come back to judge the world for their sins; the same sins he died for? What about a God who has a face that no man can see, because to see his face is to die? When you die you'll see him in heaven, but only if you were a good, God fearing person on earth? Billions of people believe these things, with no evidence or proof. This is not the case with the history of the Blackman and Original people as taught by the Honorable Elijah Muhammad.

So, what is the importance of prophecy and revelation? It is important in understanding the mind of God with regards to the eschatological events to come, and the establishing of His kingdom, which is tied to His promise to the ex-slaves in America. This is also important in understanding the time and end of Satan's rule. This is important in understanding the plot to harm Minister Farrakhan, for he is the recipient of the Divine revelation of God and the one who is challenging Satan on behalf of the Honorable Elijah Muhammad. As it was with the plot to kill the Honorable Elijah Muhammad, the plot against Minster Farrakhan will fail too. The attempt of the wicked to kill the Messenger is a death sentence to the people whom the Messenger was sent to warn. [8]

1.2   What Elijah Muhammad Teaches

The Honorable Elijah Muhammad was taught by his teacher that the *Original* Blackman is God and that for sixty-six trillion years the true knowledge of God was keep a secret. Prior to sixty-six trillion years, there was not a need to make the knowledge of God a secret. Because of the high level of madness of one God, the Honorable Elijah

---

[8] See Revelation 12:1-11. This is one of many scriptures that makes reference to the enemies of God and their attempts to kill the Messenger of Allah and his followers. The woman and her child and the war with Michael and the angels in heaven are relevant today and refer directly to Minister Farrakhan and his helpers.

Muhammad taught that this God wanted to destroy the entire planet Earth. His attempt to destroy humanity resulted in the deportation of a part of the earth now called Moon. Since then twenty-four Gods[9] (whom he also called scientists) concealed the secret of the true identity and knowledge of God. Only one from among them was permitted to rule, and his authority and wisdom lasted for 25,000 years. At the end of the 25,000 year period or cycle, another God was permitted to rule for another 25,000 years. These are the Elders mentioned in the Bible. They were divided into two groups; 12 major and 12 minor.

The knowledge of God as a man was so carefully guarded that only eleven Gods (scientists) from among the twenty-four scientists knew who the Supreme God was. This was a tradition among these men that was passed down from son to son, each having a life span of approximately 500 years. These scientists have multiple duties. One of these duties involves looking into the future with supreme mathematical precision and collecting the future events of the planet and writing them in a book. The Supreme God, Allah, studies and measures what was gathered, and judges it. What is gathered is called *history*. Although these events have not happened, they were foreseen and will take place only if it pleases these men in this supreme council. Ultimately, the decision to let these events happen is up to the Supreme Scientist. The Honorable Elijah Muhammad explains regarding the writing of the history in advance,

> We, the original nation of earth, says Allah, the Maker of everything --
> sun, moon and stars and the race called white race -- are the writers of
> the Bible and Qur-an. We make such history once every 25,000 years.
> When such history is written, it is done by twenty-four of our scientists.
> One acts as Judge or God for the others and twenty-three actually do the
> work of getting up the future of the nation, and all is put into one book
> and at intervals where such and such part or portion will come to pass,

---

[9] See Revelation 4:4; 4:10; 5:5; 5:6; 5:8; 5:11; 5:14; 7:11; 11:16; 19:4.

that people will be given that part of the book through one among that people from one of the Twelve (twelve major scientists) as it is then called a Scripture which actually means script of writing from something original or book.[10]

At intervals of time in the 25,000-year period or cycle, one of the twelve major scientists would go to the people and give wisdom to one from among the general public. The person who was blessed to receive this wisdom was called a prophet, or messenger and there were several ways in which the prophet received the message or revelation. This intervention by one of the major Scientists was to spare the general public from the eventual destruction of their own wickedness, but at its apex. True Islam in his writing *The Book of God* elaborates,

> The Scientists' duty is to guide the History of the earth in accord with the 25,000 Year Prophetic History and to fulfill the scriptures. The Bible is a book of prophecy which describes events that take us all the way into Apocalypse. As the History is written, the Twenty Four Scientist make sure it happens just as it is written. They are also responsible for imparting Wisdom, Knowledge, and Understanding to Allah's prophets and ministers.[11]

These scientists or God's are not average men. They have not been subjected to the rule and ways of Satan. They have their natural powers. Minster Farrakhan makes reference to this natural power of the Original man to see the future, but uses the term vision in comparison to dreams,

> Each one of you has the power to vision. I don't mean vision with these eyes (points to his eyes), I mean vision with the mind, to see years into the future, to see what going on, on the other part of the planet and be standing right here. You've got the power to do it and it comes to you

[10] Muhammad, *Message to the Blackman*, 108.
[11] True Islam, *The Book of God: An Encyclopedia of Proof that the Blackman is God*, (Atlanta, GA: A-Team Publishing, 2007), 180.

in snatches. You have a dream, and you will wake up from the dream knowing that you were right there in your bed, but you went somewhere last night. You had a conversation last night. You saw something and a loved one of yours; you warned them that some danger may be coming. And, sure enough the thing that you saw comes to past. Well what is that? That's a gift from God, but it belongs to you. [12]

Minister Farrakhan also makes reference to leaving the body by saying, **"You have a dream, and you will wake up from the dream knowing that you were right there in your bed, but you went somewhere last night."** I will go into greater detail about this in upcoming chapters. This natural power to see the future is lost to the average person, but regained through living a righteous and moral life. Master W. F. Muhammad, according to the Honorable Elijah Muhammad saw his future in a dream when he was six years old. In this dream he saw himself pushing, the Ford's, DuPont's, Rockefeller's, and other rulers of the world into the Lake of Fire prophesized in the scriptures.[13] For us today, the foundation of this power is rooted in the understanding of Supreme Wisdom Lessons given to the Nation of Islam in the West. Minister Farrakhan further suggests in his statement that man does not just have the ability to see the future, but also travel to the future in his mind. Then the question comes to us; what is the mind? How is it constructed? Why wait sixty-six trillion years for the true knowledge of God to come from God, in person? It took seventy-six trillion years for the first God's (originator's), Will and his mind to be made Perfect. This perfected being who is to make all things new in man is God in person, Master Fard Muhammad. Today, Master Fard Muhammad has made his messenger-messiah, the Honorable Elijah Muhammad into himself. In Revelation, He sits on the throne that the

---

[12] Louis Farrakhan. "Union of the Black and Red" YouTube. Flash video file. http://youtu.be/M_mp9Q6_Ko4 (accessed July 19, 2014).

[13] See Revelation 19:20; 20:10; 20:14 – 15.

twenty-four men sat around. This resembles the Throne of Power mentioned in the Holy Quran,[14] which is also symbolic to the Supreme One's brain power. Master Fard Muhammad wrote that New Book, that takes us through the next 10,000-years of this 25,000-year cycle of history and into an infinite world of Wisdom. He takes us into an infinite reality, a timelessness termed "Perfection".

In the very near future, there will not be a need to re-new history again because the imperfection of man will be under the power of a New Ruler (mind). What is to come is the receipt of this new book by Minister Farrakhan. He received a portion of the New Book in *English* during his *vision experience* on the Great Mother Wheel when he spoke to the Honorable Elijah Muhammad on September 17, 1985.

---

[14] See references to the Throne of Power in the Holy Quran: 7:54; 10:3; 11:7; 13:2; 20:5; 23:86; 25:59; 32:4; 39:75; 40:7; 40:15; 43:82; 57:4; 69:17; and 85:15.

1.3   *A Contemporary View*

To receive and experience a premonition or intuitive thought that is unequivocally real to the recipient is a phenomenon that has occurred for centuries among the people of the earth. What is called *revelation* is considered to be *inspired*, or revealed by a supernatural occurrence. Revelation is directly from God (Allah) who is a man, and who is indeed beyond *super-natural*. The scholars of religion understand the practicality of revelation events that prophets and figures of the Bible and Holy Quran have experienced. Dwight. J. Pentecost in his book ***Things to Come: A Study in Biblical Eschatology*** sites Gustav Friedrich Oehler's text ***Theology of the Old Testament***, on Oehler's observation of four characteristics of prophecy:

> The characteristics of Old Testament prophecy are; (1). The matter of revelation being given to the prophet in the form of intuition, the future was made to appear to them as either immediately present, complete, or all events in progress. (2). The fact that the matter of prophecy is given in the form of intuition also furnishes the reason why it always sees the realization of that matter in particular events which are complete in themselves; i.e., a prophecy may appear as just one event, but in reality there may be a two-, three-, or four fold fulfillment. (3). Since the matter of prophecy presents itself to view as a multitude of individual facts, it may sometimes appear as though single preconditions contradict each other when they are, in fact only those parts into which the ideas revealed have separated, mutually completing each other, e.g., contrasting pictures of the Messiah in states of suffering and states of glory. (4). The matter of prophecy is in form of intuition which further means as far as its form is concerned, it is on the plane of the beholder himself, i.e., the prophet spoke of the future glory in terms of his own society and experiences. [15]

Oehler's idea of prophecy identifies four basic elements:

---

[15] Pentecost, **Things to Come**, 45.

1. The immediate or present manifestation of events, and the progression of events and the completion of events witnessed through intuition.
2. The wholeness of prophecy and the multiplicity of its events.
3. The idea of "individual facts" completing each other.
4. The form of intuition and its manifestation from the witnesses' societal condition and experiences.

How relevant are these characteristics with regards to Minister Farrakhan's vision? Can we demonstrate through an observation of these rules that Minister Louis Farrakhan more than likely had a very real experience where he received revelation of future events from the Honorable Elijah Muhammad on the Wheel? C. Von Orelli's writing **Prophecy, Prophets** (Pentecost, 1965), draws attention to several observations regarding prophecy,

> (1). Prophecy may be fulfilled shortly after its delivery or at a much later date. (2.) Prophecy is ethically conditioned, that is, some of it is conditioned as to fulfillment on the behavior of the recipients. It may even be recalled. (3). Prophecy may be fulfilled successfully. (4.) We must not pedantically demand that the prophecy be fulfilled exactly as given...[16]

Prophecy should not be viewed as an event that is historical until it is fulfilled. Even then, prophecy can reoccur and fit for another time and this is called the *Law of Recurrence*. To view prophecy as history completely, can lead to making mistakes with how we understand scripture. This causes the unlearned to accept an untrue, uneducated view of the fulfillment of scriptures. This also leads to improperly viewing the one that God has raised for the people, i.e., the messenger.

---

[16] Pentecost, *Things to Come*, 45-46.

Viewing the scriptures, the Bible specifically, as a book of history and complete truth is based on romanticism, emotionalism and lies. These lies are usually ideas made up and are not based on any evidence. In the above-mentioned quote Orelli points out four clear observations about the condition of prophecy and time,

1. The time of the fulfillment of prophecy.
2. The effect of the behavior of the receiver on prophecy and the ability to beat (recall) prophecy.
3. The actual fulfillment of prophecy.
4. The expectation and the exact fulfillment of prophecy when it is pronounced.

Many people that heard the Honorable Elijah Muhammad speak on future events to come believed him. However, when the time or events passed and they did not happen, as they understood him to speak them; they doubted in him and the truth of the future events that he spoke. This happened when the Honorable Elijah Muhammad spoke of the END that would come in three years after the death of Prophet Muhammad's wife. The Honorable Elijah Muhammad said this on October 22, 1972, but was also referring to himself. [17] Many view Minister Farrakhan the same way today as those of the past viewed the Honorable Elijah Muhammad in 1972. Minister Farrakhan's

---

[17] See Theology of Time, October 22, 1972. "I'm here to talk with you on such subjects as this, which means judgment of someone or some country. This is the country that we are living in." "Some of the worldly scientists are now bearing me witness that this is the truth. They doubt if America will live another three years. This is the devil himself saying this, according to what he has learned from the Lord, sent through the mouths of his prophets and apostles that America will hardly live three more years. I bear him witness. I have not told you this, but I can show it to you in black and white. It says the end came three years after the death of Muhammad's wife; maybe you can find it. This is in the table talks of Muhammad. Also in two or three other places, by the scholars of Islam, they have described the death pretty well. I read it years ago, but I did not ever want to say anything about it until after her death, because she had many children and grandchildren and I didn't want them to know. But there is much to tell today that yesterday we didn't want to tell."

experience on the Wheel is a matter of debate with many who have heard him speak of a future meeting with the Honorable Elijah Muhammad; a man that the world views as physically dead. That is an entirely different subject and discussion. One thing to clearly point out is that what the Honorable Elijah Muhammad spoke of and what Minister Louis Farrakhan continues to repeat of his teachers' words; are not prophecies as understood by theologians, but are the direct will and command of God himself.

Pentecost continues with Orelli's point,

> (5). Many prophecies, especially those about Christ, are literally fulfilled. (6). The form and character of prophecy are conditioned by the age and location of the writer. (7). Prophecies frequently form parts of a whole and, therefore, must be compared with other prophecy. (8). The prophet sees things together which are widely separated in fulfillment.[18]

The ideas of prophecy observed by Orelli suggests; the fulfillment of Christ prophecy as complete; age and location of the one prophesying; the singularity of prophecy and the separation of events in fulfillment. These conditions along with others have significant relevance today. Minister Farrakhan was made by God, to withdraw from his active role in the Nation of Islam after the departure and assumed death of the Honorable Elijah Muhammad in 1975. This was to save his life and countless others, then and now. To outline this point in comparison to Orelli's observations of prophecy:

1. (5) The prophecy of the Honorable Elijah Muhammad as Christ has been fulfilled.

---

[18] Pentecost, *Things to Come*, 45-46.

2. (6) The form of this prophecy was conditioned on the age and location of the Honorable Elijah Muhammad in relation to the first phase of his work. (1934-1974)

3. (7) His work is the culmination of all the works of the prophets as the last Messenger of God and should be compared to the works of the prophets, but as the fulfillment of what they prophesied.

4. (8) The scope of his mission and the completion of his work although at a different time, are aligned with the Divine plan of God. These same observations can and do apply to Minister Farrakhan.

The work and the fulfillment of this divine mission will be completed through Minister Farrakhan and all of those who are with him. To just assume or take on face value that the fulfillment of all the prophecies are directly related to Minister Farrakhan and the Nation of Islam in the West, is not what I am suggesting to the reader. These truths can be verified. It can be further verified that the same prophecies are connected to Minister Farrakhan's vision experience. Jabril Muhammad in his writing *This is the One* noted,

> When we say this verifies that, we are saying that what is verified is not necessarily dependent on that which verifies it. This is not the general use of the word verify. However, when distinguished from other synonyms, verify implies: "The established correspondence of the actual facts or details to those that are given in an account or statement. When what is in question is a suspicion, fear or probability, it can be verified only in result, event, or fulfillment."…
>
> The Power (or God) establishing the facts about the Messenger to what is written of him is independent of the Power (or Gods) that produced the prophecies. Fulfillment of the prophecies verifies the scriptures. This corresponds to the deeper meaning of the word verify. In the

> general sense of the word, the scriptures verify the Messenger's identity and he verifies what it written in them of him.[19]

There are some interesting points that Muhammad mentions in the above quote:

1. When we say this verifies that, we are saying that what is verified is not necessarily dependent on that which verifies it.

When Jabril Muhammad says, "When we say this verifies that…" in context he is referring to the Bible and the Holy Quran verifying what the Honorable Elijah Muhammad teaches. Theologians of the Bible believe that that the Old Testament "type" must absolutely verify the New Testament "anti-type" in order for it to be concise. Here is where they differ in understanding of prophecy and what we are taught by the Honorable Elijah Muhammad, which is fulfillment of the prophecies.

2. The Power (or God) establishing the facts about the Messenger to what is written of him is independent of the Power (or Gods) that produced the prophecies.

As mentioned previously, the Honorable Elijah Muhammad taught that the wise scientists of Islam write history in advanced. Twenty-three write what is to come in the future, but up to 25,000 years, and the twenty-fourth is the Judge, whose name is Allah.[20] They are men. To Jabril Muhammad's point, Allah (God) is independent of the Power that produced the prophecies. In this case the Honorable Elijah Muhammad, as well as Minister Farrakhan verifies the Bible and Holy Quran (the prophets' predictions) through their work and what they have already done in America, including the effect of what they have done in America

---

[19] Jabril Muhammad, *This is the One: We need not look for another!* 3rd ed. (Phoenix, AZ: Jabril Muhammad, 1996), 100.
[20] Muhammad, *Message to the Blackman*, 109.

on the world. Even deeper, their work and mission was verified and confirmed before either of them were born. This was written of them over 15,000 years ago before the 6,000 years of scripture/history that we presently have called Bible and Holy Quran. The Honorable Elijah Muhammad and Minister Farrakhan are necessary. Both men not only fulfill portions of prophecies in the Bible and Holy Quran, but are instrumental in establishing what is called the Kingdom of heaven on earth. Jabril Muhammad continues on the point of fulfillment of prophecy,

> There is plenty of prophecy in the Bible and Holy Qur'an, which Messenger Muhammad fulfills. What makes such prophecy valid? We could quickly say his fulfillment of such prophecies makes them true. Fine. But this is not enough. To say there is prophecy in scripture, which originally came from God, is to say it was true even before it was fulfilled. Prophecies of his coming and work were true and worthy of total trust before he was born. Some people of the past knew these prophecies to be true. Moreover, the prophecies of the Bible and Qur'an were necessary. Further, the presence of Messenger Muhammad was a must. This means he is a spiritual, moral and material necessity.[21]

In the religious books of the world, the one to come in the last days comes on time. His character is forged through a multitude of trials that he is forced to overcome, all for the salvation of a lost, suffering, and rebellious people. He is extraordinarily resilient, patient, forgiving, and tolerant. He does not represent himself, he represents a greater power. This man is not a prophet, he is the Messiah. His enemies are many, and are powerful. They desire to kill the man that the prophets have talked about for thousands of years. Those who have in their hearts disdain, envy, jealously and hatred are like those mentioned in scriptures passed; they are vipers. So, how do we perceive what has been revealed,

---

[21] Muhammad, *This is the One,* 100.

or in essence, taught? Whether it is revealed through words, actions or events of governments and institutions; how do we interpret what we see as revelation? What is the basis of revelation? What is the form in which revelation comes? These are all questions that are helpful in understanding Minister Farrakhan's vision on the Wheel, September 17, 1985.

Maulana Muhammad Ali, in his book *The Religion of Islam* explains revelation,

> Revelation, we are told in the Quran, is granted to man in three forms: "And it is not vouchsafed to any mortal that Allah should speak to him, except by revelation (*wahy*) or from behind a veil, or by sending a messenger and revealing by His permission what He pleases" (42:51). The first of these three modes is called *wahy*, which is generally translated as meaning *revelation*. Since the different kinds of revelation are spoken of here, the word *wahy* is obviously used in its literal sense, its primary significance being a hasty suggestion (*al-isharat al-sari'ah*) (R.). Hence the inspired word, which enters the hearts of the prophets and of the righteous, is called *wahy* because it is like a sudden suggestion made directly to the heart of the inspired one (*ilqa-'un fi'l-rau'*). It is not a message in words but simply an idea which comes like a flash and clears up a doubt or difficulty, and it is not the result of meditation.
>
> The second mode is described as speaking from behind a veil -- a scene, carrying a deeper significance, is shown as in a vision (*kashf*), or in a dream (*ru'ya*), or words are heard by the person spoken to, as if coming from behind a veil. The third mode is that in which the angel bearing the message is sent to the recipient of the Divine revelation, and the message is delivered in words, and this is the highest form of revelation. As already stated, the angel entrusted with Divine message in words is Gabriel or the Holy Spirit, and this third mode of revelation is limited to the prophets of God only -- to men entrusted with important Divine messages to humanity -- while the first two lower forms of

revelation are common to prophets as well as those who are not prophets.[22]

The Holy Quran 42:51 reads:

"And it is not vouchsafed to a mortal that Allah should speak to him, except by revelation or from behind a veil, or by sending a messenger and revealing by his permission what He pleases."

Muhammad Ali explains the methods of revelation and the differences between them, but makes specific distinction in how they occur:

1. The two lower forms involving little change.
2. The third form involving a dramatic change while awake.

Despite these changes, Muhammad Ali describes the two lower forms as being accompanied by a *transported state of trance or vision* that is experienced while the recipient is awake or asleep.[23] The highest form is accompanied by an actual wakeful experience of "passing from one world to another" and this burdensome change is visible to the prophet or messenger and to those who see him. [24] This change bears resemblance to Jesus' transfiguration in the presence of his disciples. The manner in which the revelation comes to the messenger is important. Muhammad Ali elaborates further on Prophet Muhammad's (PBUH) experience of revelation in hadith,

---

[22] Maulana M. Ali, **The Religion of Islam.** (Columbus, OH: Ahmadiyya Anjuman Isha'at Islam, 1990), 17-19.

[23] This is not to say that Minister Farrakhan's experience is one of the lower forms and is common. His experience is one of the highest forms, which involved receiving clear instructions from God that would benefit humanity. Ali says of this: "For the delivery of the higher message which relates to the welfare of mankind, a higher form of revelation is chosen, a form in which the message is not simply an idea but is clothed in actual words. The Prophet's faculty of being spoken to by God is so highly developed that he receives the messages, not only as ideas instilled into the mind or in the form of words uttered or heard under influence of the Holy Spirit, but actually as Divine messages in words delivered through the latter." See Muhammad, *The Religion of Islam, 17.*

[24] Ali, **The Religion of Islam**,19.

"It comes to me sometimes as the ringing of a bell and this is hardest on me, then he (the angel) leaves me and I remember from him what he says; and sometimes the angel comes in the shape of a man and he talks to me and I remember what he says" (Bu. 1:1). These are the only two forms in which the Quranic revelation came to the Prophet. In both cases, the angel came to him and was seen by him; in both cases a certain message was delivered in words which he at once committed to memory. That is the essence of the whole question. The only difference between the two cases was that in one case the angel appeared in the shape of a human being and uttered the words in a soft tone as a man talks to another; in the other case, it is not stated in what form he came, but we are told that the words were uttered like the ringing of a bell, that is to say, in a harsh, hard tone, which made it a heavier task for the Prophet to receive them. But still it was the angel who brought the message, as is shown by the use of the personal pronoun *he* in the first part of the report. In both cases the Prophet was transported, as it were, to another world…[25]

The Honorable Elijah Muhammad also spoke of this manner of receiving revelation and further elaborated on how it is done, by God and others,

I will tell you. God has told me how this is done. It comes to your ears just like a bell in your telephone. It starts ringing in your ears, but you can't pick up who's on the line. *If you do have a ringing, that's me or somebody else trying to get in touch with you.* [emphasis added] I'm not trying to make you think that I am a great scientist who can pick up and tune in on you at will, God didn't raise me up to do that. I go so far as He lets me go. Regardless to the nature, the organs of nature are there to use for such purpose. David says in his Psalms, God has opened his ears that he may hear – you have it there in Psalms and I think God will bless me with the same someday when it pleases Him. I don't think David was any better than I.[26]

---

[25] Ali, *The Religion of Islam*, 21.
[26] Muhammad, *Theology of Time*, 69. My eyes have seen the defeat of my adversaries; my ears have heard the rout of my wicked foes. Psalms 92:11 New International Version.

The bell ringing that the Honorable Elijah Muhammad spoke of resembles the words of Prophet Muhammad (PBUH) as reported in a hadith:

> It comes to me sometimes as the ringing of a bell and this is hardest on me, then he (the angel) leaves me and I remember from him what he says; and sometimes the angel comes in the shape of a man and he talks to me and I remember what he says (Bu. 1:1).[27]

Minister Farrakhan was *transported* in his vision to the Great Mother Wheel. Yusuf Ali in his explanation of revelation speaks of a similar transporting to another world. [28]

> ... [I]n the other case, it is not stated in what form he came, but we are told that the words were uttered like the ringing of a bell... In both cases the Prophet was transported, as it were, to another world ...[29]

How was the Prophet transported? How was Minister Farrakhan transported? Was it in the body or out of the body? All of this and more refers to Minister Farrakhan and his vision experience.

---

[27] Ali, *The Religion of Islam*, 21.
[28] "The Holy Prophet was first *transported* to the seat of the earlier revelations in Jerusalem, and then taken through the seven heavens even to the Sublime Throne, and initiated into spiritual mysteries of the human soul struggling in Space and Time." See also Abdullah Yusuf Ali. *The Meaning of the Holy Quran*, 671.
[29] Ali, *The Religion of Islam*. 17.

This Page Intentionally Left Blank

2   Rules of Interpretation

There are rules of interpretation for the Bible and Holy Quran. The Holy Quran makes mention of the interpretation of it and warns against misinterpreting the book.

> He it is Who has revealed the Book to thee; some of its verses are decisive — they are the basis of the Book — and others are allegorical. Then those in whose hearts is perversity follow the part of it which is allegorical, seeking to mislead, and seeking to give it (their own) interpretation. And none knows its interpretation save Allah, and those firmly rooted in knowledge. They say: We believe in it, it is all from our Lord. And none mind except men of understanding.[30]

I first learned of certain rules by listening to Minister Farrakhan, in the 90's when I heard him make mention of the *Law of Double Reference*. I listened to how he explained and applied this rule, and from that point on I sought to learn more about this law and others. However, I could not find them anywhere. This was before the dawn of the internet. I then learned about *Typology* reading a book by Minister Jabril Muhammad (*Farrakhan the Traveler*) many years ago. I became intrigued by these terms and subjects, and how they are useful in scripture, as relates to understanding prophecy. I have had this fascination with the scriptures (Bible specifically) since I was 14 years old. Over the years and into my adulthood, I studied the scriptures and read as much as I could about biblical hermeneutics to gain a better understanding of the Bible and how it is interpreted. No greater understanding came to me than when I first received a copy of Message to the Blackman in America by the Honorable Elijah Muhammad. This book was and has been the foundation of my exegetical work related to

---

[30] Holy Quran 3:6.

scriptural interpretations. This keeps me in a "safety zone" so to speak, and keeps me from making mistakes with my understanding of the scriptures. Also, the modern up-to-date understanding from Minister Farrakhan.

2.1   Typology

The historical relevance of events in the past has an impact theologically on how we see and measure events of the Bible and Holy Quran typologically. The Honorable Elijah Muhammad taught that a person would be rewarded for their review and study of history. He is also known to have said that 75% of what we read in the scripture, specifically about Jesus, is prophetic and relates to him. The word *theology* has its root in two Greek words, *theos*; meaning God and *logos*; meaning; word, discourse, reason or study. Theology is the study of God. So, the importance in reviewing history and its relevance theologically lies in the fact that the study of God involves a study of history. The Honorable Elijah Muhammad taught that *We* make history and that *We* see it before it happens.[31] "We" represents the Gods (scientists) who are original people mentioned previously. Regarding the divine fulfillment of history Tynnetta Muhammad suggests,

> Dear readers, nothing happens by chance; everything of our present and future has long been prepared and we are walking into the footsteps of those who went before us written from the most ancient times. As the Honorable Elijah Muhammad taught us, everything about ourselves is written in a book. Some things we can escape, while others are a part of our destiny.[32]

---

[31] Muhammad, *Message to the Blackman*, 108.
32 Tynnetta Muhammad, "Unveiling the Number 19: The Sign of Egypt—On the Heels of a Death Plot", *Final Call Online*, March 22, 2010, www.finalcall.com/artman/publish/Columns_4/article_6834.shtml

Typology is a methodology used to allow students to gain understanding of the scriptures through the contrast and comparison of scriptural characters based on time, events, and the overall purpose of God's plan for humanity, i.e., prophecy. Typology is an old methodology that is not comprehensively taught in most seminaries. So, the average student of the Bible will probably never come into contact with typology as a method of interpreting scripture. This is largely due to the scholars misunderstanding of what they are interpreting and the time that they are associating with their interpretation.

Leaders of religious schools of thought are usually the means by which most people gain insight into scriptures. Students of seminaries are taught biblical exegesis, and the continuity of Old and New Testament, but are not taught it in a modern context, so they miss the future representative of revelation by their association with an out dated historical one. The idea of revelation, past and present are seen through what are termed *types* and the *antitypes*. Therefore, biblical typology is consider by theologians as a methodology that is limited to only Old and New Testaments, meaning that the type itself is limited to the Old Testament whereas the anti-type to the New Testament.

Type - In theology; referring to a person, place or institution that pre-figures a future person, place or event. This term is often meant to show the relationship between Old Testament and New Testament figures.

I disagree and will offer another approach to this that I will elaborate on further. Stanley Gundry explains in his article *Typology as a means of interpretation: Past and Present,*

In the New Testament itself the saving events of the Gospel were regarded as the antitypes of the events, institutions, and certain persons of the Old Testament, the correspondence often being mentioned in rather subtle and indirect ways. Faced with the task of apologetics, post-apostolic Christians were quick to follow the lead of the New Testament writers. One of their most pressing tasks was to demonstrate the underlying agreement and continuity between the Old Testament, properly understood, and Christianity and its claims. The unity of the Bible was the fundamental premise.

The whole Bible spoke directly of Christ, in prophecy and in type. While the historical context and grammatical meaning of the Old Testament texts was to be sought out and adhered to, for the events would have had no validity if they had not actually happened, it was the foreshadowing of Christ that was of the greatest importance. This unity transcended all diversity present in scripture. Though there was diversity of opinion between the Alexandrian and Antiochene exegetes as to the importance of literal exegesis, they were united on the importance of the witness of all scripture to Christ, and typological exegesis of scripture was one means of seeing that unity and witness.[33]

Here Gundry mentions that the post-apologetics like the apologetics before them attempted to rationalize the agreement with Old and New Testament and establish a foundational unity of both. The continuity and witness of the scriptures of the Bible are just as relevant today as they were centuries ago.[34] The messianic figure that is to come and that was spoken of centuries ago can be witnessed through a study

---

[33] Stanley N. Gundry, "Typology as a means of interpretation: past and present." *Journal of the Evangelical Theological Society* 12, no. 4 (Fall 1969): 234.

[34] I would have to include that according to Gundry, "...One of their most pressing tasks was to demonstrate the underlying agreement and continuity between the Old Testament, properly understood, and Christianity and its claims. The unity of the Bible was the fundamental premise." Early Christian attempts to create continuity between Old and New Testament is partly the reason why typology as a form of exegesis is used. When used the way that Gundry and others suggests; regarding prophecy, typological references are limited to the Bible. All the prophets had one message, from the same God, and made no distinctions between the messages from God. So, the attempt to create "continuity" was an attempt to "make sense" and give meaning to Christian faith and traditions as a whole. However, the Old Testament, evolved from Jewish tradition, which evolved from Islamic revelation given to the Jews by Moses; who was a Muslim. Many would disagree, but this is a fact. Although, I do believe that the continuity of the Old and New Testament is relevant, I also believe that the way it is used continues to propagate an outdated dogmatic approach to Christianity as a whole.

of the type and anti-type figures of the scriptures, but more specifically, the Honorable Elijah Muhammad and Minister Louis Farrakhan. The unity of the scriptures points to Christ. This is not foreign to the scholars of religion, but it is an absolute necessity in understanding the eschatological events to come, since what "is to come" is making reference to the future.

Anti-Type – Person, place, institution or incident that mirrors or fulfills a historical person, place, institution or occurrence.

These events are seen by scholars as having a traditional/historical root in scripture that the contemporary view rest firmly upon and this view draws on history as a point of reference to validate present and future realities. Joseph P. Cahill in his writing, ***Hermeneutical implications of Typology*** explains,

> Typology, however, is but one specific mode of the larger category of inter-pretation, one in which a present event, person, situation, or thing suggests a likeness to an event, person, situation, or thing of the past. The typological conjunction is generically parallel to the hermeneutic work of the Yahwist, the Elohist, the Deuteronomist, the prophets, and, of course, the formers of the gospel tradition… So typology, as one form of interpretation, is rooted not simply in the universal experience where one sees new meaning in a past event in the light of a present experience but rather in the hermeneutical nature of the biblical books. For the basic impe-tus in the writing and assembling of the biblical books is to understand present experience in the light of a past tradition by reinterpreting the past tradition so that it is relevant to the contemporary situation. This constitutes the ever-permanent and ever-expanding

hermeneutical circle that gives a very unusual unity to the Christian Bible and still suggests that the Bible is a hermeneutical book.[35]

Both Cahill and Gundry suggest that typology is used to show the "unity" or "continuity" of the Bible. I completely understand this perspective since their approach to typology is limited to the Bible. However Cahill acknowledges in the above quote,

> The typological conjunction is generically parallel to the hermeneutic work of the Yahwist, the Elohist, the Deuteronomist, the prophets, and, of course, the formers of the gospel tradition...

Here Cahill recognizes the early hermeneutical work of the Yahwist, Elohist and Deuteronomist. This shows us that the hermeneutical observation of Christianity has a basis somewhere else, and has evolved and was not absent of influence from other source material or traditions. I make this point because my approach to the subject of Minister Farrakhan's vision is such that it justifies an explanation. Some will not acknowledge this view, much less the way that the Bible is referenced on this subject. My hermeneutical observation of the Bible and the interpretation of the Holy Quran, including my use of typology are not metaphorical, but prophetic and rooted in science.

⊘ *Yahwist* - One of the believed sources of a portion of the Hebrew canon; Pentateuch (first five books of the Bible). The basis for recognizing a component of the Pentateuch as the writing of the *Yawhist*.

---

[35] Joseph P. Cahill. "Hermeneutical implications of typology." *Catholic Biblical Quarterly* 44, no. 2 (April 1982): 267.

The Bible is considered to be in *encyclopedic form,* beginning with creation and ending with apocalypse shaped into a divine unity.[36] However, if the Bible is inspired then the process of interpretation must be inspired also.[37] Who inspired the prophets? Where did they receive the wisdom of prophecy? As mentioned, the Bible is a hermeneutical book.[38] There is a danger when interpreting scriptures, so a careful and respectful approach must be considered since misunderstanding may lead to misinterpreting scriptures. This can lead to making allegorical references to the scriptures that do not apply.[39] What Gundry calls allegory was spread by the Augustinian[40] interpretation and exegetical work of the Bible up to Protestant Reformation, and it was purely allegorical.

Elohist - One of the believed sources that comprise the original elements of the Pentateuch (first five books of the Bible). The source for recognizing a component of the Pentateuch as the writing of the Elohist.

Although Calvinist and Lutheran interpretation did not have a specific methodology for typological insight, the Reformed movements view reestablished typology as a premiere methodology of exegesis.[41]

---

[36] Cahill. "Hermeneutical implications of typology.", 270.

[37] Ibid.

[38] "... [H]ermeneutics, the study of interpretation or the quest for meaning. This employs various approaches to written documents; each called a "criticism", e.g., Textual Criticism, Historical Criticism, and Source Criticism." This criticism is a careful analysis of the text and should include the other types of criticism that Brown mentioned that I did not include in this writing. Those criticisms are: Form Criticism; Canonical Criticism; Structuralism (Semiotics), Narrative Criticism; Rhetorical Criticism; Social Criticism and Advocacy Criticism. Raymond Brown. *Introduction to the New Testament,* (New York, NY: Bantam, Doubleday, Dell Publishing, 1ed.1997) 20.

[39] Gundry, "Typology as a means of interpretation", 235.

[40] This is specific to Augustine of Hippo and his philosophical and theological views and its influence on the Calvinists and Protestant Reformation.

[41] Gundry, "Typology as a means of interpretation", 235-36. Originally with Martin Luther and John Calvin's views of scripture, typology was not a practice "coined" or methodology developed and used. However as Gundry mentions, it was reestablished by the Reformed movements, who were greatly influenced by Luther and Calvin's writings, .i.e., theology and philosophy.

As mentioned previously, the events of the Bible, particularly the Old Testament are relevant and foreshadow the events of the New Testament. These events have special importance, but as types indicating when God would come to establish his New Covenant.[42] Charles Fritsch in his writing, **Biblical Typology** defines a type as,

> ... [A]n institution, historical event or person, ordained by God, which effectively prefigures some truth connected with Christianity [43]

Although Fritsch's definition of type makes a specific connection to Christianity, this principle is applicable where a messianic figure is to return and establish a kingdom of eternal peace. Fritsch explains types in relation to allegories in his observation,

> ... [A] type differs from an allegory, a distinction which is not always observed. For an allegory is a fictitious narrative, or to put it less bluntly, in an allegory the historical truth of the narrative dealt with may or may not be accepted, whereas in typology, the fulfillment of the antitype can only be understood in the light of the reality of the original type.[44]

Here are several points that we should consider typologically:

1. Minister Louis Farrakhan's work can only be understood in light of the Honorable Elijah Muhammad's mission. This work can be observed in scripture; Bible and Holy Quran.

2. Minister Louis Farrakhan's work is an extension and continuation of the work of his teacher. Both men are written of in the scriptures, and this partnership can be seen in the lives of certain scriptural characters.

---

[42] W. H. Lampe, "*The Reasonableness of Typology*," in **Essays on Typology** (Alec R. Allenson INC., 1957), 10.
[43] Charles T. Fritsch. "Biblical typology." *Bibliotheca sacra* 104, no. 414 (April 1947): 214.
[44] Ibid.,

3. Minister Louis Farrakhan's declaration that the Honorable Elijah Muhammad is physically alive is the most profound declaration of faith, next to the Honorable Elijah Muhammad's declaration that he (Honorable Elijah Muhammad) was taught by Almighty God. This too is written in the Bible and Holy Quran and is probably the most profound of all typological references, since it relates to ascension and the return of Jesus Christ, and more.

There must be a divine connection between the type and the anti-type that is rooted in historical truth whereas the allegory historically, may not make that connection and is imaginative.[45] The Honorable Elijah Muhammad has proven the effectiveness of his truth to the world through the bearing of witness of Master Fard Muhammad as God. His work has established the strength of his claims, and the basis of his work demonstrates; if we view the scriptures that he (Honorable Elijah Muhammad) is divinely connected to Minister Louis Farrakhan and the fulfillment of prophecy. Thus the type prefigures the anti-type and is connected to it and is fully understood through the anti-type.[46] Minister Farrakhan affirms that the Honorable Elijah Muhammad is alive! These statements are not allegorical or symbolic. His declaration speaks to the deepest testimony of faith and love for God and his teacher. Through them both, he is empowered. Those who take his words for allegory are unlearned on this subject. There are others who know the truth of scripture and understand Minister Farrakhan and his divine mission and the proper scriptural interpretation, but are moved by the spirit of arrogance, and in some instances the spirit of Satan, and teach other than the truth. The Holy Quran speaks of this and also the allegorical aspects of interpretation:

---

[45] Charles T. Fritsch. "Biblical typology." Bibliotheca sacra 104, no. 414 (April 1947): 214.
[46] Charles T. Fritsch. "Biblical typology." Bibliotheca sacra 104, no. 414 (April 1947): 215.

He it is Who has revealed the Book to thee; some of its verses are decisive — they are the basis of the Book — and others are allegorical. Then those in whose hearts is perversity follow the part of it which is allegorical, seeking to mislead, and seeking to give it (their own) interpretation. And none knows its interpretation save Allah, and those firmly rooted in knowledge. They say: We believe in it, it is all from our Lord. And none mind except men of understanding.[47]

When explaining the difference between typology and prophecy Fritsch writes,

Typology differs from prophecy in the strict sense of the term only in the means of prediction. Prophecy predicts mainly by means of the word, whereas typology predicts by institution, act or person. Herein lies also the difference between typology and symbolism, or between a type and a symbol. The symbol, whatever form it may take, merely teaches a truth, without predicting an actual realization of that truth. The symbolic actions of the prophets which were prophetic in character, were always accompanied by the interpretative word.[48]

The type manifests truth that is redemptive, whether an institution, place, or person, the type is representative of a divine meaning and purpose that is to be fulfilled through the antitype. The type prefigures the anti-type and the truth that comes with the type validates the anti-type.[49] The type must be redemptive in its time and in the time of the fulfillment of the anti-type.[50] The Honorable Elijah Muhammad and

---

[47] Holy Quran 3:7, See Maulana Muhammad Ali's translation of the Holy Quran, footnote 387. "...when it is stated that the whole of the book is *mukham,* the meaning is that all of its verses are decisive, and when the Quran is called *mutashabih* (39:23), the meaning of it is that all of it is *conformable in its various parts.* In the verse under discussion is laid down the important principle how verses susceptible to different interpretations may be interpreted so that a decisive significance can be attached to them. The Quran we are told, establishes certain principles in clear words which are to be taken as the basis, while there are statements made in allegorical words or susceptible to different meanings, the interpretation of which must be in consonance, with the other parts and the spirit of the Book. In fact, this is true with every writing. When a certain law is laid down in a book in unmistakable words, any statement carrying a doubtful significance or one which is apparently opposed to the law must be interpreted subject to the principle enunciated."
[48] Fritsch, "Biblical Typology." 215-216.
[49] Ibid.," 220.
[50] Ibid., 221.

Minister Farrakhan have a significant importance to the typological references in the scriptures today; Bible and Holy Quran. Their redemptive work is just one of many qualifiers verifying the divinity of them both. In *The typological use of the Old Testament in the New Testament,* Walter R. Roehrs suggests,

> … [T]he term "typology" has come to be used generally as the concept denoting the predicted con-summation of God's plan to redeem lost mankind. It does have this advantage over other Biblical synonyms, in that it appears in the compound noun "antitype" to designate the fulfillment of what was prefigured …[51]

Roehrs also explains the relationship between various instances when referring to the word type:

> The Greek word *typos* is translated by a variety of English equivalents… It always denotes a reciprocal relationship between two objects, actions, or concepts having a specified feature in common. Their resemblance to one another, however, is not accidental but is produced by a deliberate purpose and design.[52]

Typology therefore is rooted in the power of God to bring understanding of His purpose to a suffering people who have gone astray from the path of righteousness. Who is Louis Farrakhan that the resemblance of the Honorable Elijah Muhammad is so clear, that when you see him you see Elijah Muhammad? This resemblance is produced by the "deliberate purpose and design" of Allah (God), and the continued obedience of Minister Farrakhan to his teacher. The preparation that it takes to make a man like Minister Farrakhan goes far beyond his physical birth.

---

[51] Walter R. Roehrs, "The typological use of the Old Testament in the New Testament." *Concordia Journal* 10, no. 6 (November 1984): 213.

[52] Roehrs, "The typological use of the Old Testament ", 214.

We can agree that every human being who is a believer in a 'Supreme Being', has the belief in mind that they (in one way or another) are being guided and made better by God directly. This is often viewed in relationship to the scriptures that the prophets brought and the wisdom that a person gets from them. In some way people believe that they have a personal relationship with God. They also believe, and it is accepted that the two books Bible and Holy Quran are from God. Even though God did not write these scriptures himself; He authorized them. It is accepted that he is the author and is behind their production. If this is true, and men have been written of in both Bible and Holy Quran before they were born; what about today? The Old and New Testaments of the Bible, as well as the scriptures of the Holy Quran were established by Allah (God) with Minister Farrakhan in mind.

2.2   *Laws and Rules of Interpretation*

From a typological perspective, there are parallel meanings to the events, and persons mentioned in scripture that are somewhat *double* or even *multiple* in their appearance. This is a principle that is important when determining the relevance of prophesies:

> Few laws are more important to observe in the interpretation of prophetic Scriptures than the law of double reference. Two events, widely separated as to the time of their fulfillment, may be brought together into the scope of one prophecy. This was done because the prophet had a message for his own day as well as for a future time. By brining two widely separated events into the scope of the prophecy both purposes could be fulfilled.[53]

Prophecies usually have multiple meanings as mentioned by Pentecost,

---

[53] Pentecost, *Things to Come*, 46.

The same prophecies frequently have a double meaning, and refer to different events, the one near, the other remote; the one temporal, the other spiritual or perhaps eternal. The prophets thus having events in view, their expressions may be partly applicable to one, and partly to another, and it is not always easy to make the transitions. What has not been fulfilled in the first, we must apply to the second; and what has already been fulfilled, may often be considered as typical of what remains to be accomplished.[54]

This type of double reference can be applied to Minister Farrakhan and the Honorable Elijah Muhammad as with the Honorable Elijah Muhammad and Master W. Fard Muhammad. Therefore, it is proper to say that the Honorable Elijah Muhammad is the Mahdi and has been given power as God over pharaoh and his people. This is seen in scripture and is also demonstrated in the work of the Honorable Elijah Muhammad.[55]

Double Reference – The principle by which two events or people that are divinely connected in type, refer to one another in meaning, purpose and fulfillment.

Would it be appropriate to say by applying this rule that Minister Farrakhan is the Messiah? He certainly without doubt represents Aaron. It was Aaron who was chosen by Allah (God) to assist Moses in his absence. Aaron was the first *high priest* in Leviticus. It was Aaron's covenant with Allah (God) as a representative of Moses that permitted him to walk into the Holy of Holies and establish the Day of Atonement,

---

[54] Pentecost, *Things to Come*, 46-47.
[55] "And the LORD said unto Moses, See, I have made thee a god to Pharaoh: and Aaron thy brother shall be thy prophet. Thou shalt speak all that I command thee: and Aaron thy brother shall speak unto Pharaoh, that he send the children of Israel out of his land." Exodus 7:1-2.

through the Order of Melchizedek.[56] This is the same Melchizedek that met with Abram and blessed him. David came through this Order.[57]

Jesus according to the Bible came through this elite Order, but many did not understand. This refers to the Honorable Elijah Muhammad and also applies to Minister Farrakhan, not the Prophet Jesus of two thousand years ago. Hebrews 5:7-13 clearly explains this and further explains why and warns of an eventual falling away:

> During the days of Jesus' life on earth, he offered up prayers and petitions with loud cries and tears to the one who could save him from death, and he was heard because of his reverent submission. Although he was a son, he learned obedience from what he suffered and, once made perfect, he became the source of eternal salvation for all who obey him and was designated by God to be high priest in the order of Melchizedek. We have much to say about this, but it is hard to explain because you are slow to learn. In fact, though by this time you ought to be teachers, you need someone to teach you the elementary truths of God's word all over again. You need milk, not solid food! Anyone who lives on milk, being still an infant, is not acquainted with the teaching about righteousness.

These events are examples of how double references can be viewed in scripture between two people who are similar in work and function, but in a different time. In this case, the prophecy applies to the Honorable Elijah Muhammad and Minister Farrakhan equally. The Honorable Elijah Muhammad at this point does not represent Moses to the people as he did when he was present working in America. He has ascended, and now serves a different role and function, as Minister Farrakhan does too. This speaks to the fulfillment of Minister Farrakhan's destiny and identity as Messiah and much more. This is debated by the scholars as the *Messianic Secret*, except that they argue

---

[56] Genesis 14:17-19.
[57] Psalm 110:3-5.

about the Prophet Jesus of two thousand years ago instead of the living example in front of their faces.

Diagram 1. shows the relationship between *events* or *types* of prophecy and their fulfillment. The double reference that applies to Event 1 and 2 (types) have what I termed a **Transitional Dependency**[58] that affects the outcome or fulfillment of Event 3; the antitype.

Transitional Dependency - The transitioning of functions, roles, and identities in relation to types and anti-types and their dependency on each other in the fulfillment of scripture.

Transitional Dependency is the working relationship between types, from the inception of prophesy to the transitioning of fulfillment, including the dependency that the types have on each other. During the transition period, the first two types are fulfilled by the third type (antitype) and this is what I will term *"multiplicity"*. There are *multiple* dependencies in the fulfillment of types even when the anti-type appears to have fulfilled the other types (See Diagram 1). This is not the same as the *Three-Fold Principle*, which is the revelation of scripture as it pertains to the past, present and future.

As mentioned previously, Pentecost explained the multiplicity of fulfillment and prophesies in the second element of prophecy:

> The fact that the matter of prophecy is given in the form of intuition also furnishes the reason why it always sees the realization of that matter in particular events which are complete in themselves; i.e., a prophecy may appear as just one event, but in reality there may be a two-, three-, or four fold fulfillment.[59]

---

[58] I use this term to explain the relationship of type and anti-types and their dependency on each other, but specifically in my observation of the work of Minister Farrakhan and the Honorable Elijah Muhammad.

[59] Pentecost, *Things to Come*, 45.

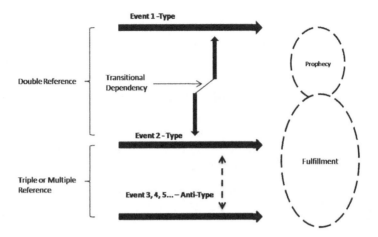

Diagram 1: Transitional Dependency of Type and Anti-type (Diagram by M.T. Muhammad)

Cahill outlines what he considers to be the *characteristics of typology:*

1. In all instances of typology there is historical continuity between type and antitype. The work of Adam and of Christ occurs in a temporally-united sequence, a temporal order. There is an intrinsic historical connection, so much so that it would seem that the creation of Adam almost necessitates the sending of Christ. The type looks forward though the authors and the actors do not understand the typological significance.

2. The type represents an acceptable level of truth in its own time and place but there are always occasional hints of more to come which are then verified by the antitype which intensifies and augments the truth.

3. All the figures or types in the OT coalesce into the one antitype, the person of Christ who is the one God, the one man, the one Lamb, the one tree of life, the one temple. There is a religious and poetic identification of type and antitype. The antitype realizes the eschatological dimensions of the biblical promises and suggests that "entry into Paradise is presented not as something kept for the last day, but as realized here and now in Christ," thus suggesting a tension at the very heart of human existence, fulfillment, and promise. This reminds

the interpreter that typology is not an exegetical method but rather the result of a conviction that salvation had taken place in the end-time through Jesus Christ.[60]

The above mentioned is why Cahill suggests that typology is not an exegetical method. The fourth characteristic described by Cahill is what scholars have called *creative vision* and suggests that this form of typology links the present and the past with a typological perception that is divine.[61] This divine perception links the type and the anti-type into an order that imposes itself on the historical events of the past and transforms the history of the past into a form of Theophany.[62] This form called Theophany is when God appears to a person, either by vision, or in person. This was demonstrated in September 1931 when the Honorable Elijah Muhammad met Master Fard Muhammad and once again when Minister Farrakhan met with the Honorable Elijah Muhammad in his vision experience on the Wheel.

Hermeneutical interpretations of typology centers on,

1. The nature of history
2. The minds ability to comprehend the prophecy
3. The student's commitment to understanding scriptural traditions

Concentrated study of God's wisdom in scripture, including the history and traditions are important, and how the scriptures are manifested is critical. Typological events may appear random, but typology sees the divine connection to a supreme God, thus Divine insight is required to have perception of the connection between the past and the present, and

---

[60] Cahill, "Hermeneutical implications of typology." 273.
[61] Ibid.
[62] Ibid., 275.

the spiritual and the carnal.[63] The process of typology shows that tradition does not operate alone, but must include a spiritual and magnetic perspective during interpretation that is a part of divine revelation.[64] The study of types involves a divine purpose manifested in scripture, which is rooted in the revelation of God to man and the redemption of man by God.[65] Fritsch explains:

> … [T]ypology is not a matter of collecting all of the resemblances between the Old and New Testaments, but rather of understanding the underlying redemptive and revelational [sic] process which begins in the Old Testament and finds its fulfillment in the New.[66]

There are other important rules that will help student explore the scriptures with a different view that gives insight into revelation and insight into the time of prophecy. It is also important to understand the relationship of Bible and Holy Quran and even closer, the understanding of the scriptures in these books separately.

[63] Cahill, "Hermeneutical implications of typology." 275.
[64] Ibid., 278.
[65] Fritsch, "Biblical Typology", 219.
[66] Ibid., 220.

This Page Intentionally Left Blank

3   The Mother Plane, Prophets, and Visions from God

3.1   *Visions from God, the Wheel, and Its Power*

This chapter offers some insight on the Bible and makes the connection of the divine role and purpose of the Mother Plane, including its relationship to Minister Farrakhan. The purpose of the use of typology here involves providing understanding on specific scriptures of the Bible, linking them to the redemptive plan of God today, but as taught by the Honorable Elijah Muhammad. There were many Close Encounters with the wheels by the prophets in the Bible. These encounters are *types* that foreshadow events and experiences today and they are directly connected to Minister Farrakhan and the Nation of Islam. Abraham, Ezekiel, Jesus and other Biblical characters appear to have had close encounters with the Wheel. It is very important that the reader understands that so called Unidentified Flying Objects (UFO) or flying saucers are not new to the planet earth and that the knowledge, wisdom, and technology on these wheels are far greater than what is present in this world today. Minister Farrakhan's vision took place on the Mother Wheel, which is viewed by many as an alien UFO. The Wheel exercises unparalleled and unimaginable power. This is the same power that backed the Honorable Elijah Muhammad, and it is the same power that backs Minister Farrakhan and the Nation of Islam.

The ongoing controversy of so-called UFO's has caused many people to question the reality of this phenomenon and also the validity of Minister Farrakhan's announcement and vision experience. Despite thousands of witnesses and sightings, the question remains; Are UFO's real? This is an important point to understand when approaching Minister Farrakhan's experience. In the midst of all the controversy, it has not been brought forth in a public discourse (except by the Nation of Islam) what the Honorable Elijah Muhammad has taught his followers on the subject since the 1930's. These UFO's are not "unidentified" but are "identified" and are in fact a result of the majesty of Master W. F. Muhammad (Elijah Muhammad's teacher).

According to the Honorable Elijah Muhammad, these objects were made on earth by the command and authority of Master W. F. Muhammad. Master W. F. Muhammad taught the Honorable Elijah Muhammad the origin of these wheel shaped space craft. In fact he showed them to him. The Honorable Elijah Muhammad taught that this plane is the Mother of all planes, because it is the type of plane that was used before the making of this present world.[67] The world media has covered all types of stories, and ufologists have interviewed thousands of people who have claimed to see the Wheel and its smaller planes.[68] There are thousands of publically viewable videos showing these wheels, and many governments throughout the world have opened their archives to the public. To leak the truth of the Mother Plane or Wheel, is to confirm what Minister Farrakhan has taught publicly on the subject; especially since his announcement that he visited this Wheel in 1985, and all that he has taught recently in his 58 week lectures series, *The Time and What Must be Done*. It will further confirm that everything Minister Farrakhan has taught about the Honorable Elijah Muhammad being PHYSICALLY alive on the Great Mother Wheel is true.

---

[67] Elijah Muhammad, *The Fall of America.* (Chicago, IL: Muhammad's Temple 2.1973), 236.

[68] Captain Kenju Terauchi, an airplane pilot for Japan Airline also had a spectacular encounter with the modern Mother Plane built by Master Fard Muhammad. On November 17th, 1986 while on flying flight JAL1628, Captain Terauchi (a veteran pilot of 29 years), saw the Wheel and said in his testimony, "It was very big one or two times bigger than an aircraft carrier." He watched the aircraft for 6 minutes before reporting it, but encountered it for at least 30 minutes. (See Figures 2-3) With the permission of the FAA he maneuvered his airplane and was able to get a better view of the object. As the object followed him, Terauchi reported that it came to a complete stop in the air. The FAA and the US Air Force noted that they were able to identify the airplane and another object on their radars.

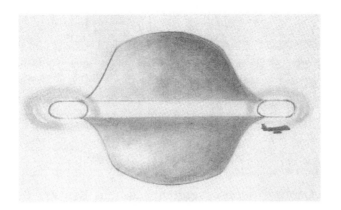

Figure 2: Artist rendition of the Mother Plane as seen by Capt. Kenju Terauchi

The Honorable Elijah Muhammad taught for 44 years that what the world calls "unidentified" are in fact "identified" wheels and have been on the planet for many years, even before the present day Wheel made by Master Fard Muhammad.

> The same type of plane was used by the Original God to put mountains on His planet. Allah (God) Who came in the person of Master Fard Muhammad, to Whom all Praises are due forever, is wiser than any god before Him as the Bible and Holy Quran teach us. He taught me that this plane will be used to raise mountains on the planet (earth). The mountains that he will put on the earth will not be very high. He will raise these mountains to a height of one (1) mile over the United States of America.[69]

The Honorable Elijah Muhammad spoke of having an intimate relationship with the creator of the Mother Wheel, who he said is God in person. Although religions throughout the world often indicate in their history that their communities, prophets, sages, and warner's encountered "extraterrestrial" flying objects and even beings; Elijah Muhammad and the Nation of Islam have been ridiculed on this subject.

---

[69] Muhammad, *The Fall of America*, 236.

Ilia Rashad Muhammad, in his writing *UFO's and the Nation of Islam: The Source, Proof, and Reality of the Wheels* points out,

> If theologians acknowledge UFO's as a reality, they would have to acknowledge the entity that introduced these crafts to the modern world. To do so would force religions to accept the fact that a mild manner Black man from Georgia may have actually met the Supreme Being.[70]

Does what the Honorable Elijah Muhammad teach have any relevance to the discussions of these sightings around the world? Does his teaching on the subject of these flying wheels impact the religious world and the prophecies in any way? Absolutely! There are many skeptics and doubters of the reality of the Mother Plane. Why hasn't the Honorable Elijah Muhammad's teachings been considered? In some instances it is arrogance. Sometimes it is ignorance. In the ufologist's community it is not considered that Black people, (descendants of slaves) may be connected to the wheel like ships appearing all over America. However, their lack of consideration of what the Honorable Elijah Muhammad teaches on these wheels does not dismiss the fact that the Nation of Islam was the first to announce, offer and confirm the knowledge of these flying objects. Not only as an integral part of its theology, but also as the leading subject matter experts addressing many questions that modern religion, science and education have yet to answer.[71] Some of this knowledge refers specifically to the prophecies of the Bible and Holy Quran. These prophecies include men and women, and in general nations that will experience sightings, and first hand encounters with these objects. Minister Farrakhan's vision experience on the little wheels and the BIG Wheel is such an encounter. This was

---

[70] Ilia Rashad Muhammad, **UFO's and The Nation of Islam: The Source, Proof, and Reality of the Wheels**. (Memphis, TN: Nation Brothers. 2013), 6,
[71] Ibid., 7.

seen in the history of Prophet Muhammad over 1,400 years ago in his *Night Journey.* Tynnetta Muhammad elaborates,

> The sign of Muhammad's ascension into the seventh heavens over 1,400 years ago took place at this same sacred sight and serves as a sign of the Night Journey and Ascension of the Honorable Elijah Muhammad in 1975. Ten years later, the Honorable Minister Louis Farrakhan experienced his ascension into a great Metallic Wheel and City in the sky called the Mother Plane in Tepoztlan, Mexico in 1985. Note that the number and the date 1975, contains (975) which equals Surah 97, containing five verses. This Surah is entitled, "The Night of Majesty." From the date 975, we have the foundation of Al-Azhar Mosque and University in Cairo, Egypt. Counting forward 1,000 years, we come to the date of the Honorable Elijah Muhammad's departure in 1975. The one thousandth month referred to in this chapter equals approximately 83 years in a century that equals nearly the same time when the Honorable Minister Farrakhan had his own Night Journey to the Great Mother Plane where he communed with the Honorable Elijah Muhammad.[72]

This type of revelation and sign of the Mother Plane and its divine connection to Minister Farrakhan and the Honorable Elijah Muhammad can be seen throughout history.

3.2   The Wheel and the Prophecies of the Bible

Minister Farrakhan's vision experience bears witness that the Honorable Elijah Muhammad is physically alive and is the basis of his declaration that his teacher is the exalted Christ of Almighty God. This reality is concealed in the true identity of the prophetic figure called Jesus. I will elaborate on this later in this writing.

---

[72] Tynnetta Muhammad, Unveiling the Number 19: Bright Object Photographed Over the Dome of the Rock in Jerusalem—Sign of the Changeover of Worlds, *FinalCall.Com*, 2/14/2011. http://www.finalcall.com/artman/publish/Columns_4/article_7611.shtml

But Nay I call to witness the stars, That run their course (and) hide themselves, And the night when it departs, And the morning when it brightens, Most surely it is the word of an honoured Apostle, The possessor of strength, having an honourable place with the Lord of Dominion, One (to be) obeyed and faithful in trust. And your companion is not gone mad. And of the truth he saw himself on the clear horizon. Nor of the unseen is he a tenacious concealer. Nor is it the word of the cursed devil.[73]

In vision or dream experiences of the characters in the Bible; the visions are usually followed by the appearance of a flying object or saucer like vehicle observed as a sign of God's power. This power is often shown to the prophet as a sign of God's power to destroy His enemies and save His people.[74] This type of Wheel is the same type that Abraham witnessed when he fell into a deep sleep and experienced a vision or dream, which soon followed with communication from God.[75] Genesis 15:17 appears to be the first sighting or experience with a flying object in the Bible by a prophet. These both have striking similarities to a sighting by Roman historian Julio Obsequens as documented in his book "Prodigiorum Liber" or Book of Prodigies.

"Something like a sort of weapon, or missile, rose with a great noise from the earth and soared into the sky."

---

[73] **Holy Quran 81:15-25.** This is the 1917 translation of Mualvi Muhammad Ali. This edition is the first translated edition given to the Honorable Elijah Muhammad by Master Fard Muhammad according to the Honorable Elijah Muhammad words, August 20, 1972.

[74] **Numbers 12:5 NIV** - Now Moses was a very humble man, more humble than anyone else on the face of the earth.) At once the LORD said to Moses, Aaron and Miriam, "Come out to the tent of meeting, all three of you." So the three of them went out. Then the LORD came down in a pillar of cloud; he stood at the entrance to the tent and summoned Aaron and Miriam. When the two of them stepped forward, he said, "Listen to my words: "When there is a prophet among you, I, the LORD, reveal myself to them in visions, I speak to them in dreams.

[75] See **Genesis 15:12 – 17**.

This craft also has the appearance of what is called in the Bible, "a flying roll".[76] This flying roll was described as being "*the length thereof is twenty cubits, and the breadth thereof ten cubits*", which is thirty-five (35) feet long and eighteen feet in breadth. In Exodus 13:21-22, the flying craft changed in appearance by day and night. This has been reported throughout the earth where witnesses have seen very large clouds that seem to have masked some type of object. The mother Wheel or ship is the most mysterious of wheels in the way of military science and is made to work as a military device.[77] In the book of Exodus the object that appeared followed the Israelites and protected them.[78] This was not an ethereal experience but a real prophetic one. Elijah Muhammad prophetically fulfilled this type of protection from God, as does Minister Farrakhan, and Original people in America. This craft was controlled by living beings that Moses was familiar with intimately.

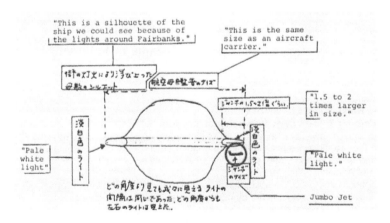

Figure 3: Drawing by Capt. Kenju Terauchi of the Mother Plane with translated notes, November 1986.

---

[76] See **Zechariah 5:1-2**, "Then I turned, and lifted up mine eyes, and looked, and behold a flying roll. And he said unto me, What seest thou? And I answered, I see a flying roll; the length thereof is twenty cubits, and the breadth thereof ten cubits."
[77] Elijah Muhammad et al., "Inside of Ezekiel's Wheel - Part V," *Muhammad Speaks*, September 21, 1973.
[78] See **Exodus 14:19-20**.

This dreadful plane is a sign and will be used to destroy the wicked rulers who oppose God and the righteous. [79] In Exodus 14:24, the Lord watch the Egyptians "through the pillar of fire and of the cloud" and disrupted their plans against Moses. [80] The people witnessed these flying vessels in the sky and were moved by their presence. These wheels stayed for long periods of time, as they do today and come and go as they please. [81] They provided assistance to the people of God in the way of deliverance. [82] In 2Samuel 22:10, God flew on a cherub on the winds, [83] which also represents some type of flight. In Psalm 66:32-33 God rides on the heavens. [84] How could this be possible if God was not in some sort of vehicle? The Honorable Elijah Muhammad taught that God is a man and that He can be nothing else, except a man. [85] In the Bible God is witnessed by the people as always in flight, in the air, on clouds, in clouds and demonstrating power from the heavens. Bible and Holy Quran use symbols and codes to describe the characteristics of God and the vessel that He travels in. It is described as a bird in Isaiah, [86] and as an eagle in Jeremiah. [87]

---

[79] Muhammad, *The Fall of America*, 236.

[80] Also see **Nehemiah 9:12**

[81] See **Numbers 9:20-21 (New International Version)** – "Sometimes the cloud was over the tabernacle only a few days; at the LORD's command they would encamp, and then at his command they would set out. Sometimes the cloud stayed only from evening till morning, and when it lifted in the morning, they set out. Whether by day or by night, whenever the cloud lifted, they set out." Also see Isaiah 19:1, Numbers 9:17; 10:11; 11:17; 11:25; 12:5

[82] See **Deuteronomy 1:33** "In spite of this, you did not trust in the LORD your God, who went ahead of you on your journey, in fire by night and in a cloud by day, to search out places for you to camp and to show you the way you should go."

[83] See **Samuel 22:10-11 (NIV)**, "He parted the heavens and came down; dark clouds were under his feet. He mounted the cherubim and flew; he soared on the wings of the wind." Also see, **Psalms 18:10**.

[84] See **Psalm 66:32-33**, "Sing to God, you kingdoms of the earth, sing praise to the Lord, to him who rides across the highest heavens, the ancient heavens, who thunders with mighty voice."

[85] Muhammad, *Message to the Blackman*, 6.

[86] See **Isaiah 35:5** "Like birds hovering overhead, the LORD Almighty will shield Jerusalem; he will shield it and deliver it, he will 'pass over' it and will rescue it." See Isaiah 60:8 "Who are these that fly along like clouds, like doves to their nests?"

[87] **Jeremiah 48:40 (KJV)** "For thus saith the LORD; Behold, he shall fly as an eagle, and shall spread his wings over Moab." **Isaiah 49:22 (KJV)**, "Behold, he shall come up and fly as the eagle, and spread his wings over Bozrah: and at that day shall the heart of the mighty men of Edom be as the heart of a woman in her pangs."

In the year that King Uzziah died, I saw the Lord, high and exalted, seated on a throne; and the train of his robe filled the temple. Above him were seraphim, each with six wings: With two wings they covered their faces, with two they covered their feet, and with two they were flying.[88]

These vehicles carried the hosts of God as it did with Gabriel and witnessed by Daniel as the angel Gabriel was taken up onto the Wheel.[89] This has a similar reference to Minister Farrakhan's vision experience where his companions, witnessed him go to the Wheel. As Gabriel goes up, God also comes down in the visions of Daniel, which shows that the Holy One "comes" down, but from what?[90] How did Daniel see the Holy One come down from heaven? Who is the Holy One? Certainly this has many meanings, but in order for the Holy One to come down; he must be coming from a place that is high. The Honorable Elijah Muhammad said of this Holy One;

> …Habakkuk saw the Holy One from Mount Paran. This is also earthly, somewhere in Arabia. Here the Bible makes a difference between God and another person who is called the Holy One. Which one should we take for our God? For one is called God, while another One is called Holy One. The Holy One: His glory covered the heavens and the earth was full of His praise. It has been a long time since the earth was full of praise for a Holy One.[91]

> **Daniel 4:23 NIV-** Your Majesty saw a holy one, a messenger, coming down from heaven and saying, 'Cut down the tree and destroy it, but leave the stump, bound with iron and bronze, in the grass of the field, while its roots remain in the ground. Let him be drenched with the dew

---

[88] See **Isaiah 6:1-2**.
[89] **Daniel 9:21 (KJV)** – "Yea, whiles I was speaking in prayer, even the man Gabriel, whom I had seen in the vision at the beginning, being caused to fly swiftly, touched me about the time of the evening oblation."
[90] **Daniel 4:13 (KJV)** "I saw in the visions of my head upon my bed, and, behold, a watcher and an holy one came down from heaven."
[91] Muhammad, **Message to the Blackman**, 7.

of heaven; let him live with the wild animals, until seven times pass by for him.'

Jesus is one of the key characters in the Bible, who interacts with flying vehicles in the sky. Like Ezekiel, Jesus sees the vehicle, but has a more intimate experience like the prophet Elijah and is actually taken up onto the flying vehicle. Like Moses though, Jesus returns in the same flying object. The references are identified as "coming in a cloud", all of this which is to take place in the last days, or the end of time.[92] In Matthew 26:24, the same Jesus is seen having power of the Lord, but "coming down" in the clouds and as a ghost, but as the Son of Man. The phrase "Son of Man" in its Aramaic *"bar enash"* means *human being*.[93] In Mark 14:62 while Jesus was before the Sanhedrin, the high priest ask if he was the Christ. This question was proposed before his crucifixion in Mark. Even here, Jesus makes specific reference to a Mighty One, coming to them on the clouds of heaven.

> **Mark 14:57-62 (NIV)** -Then some stood up and gave this false testimony against him: "We heard him say, 'I will destroy this temple made with human hands and in three days will build another, not made with hands.'" Yet even then their testimony did not agree. Then the high priest stood up before them and asked Jesus, "Are you not going to answer? What is this testimony that these men are bringing against you?" But Jesus remained silent and gave no answer. Again the high priest asked him, "Are you the Messiah, the Son of the Blessed One?" "I

---

[92] See **Matthew 24:30**, "Then will appear the sign of the Son of Man in heaven. And then all the peoples of the earth will mourn when they see the Son of Man coming on the clouds of heaven, with power and great glory." Also, **Daniel 7:13 NIV** - "In my vision at night I looked, and there before me was one like a son of man, coming with the clouds of heaven. He approached the Ancient of Days and was led into his presence.

[93] Also see; **Matthew 26:64 NIV** – "You have said so," Jesus replied. "But I say to all of you: From now on you will see the Son of Man sitting at the right hand of the Mighty One and coming on the clouds of heaven." **Mark 13:26 NIV**- "At that time people will see the Son of Man coming in clouds with great power and glory. And he will send his angels and gather his elect from the four winds, from the ends of the earth to the ends of the heavens"

am," said Jesus. "And you will see the Son of Man sitting at the right hand of the Mighty One and coming on the clouds of heaven."

This makes specific reference to a future event that is to take place. This is not a historical event. Who is the "Blessed One"? Why in Mark's account, would Jesus acknowledge that he was the Christ prior to ascension? In Luke there is a similar event that takes place with the appearance of the Son of Man in the clouds.

> **Luke 21:25-27 (NIV)** - There will be signs in the sun, moon and stars. On the earth, nations will be in anguish and perplexity at the roaring and tossing of the sea. People will faint from terror, apprehensive of what is coming on the world, for the heavenly bodies will be shaken. At that time they will see the Son of Man coming in a cloud with power and great glory.

The Honorable Elijah Muhammad taught of the great military power of the Wheel and also of its power to create and heal. He explained that the Wheel will be used to destroy the wicked and that the wicked rulers of the earth have this knowledge and work to try to shoot down the Mother Wheel and its smaller wheels. In the Bible the wicked were aware of God's presence and were always told by His prophets of the great power of God in the sky.

> Now the white man has cast his eyes into space (the sky), to conquer it, and he is doing that. The white race, having knowledge of what they may expect today, they are spending billions of dollars on space travel. He has now brought the moon to him and seen some of the stars. The main thing I guess you are thinking is: Can he win against God, if God and His Prophets have foretold the outcome of this battle in the sky? It is impossible for the white race to win. What makes it impossible for them to win is because they have not the power of the forces of nature,

while the power of the forces of nature is in the Hands of God making it impossible for the white man to win a war of this sort.[94]

In 1Thessalonians[95] it further speaks to the divine connection of the righteous to these wheels by clearly describing a meeting with the "Lord in the air." This is another aspect of the teaching of the Honorable Elijah Muhammad that should be carefully analyzed. His "departure" or escape to Master Fard Muhammad, on the Wheel, was masterly arranged by God himself. The alleged death of Elijah Muhammad confused the entire world. This ascension or meeting of the Lord "in the air" will also happen with Minister Farrakhan, a second time just as it was when Jesus ascended. [96] Ezekiel, the prophet of the 6th century, experienced seven visions during a twenty-two year period; from 593 to 571 BCE, during exile in Babylon.[97] Several of these visions were specific to his vision experience with what is termed a "Wheel". The Honorable Elijah Muhammad explains;

> The vision of Ezekiel's wheel in a wheel in the sky is true if carefully understood. There is a similar wheel in the sky today which very well answers the description of Ezekiel's vision. This wheel corresponds in a way with the sphere of spheres called the universe. The Maker of the universe is Allah (God) the Father of the Black nation which includes the brown, yellow, and red people. The Great Wheel which many of us see in the sky today is not so much a wheel as one may think in such terms, but rather a place made like a wheel. The like of this wheel-like plane was never seen before. You cannot build one like it and get the same results. Your brains are limited. If you would make one to look like it, you could not get it up off the earth into outer space. The similar Ezekiel's wheel is a masterpiece of mechanics. Maybe I should not say the wheel is similar to Ezekiel's vision of a wheel, but that Ezekiel's vision has become a reality. His vision of the wheel included hints on the Great Wisdom of Almighty God (Allah); that really He is the Maker

---

[94] Elijah Muhammad, *The Mother Plane* (Cleveland, OH: Secretarius Memps Publications, 1995), 2.
[95] See **1Thessalonians** 4:15-17.
[96] Also see; Hebrews 8:1; Revelation 1:7; Jeremiah 4:13;
[97] See Ezekiel 1:1 NIV.

of the universe, and reveals just where and how the decisive battle would take place (in the sky).[98]

What makes his experience even worth discussing? Why is it of any importance if this vision/experience happened thousands of years ago? Ezekiel's vision is not like the common experiences of other prophets, especially since it occurred on the exact same month and day of Minister Farrakhan's vision; September 17th.[99] There are ongoing discussions among theologians, scientist and scholars about the unique experience of the Prophet Ezekiel, since his prophecies are the most dated, and most descriptive of any of the scriptures in the Old Testament. The Lord even instructs Ezekiel to record specific dates and sends him out to warn the people.[100] The Honorable Elijah Muhammad was shown this Wheel and has described this Wheel in great detail. He not only describes the shape, make and other details of the Wheel, he also elaborates on the purpose of the Wheel and the pilots,

> The present wheel-shaped plane known as the Mother of Planes is one-half mile of a half mile and is the largest mechanical man-made object in the sky. It is a small human planet made for the purpose of destroying the present world of the enemies of Allah. The cost to build such a plane is staggering! The finest brains were used to build it. It is capable of staying in outer space six to twelve months at a time without coming into the earth's gravity. It carried fifteen hundred bombing planes with most deadliest explosives the type used in bringing up mountains on the earth. The very same method is to be used in the destruction of this world. The bombs are equipped with motors and the toughest of steel was used in making them. This steel drills and takes the bombs into the

---

[98] Muhammad, *Message to the Blackman,* 290.
[99] See Ezekiel 8:1-4. Most scholars and theologians agree that, "In the sixth month on the fifth day", represented in the modern Gregorian calendar, September 17th, 592. According to scholars Kenneth L. Baker, John H. Stek (with contributions from Mark Hillmer) in the revised edition of the NIV Study Bible; the prophecy mentioned in Ezekiel can be "dated with considerable precision." They agree that modern scholarship using archaeology (Babylonian annals on cuneiform tablets) and astronomy (precise dates of eclipse found in ancient archives) can provide *precise modern calendar equivalents.*
[100] See Ezekiel 24:2.

earth at a depth of one mile and is timed not to explode until it reaches one mile into the earth. This explosion produces a mountain one mile high; not one bomb will fall into water. They will all fall on cities. As Ezekiel saw and heard in his vision of it (Chapter 10:2) the plane is terrible. It is seen but do not think of trying to attack it. That would be suicide! The small circular-made planes called flying saucers, which are so much talked of being seen, could be from this Mother Plane. This is only one of the things in store for the white man's evil world. Believe it or believe it not! This is to warn you and me to fly to our own God and people.[101]

To reiterate, next to what was taught by the Honorable Elijah Muhammad, Ezekiel's experience is one of the most descriptive sightings ever documented; except it was a vision. A vision experience does not discredit the authenticity of the sighting. This type of experience like Minister Farrakhan's experience is very powerful. In Ezekiel 1:19, the Wheel according to Ezekiel had control over the four creatures and according to the Honorable Elijah Muhammad these four creatures are Gods chosen people.

There are five great powers of the nations of the earth. These five Powers are the Black, Brown, Yellow, Red and White. Of the four Original Powers, the Red is not an equal Power. The vision shows the four creatures being lifted up from the earth. When the wheel was lifted up, they were lifted up and when the wheel stood, they stood. This means that they waited upon the movement of the wheel.[102]

In Ezekiel 10:2, God spoke to a man clothed in linen, "Go in among the wheels beneath the cherubim. Fill your hands with burning coals from among the cherubim and scatter them over the city." Ezekiel then says, "And as I watched, he went in." Elijah Muhammad explains;

[101] Muhammad, **Message to the Blackman,** 291.
[102] Muhammad, **The Fall of America,** 238.

In Ezekiel's vision concerning the wheel, he said that he heard the voice of one tell the other to take coals of fire and to scatter it over the cities; this means bombs. It could mean fire too, however. The Plane is to drop bombs which would automatically be timed to burrow quickly to a position of one mile below the surface of the earth where they are timed to explode. Allah (God) taught me that these bombs are not to be dropped into water. They are to be dropped only on the cities. It will be the work of the wheel. The wheel is the power of the four creatures, namely the four colors of the Black man (Black, brown, yellow and red). The Red Indian is to benefit also from the judgment of the world.[103]

Like Ezekiel, in the Book of Exodus over 3,500 years ago, Moses had an encounter with a flying object while fleeing Pharaoh who sought to kill the children of Israel. This Wheel appeared for the protection of Moses. This was not a historical incident, but represents the prophetic reality. The fulfillment of these Biblical references has a "double reference". Also, a "transitional dependency", as they are fulfilled in the work of the Honorable Elijah Muhammad and will continue to be fulfilled in Minister Farrakhan.[104] Nine hundred (900) years before Jesus, Prophet Elijah had an experience where he was taken up into one of the flying objects. He was completely aware of his meeting with his Lord, which further confirms prophetically, that one in the future like the Prophet Elijah would have an intimate relationship with the beings of these Wheels.

> **2Kings 2:1-11 NIV-** When the LORD was about to take Elijah up to heaven in a whirlwind, Elijah and Elisha were on their way from Gilgal. Elijah said to Elisha, "Stay here; the LORD has sent me to Bethel." But Elisha said, "As surely as the LORD lives and as you live, I will not

---

[103] Muhammad, *The Fall of America,* 238-39. Also see, Ezekiel 1:19; 3:12-14; 8:3-4; 10:15 -19; 11:1; 43:3-5.

[104] See **Numbers** 14:14 NIV- "And they will tell the inhabitants of this land about it. They have already heard that you, LORD, are with these people and that you, LORD, have been seen face to face, that your cloud stays over them, and that you go before them in a pillar of cloud by day and a pillar of fire by night." Also see, **Exodus** 13: 21-22; 14:19-24; 16:10; 19:9; 19:16; 24:15-18; 33:9; 34:5; 40:34-38. **Numbers** 9:15-18; 9:22; 10:11-15; 10:34-38; 16:42-45; 11:25.

leave you." So they went down to Bethel. The company of the prophets at Bethel came out to Elisha and asked, "Do you know that the LORD is going to take your master from you today?"

Figure 4: Betsy Jean Farrakhan describes here sighting of a Baby Plane. Photo from *Is It Possible that the Honorable Elijah Muhammad is Physically Alive*, by Jabril Muhammad.

"Yes, I know," Elisha replied, "so be quiet." Then Elijah said to him, "Stay here, Elisha; the LORD has sent me to Jericho." And he replied, "As surely as the LORD lives and as you live, I will not leave you." So they went to Jericho. The company of the prophets at Jericho went up to Elisha and asked him, "Do you know that the LORD is going to take your master from you today?" "Yes, I know," he replied, "so be quiet." Then Elijah said to him, "Stay here; the LORD has sent me to the Jordan." And he replied, "As surely as the LORD lives and as you live, I will not leave you." So the two of them walked on. Fifty men from the company of the prophets went and stood at a distance, facing the place where Elijah and Elisha had stopped at the Jordan. Elijah took his cloak, rolled it up and struck the water with it. The water divided to the right and to the left, and the two of them crossed over on dry ground. When they had crossed, Elijah said to Elisha, "Tell me, what can I do for you before I am taken from you?" "Let me inherit a double portion of your spirit," Elisha replied. "You have asked a difficult thing," Elijah said, "yet if you see me when I am taken from you, it will be yours— otherwise, it will not." As they were walking along and talking together, suddenly a chariot of fire and horses of fire appeared and separated the two of them, and Elijah went up to heaven in a whirlwind.

This event cited above was not something that happened almost 3000 years ago, but it foreshadows a future event that has taken place and will reoccur in the very near future. But, if there were a slight possibility that this did occur about 3,000 years ago, it only confirms and shows that the flying objects did exists. Ezekiel's intimate experience with God in the inner sanctum (Ezekiel 8:16) parallels what the Honorable Elijah Muhammad taught about the twenty-four scientists of Islam, mentioned in the New Testament.[105] But, here an extra person is included, like in Revelation 4.

> He then brought me into the inner court of the house of the LORD, and there at the entrance to the temple, between the portico and the altar, were about twenty-five men. With their backs toward the temple of the LORD and their faces toward the east, they were bowing down to the sun in the east.

These twenty-four elders, who were seen prostrating towards the east (as Muslims) represent God and the scientists that assist him. Ezekiel saw this just as John the Revelator, but centuries before him. In John's account, he describes a man entering heaven, and with great detail provides a description of what he witnessed.

> After this I looked, and there before me was a door standing open in heaven. And the voice I had first heard speaking to me like a trumpet said, "Come up here, and I will show you what must take place after this." At once I was in the Spirit, and there before me was a throne in heaven with someone sitting on it. And the one who sat there had the appearance of jasper and ruby. A rainbow that shone like an emerald encircled the throne. Surrounding the throne were twenty-four

---

[105] See Ezekiel 11:1. Here as with 8:16, the same twenty-five men are also witnessed in the house of the Lord facing the east.

other thrones, and seated on them were twenty-four elders. They were dressed in white and had crowns of gold on their heads. From the throne came flashes of lightning, rumblings and peals of thunder. In front of the throne, seven lamps were blazing. These are the seven spirits of God. Also in front of the throne there was what looked like a sea of glass, clear as crystal.[106]

Jesus and Prophet Muhammad had two of the most profound revelatory experiences in religion. Muhammad's night journey, although considered a spiritual experience by theologians and scholars, represents an encounter where the prophet not only traveled to Allah (God), but he also received revelation, and instructions related to the future of the Muslims and the world of Islam. The experience of the character Jesus in the Bible, similar to Prophet Muhammad was revelatory in nature and one where he received personal empowerment from God. This power extended to his disciples. Jesus' relationship to God in the Bible is so intimate that God places him over all things, except himself.

The Honorable Elijah Muhammad taught that out of all the history, the life of Prophet Jesus was the most confusing. He further taught, that if Black people knew the true knowledge of Jesus that they would be raised (enlightened) spiritually, overnight. What makes the historical figure Jesus so important? Why is a prophet that has been dead for over 2,000 years relevant to the spiritual rise of an entire race of people, and ultimately the entire world? This Jesus figure is raised to sit and rule the entire universe, by the permission of Allah (God).

In Matthew 28:1-4, Mary Magdalene and another Mary went to the tomb and saw Jesus come down from Heaven, others saw him come down too and his appearance frightened them. How did he come down from heaven? Was it on a flying vehicle? This was the return of Jesus

---

[106] See Revelation 4:1-6

after the crucifixion. But in Mark 16: 17-21, the disciples see Jesus go away as he is taken up into heaven and sat at the right hand of God. In Luke 2:11-17, at the birth of Jesus the angels came from heaven and spoke to the shepherds and told them of the birth of the Messiah. Where did the angels come from? Throughout the New Testament Jesus is "taken up" into heaven. How?[107] In John 16:55-66, Jesus instructed the disciples to teach what he was teaching and the disciples doubted that the people would understand. Jesus sensed their disbelief and spoke of his ascension, which he also knew some doubted. The language of the Bible, "ascend", "descend", "taken-up", and "comes down", is found throughout the New Testament.[108] These references are prophetic and are not specific to spirits only, but men.

---

[107] See Luke 24:45-51; Acts 1:1-2; 1:9-11; 1:22; Acts 10:10-16; 11:1-5; for Peters vision of the wheel; See 2Corinthians 12:4, Paul's experience of a man taken into Paradise; Jesus ascends in Ephesians 4:8; 1Peter 3:22.
[108] Also see, Revelation 3:12; 7:2; 11:11-12; 14:14 -16; 18:1; 20:1; 20:9; 21:10; Mark 1:10; 9:7-8, Luke 2:8-9; 3:21-22; 22:43. John 1:32; 1:51; 3:31; 6:33; 6:38; 6:51; 6:58. 1Thessalonians 4:16; 1Peter 1:12, 1Chronicles 21:16; Matthew 17:5.

This Page Intentionally Left Blank

4   Close Encounters of Antiquity

4.1   *Communication, Technology and History of Wheels*

Throughout history there have been cases of Close Encounters with flying objects from the sky. These objects often interacted with the people and this has been seen in historical writings, art, folklore, and in the oral traditions of various cultures, passed down from generation to generation. For a person who is less familiar with the Nation of Islam's teaching, this chapter will bring some understanding of just a few encounters with so-called UFO's in history. The significance of this topic is to show that, these flying objects are not new to our planet and through advanced communication they have interacted with the public. These flying objects are not fictitious. This is serious study and subject throughout the world. Governments have spent billions of dollars in research, and many people have spent their lives cataloging the countless "sightings" of eye witnesses of these UFO's. As a result of the increasing interests over the years, there are developed terms by which to identify the numerous types of encounters with the so-called UFO's. These are termed *Close Encounters*, and there are different *kinds* of encounters.

First Kind – A sighting of a so-called unidentified flying object (UFO) in a distance of at least 500 feet away that shows viewable details.

Second Kind – An event in which a person experiences physical effects of an encounter. Any physical trace of an encounter, including physiological effects, electronic interference, physical impressions on the earth surface, etc…

Third Kind - An encounter where living creatures/humanoids or occupants of a so-called UFO are present.

Fourth Kind – When a human is abducted or seized by a so-called UFO or its inhabitants. This includes non-abduction cases when dream or paranormal events are associated with the encounter.

Fifth Kind - An encounter with a so-called UFO that involves direct communication between extraterrestrials and humans. This is also called bilateral contact, which starts through some form of human-initiated communication with extraterrestrial intelligence.

These objects that are seen darting across the skies of the earth are not from another planet, but are from this planet earth. No one prior to the Honorable Elijah Muhammad taught of these space crafts, flying saucers, or so-called UFO's, until he began to speak on them in the 1930's. In fact the US did not begin to acknowledge the possibility that they even existed until the late 1940's, years after the Honorable Elijah Muhammad made mention of them. The Honorable Elijah Muhammad taught that Master Fard Muhammad made this Mother Wheel himself, and completed it in 1929. He used the finest minds of the world to build it in secret. He paid large sums of money in gold to complete this magnificent humanly built planet. History shows that these wheels have been seen for centuries. The US investigation of UFO occurrences grew from the first publically reported sighting in 1947 to the US Air Force's *Project Sign*, then to *Project Grudge* and then to the ever popular and longest lived US research inquiry on UFO's, *Project Blue Book.*[109] A *History.com* review elaborates,

> From 1952 to 1969 Project Blue Book compiled reports of more than 12,000 sightings or events, each of which was ultimately classified as (1) "identified" with a known astronomical, atmospheric, or artificial (human-caused) phenomenon or (2) "unidentified." The latter category, approximately 6 percent of the total, included cases for which there was insufficient information to make an identification with a known phenomenon.[110]

The facts show that the Honorable Elijah Muhammad was correct about the origin of these wheels, and if this is the case the facts will also show that Minister Farrakhan is connected to them too and has encountered them in the most supreme and divine way.

The ancient Samarians in their writings show advanced aircrafts of about 50,000 years ago. Alexander the Great observed flying objects in 329 BCE. The tenth Egyptian pharaoh of the 18th dynasty (Akhenaton) experienced and encountered what many consider to be extraterrestrial beings; close encounter of the Third Kind or possibly the Fifth Kind. Akhenaton (Amenhotep IV) during his reign established the worship of One God or Aten/Aton. This was represented by a Sun disk with 19 rays, and Akhenaton, along with his wife Nefertiti established the monotheistic worship of God. This drastic move away from Ma' at caused Akhenaton to be considered a heretic.[111] This eventually led to him being dethroned, along with the mysterious disappearance of his body[112] including his immediate family. The revolutionary reign of

---

[109] "History of UFO's" History.Com. Accessed July 2, 2014. http://www.history.com/topics/history-of-ufos

[110] History, "History of UFO's".

[111] Claire Gibson, *The Hidden Life of Ancient Egypt: Decoding the Secrets of a Lost* (New York: Fall River Press, 2009), 74.

[112] Ian Shaw and Paul Nicholson, *The Dictionary of Ancient Egypt* (New York, NY: Harry N. Abrams, Inc., 1995), 21.

Akhenaton has changed the face of Egypt. According to Tynnetta Muhammad,

> Akhenaton launched an unexpected and revolutionary period in Egypt, which was a direct threat to the Ammon priesthood and all other dynasties. According to the history of that period, Akhenaton died or was killed by his contemporaries after only 17 years of ruling with his Queen Nefertiti. Tutankhamun, along with another young boy named Smenkare, were regents of Akhenaton to be anointed as ruler after him. Smenkare was erased from the scene, leaving Tutankhamun as the "boy king." There is suspicion surrounding the fact that he was forced to return to the order of the Ammon priesthood, only to die shortly thereafter.[113]

There are also talks of Akhenaton's revolutionary change being of divine intervention, or extraterrestrial intervention. It has even been said that Akhenaton was of extraterrestrial birth and his birth prefigured the symbolic virgin birth of Jesus. I personally do not see these *extraterrestrials* as meaning from another planet, but from an elect circle of Gods. The elongated shape of his and his families heads have been compared to the 13 Crystal Skulls, similar to the Mayan and Incan people. These skulls may have a connection to the 13 tribes, and the one lost God tribe of Shabazz. These skulls are known to hold an advance technology that is being reawakened, and this is also connected to the region of the Himalayas near Tibet. This has great relevance to the teachings of the Honorable Elijah Muhammad. This also has significance to telepathic communication, and is a sign of the rulership of the Honorable Elijah Muhammad as the exalted Christ. How? The history and signs left by the ancients were clues for future generations.

---

[113] Tynnetta Muhammad, "Unveiling the Number 19: Tracing King Tut's Genealogy and the 18th Dynastic Age to Their Black Descendants Living in America Today," *FinalCall.Com*, June 21, 2006.
http://www.finalcall.com/artman/publish/Columns_4/Tracing_King_Tut_s_Genealogy_by_Mother_Tynnetta_Mu_2710.shtml

The power of the Crystal Skulls and the minds ability to transfer thought is an ancient practice. The transformation of the original people and the entire human family is taking place as the knowledge and power of the Crystal Skulls are revealed. All of this we can point back to the Honorable Elijah Muhammad and Minister Farrakhan's communication and experience on the Wheel.[114]

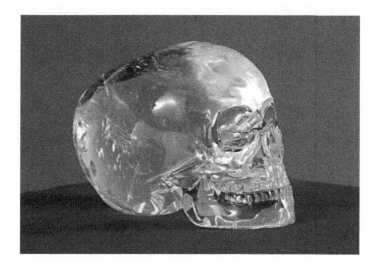

Figure 5: Photo of a Crystal Skull. It is known and debated that multiple skulls like the one pictured above exists, but how they are made and by whom is unknown by modern science and technology.

---

[114] Tynnetta Muhammad, "Unveiling the Number 19: The Meaning of the Crystal Skull and the Expansion of Spiritual Consciousness," *FinalCall.Com*, May 14, 2007.
http://www.finalcall.com/artman/publish/Columns_4/My_Living_Testimony_by_Mother_Tynetta_Muhammad_3469.shtml

Figure 6: Akhenaton, Nefertiti, and children basking in the 19 ray Sun disk.

In Mali, West Africa, the Dogon people (of Egyptian decent) record a history back thousands of years to 3200 BC, telling of their encounters of people from the sky. In the Dogon traditions, the star Sirius has a companion star that cannot be seen by the human eye. This companion star has an elliptical orbit around the visible Sirius of about 50 years. This star is called by scientist, Sirius B, and was first photographed in 1970 by a large telescope. How did the Dogon know that this star existed without modern technology? In the oral traditions of the Dogon, a race of beings called the Nommos visited the Earth 5,000 thousand years ago from the Sirius system. These masters are also called *Etheric Sirians*.

The Nommos gave the Dogon the knowledge of Sirius A and B and this has been passed down in the oral traditions of the Dogon for thousands of years. The Dogon teach of these beings coming to earth in *three legged* vehicles. These vehicles resemble the three legged vehicle that Minister Farrakhan saw and was carried on in his vision experience. This is also demonstrated in the Dogon rituals and dance. As far back as the 13th century the Dogon have celebrated the cycle of Sirius A and B. Western scientists did not witness these stars until the 19th century.

The Dogon have also been aware that planets rotate around the sun in elliptical orbits, and that Jupiter has four moons and they have been aware of the rings of Saturn for centuries. Sirius was also observed and revered by the ancient Egyptians.

My point at this juncture is that the ability to "see" is not limited to the physical eye. Also, the history of the planet earth includes untold stories of phenomena that include technology, science, mathematics, and more. There is a greater power in this world that exists, greater than the power of this modern world. The power that backs Minister Farrakhan and the Nation of Islam is connected to this ancient history and power. For centuries this power has been revealed and witnessed, and in most cases the "major" happenings of this world have been guided and permitted by this great power and elect group of men.

For example, in the Supreme Wisdom Lessons of the Nation of Islam it states: "Why did we let half-original man, Columbus, discover the Poor Part of the planet Earth?" [115] When someone reads this question, the first thing that may come to mind is, "Who's speaking?" The 'we' speaking represents these wise Gods of the elect circle that are also called wise scientist of Islam. When we observe the diary of Christopher Columbus, [116] it seems that there may have been divine intervention of one of the little wheels in his landing on the shores of what is now called North America. This is directly related to the above question asked by Master Fard Muhammad to the Honorable Elijah Muhammad. A part of the Honorable Elijah Muhammad's answer reads,

---

[115] Master Fard Muhammad, *The Supreme Wisdom* (Chicago: The Final Call Inc., 1995), 11.
[116] Christopher Columbus, Christopher Columbus: Extracts from Journal, *The ORB: Online Reference Book for Medieval Studies.* 3/1996.
http://www.fordham.edu/halsall/source/Columbus1.html - Published by Paul Halsall

> Because the Original Man is God and Owner of the Earth and knows
> every square inch of it, and has chosen the Best Part. He did not care
> about the Poor Part...

Did Christopher Columbus and his crew see a wheel in the sky, and were they guided by a strange illuminated wheel? It has been readily accepted by many scientists that Columbus' experience and the movement of what he and his companions described as a "waxed candle" light in the middle of the ocean, was a flying object in the sky. In the early work of Elijah Muhammad, it is a fact that US federal agencies spied and raided the temples of the Nation of Islam. They stole many documents about the Wheel and have been using the knowledge contained in these documents to advance their technology.[117]

The technology of the Wheel is superior to any technology known to this modern world. A part of this technology is directly related to the wheel's power to heal; power to raise the consciousness or spiritual frequency, and magnetic frequency of anyone who encounters it.[118] The experience of Mexican ufologist and photographer, Carlos Diaz is an example, as he was taken up on one of the wheels one morning in January 1981. This is a fascinating example of a Close Encounter of the Fourth Kind with the Wheel and its occupants. This encounter sheds light on the supreme power of the Wheel and the technology used to recreate the human body. This experience also verifies the ability of the Wheel to communicate. Tynnetta Muhammad explains in her article *Unveiling the Number 19*,

---

[117] Tynnetta Muhammad, Unveiling the Number 19: Revisiting the Honorable Minister Louis Farrakhan's Vision-Like Experience On the Great Mother's Wheel and Its Connection to Us Today, *FinalCall.Com*, Sep 23, 2010.
http://www.finalcall.com/artman/publish/Columns_4/article_7303.shtml

[118] Tynnetta Muhammad, Unveiling the Number 19: The Power of Prayer: Reflections on Minister Farrakhan's Stages of Recovery, *FinalCall.Com*, 2/9/2007.
http://www.finalcall.com/artman/publish/Columns_4/The_Power_of_Prayer_Reflections_on_Minister_Farrak_3246.shtml

...I envisioned a particular prayer service focusing on the appearance of this Divine Light, visible high in the sky on a particular day in the Mexican village of Tepoztlan, in the latter part of September 2001, viewed by the Honorable Minister Louis Farrakhan and several witnesses. Among the witnesses was Mr. Carlos Diaz, who has photographed this extraordinary phenomenon of ships of light in Tepoztlan for more than 20 years and has firsthand information concerning the essence of this conscious light. In a recent meeting with Mr. Diaz, accompanied by several members of my family in Tepoztlan, in the latter part of December, 2006, he unveiled more deepening insights about the work of these ships of light and their effect upon the human psyche. He explained that the image of light and its force field, coming from the outside, must be drawn inwardly for purification and healing. When this is accomplished, we become the vessels of light in its broadest expression of unconditional and universal love. At this vibratory rate or frequency, the light itself emits sound and is capable of reconstructing the cells of our body so that we become ageless and are transformed into light bodies that produce a resonance field of healing that extends throughout our entire planet.[119]

What Minister Farrakhan received contains a healing power to raise the vibratory rate of human consciousness. We become transformed by the infinite wisdom of God and grow into *light* beings that become ageless. This happens as a result of studying the new wisdom of the New Book (teaching). The whereabouts of the Wheel is unknown to the public, but it shows itself when it pleases. The ancients were also witnesses of wheels similar to the one built by Master Fard Muhammad. In ancient cultures, the Chinese, Egyptians, Hindus, Buddhists, and others believed in an advanced civilization occupied by an advanced people who reside in the center of the earth. This idea falls right in line

---

[119] Tynnetta Muhammad, Unveiling the Number 19: The Power of Prayer: Reflections on Minister Farrakhan's Stages of Recovery, *FinalCall.Com*, 2/9/2007.
http://www.finalcall.com/artman/publish/Columns_4/The_Power_of_Prayer_Reflections_on_Mini
ster_Farrak_3246.shtml

with other great advanced lost civilizations like Atlantis, Lumeria, Agartha, and Shamballah.

Dr. Raymond Bernard describes two of these subterranean places,

> The word "Agharta" is of Buddhist origin. It refers to the Subterranean World or Empire in whose existence all true Buddhists fervently believe. They also believe that this Subterranean World has millions of inhabitants and many cities, all under the supreme domination of the subterranean world capital, Shamballah, where dwells the Supreme Ruler of this Empire, known in the Orient as the King of the World. It is believed that he gave his orders to the Dalai Lama of Tibet, who was his terrestrial representative, his messages being transmitted through certain secret tunnels connecting the Subterranean World with Tibet.[120]

These civilizations are known to have had advanced technologies far greater than the present world. Master Fard Muhammad used advanced technology unknown to the present world to build the current Mother Plane. In a set of lessons called the *Actual Facts* written by Master Fard Muhammad for the Nation of Islam in the West, it is taught that Mount Everest is 29,141 feet high. Mount Everest is located in the Himalayas and borders Tibet, the same location where it is believed that tunnels to subterranean worlds exists, also as mentioned previously, the connection with the Crystal Skulls. In the ancient teaching of the Maya, Quetzalcoatl or Kukulcan was a white bearded, tall subterranean being who visited the Maya on a space craft from the center of the earth. A lie was proposed that he was a tall *white* God. This is related to the conquering of the Spaniards of the original people and today still, the

---

[120] Dr. Raymond Bernard, **The Hollow Earth** (New York: Fieldcrest Publishing Co. Inc., 1996), 92, Shamballah is also known as the City of Allah. Dr. Bernard in his observations also makes reference to the Eskimos and Mongolians as being descendants of the original inhabitants of this world beneath the earth.

imposing of the European influences on the darker people of Mexico and areas of South America.[121]

4.2   *Beneath our Planet: The Hollow Earth*

The Root of Civilization is in Arabia at the Holy City (Mecca) which means where wisdom and knowledge of the original man first started when the Planet was found. – **Supreme Wisdom, Lost Found Muslim Lesson #1, Lesson #4**

In the above statement, which is a part of the answer to a question asked to the Honorable Elijah Muhammad by his teacher; what does it mean, "When the Planet was found"? Another question that comes to mind is where was the original man before he "found" the Planet? These questions open up a world of ideas that are not common to the general public. Was the Planet found after the great separation or deportation of the moon from the Earth sixty six trillion years ago, that the Honorable Elijah Muhammad taught about? Did the original man inhabit another part of the planet during this explosion? One idea that has been debated for years is that the earth is hollow. This *Hollow Earth* theory has created an ongoing debate about what lies beneath the earth.

The Honorable Elijah Muhammad taught that the people on Mars can hide themselves and live inside or beneath their planet. How far fetch is the idea that there are passage ways into a subterranean world beneath the crust of the earth? There is a school of thought that teaches that there are numerous portals and passage ways for intergalactic travel of the flying objects often seen in the sky. Tynnetta Muhammad elaborates,

---

[121] Hubatz Men, *Secrets of Mayan Science/Religion* (Santa Fe, N.M.: Bear & Company, 1989), 109-10.

During one of the Most Honorable Elijah Muhammad's Dinner Talks at the Palace in 1974, he began speaking on the subject of Mars, its people and type of civilization. He spoke in such a soft tone that only perhaps a few of us seated near him could hear with clarity. He began speaking about Allah's promise to allow him to see the people on Mars. In earlier discussions on this subject of Mars, he spoke about the Martian's ability to hide and conceal themselves underground so that no one would even know that they were there. This immediately brought to mind his earlier discussions about two places on earth where people could hide and conceal themselves for a long period of time without being detected. I further thought that perhaps our entire planetary system, including our own planet earth, contains many hiding places with physical coordinates that connects us from one planet to the other utilizing polar caps which may lead into a subterranean world beneath the surface. These words connect to the subject we are currently discussing about the possibility of a Hollow Earth with a concave entrance through the poles that extends itself into some kind of subterranean world or civilization exhibiting an advanced technology which could include the manufacturing of space craft we identify today as UFOs. These crafts would then be categorized as coming from within our earth rather than from outer planets or galaxies.[122]

Geologist and explorers have sought to settle the dispute of the existence inhabitants in the interior of the earth. What is called the world's greatest geological discovery has been credited to Rear Admiral Richard E. Byrd of the United Sates Navy. Byrd led one of the United States largest expeditions to Antarctica, which was one of his five trips to Antarctica. The expedition was called operation *High Jump* and was meant to establish an Antarctic research base called Little America. He was provided with a team called Task Force 68 which included 4,700 men, 13 ships, and 25 aircraft. During this expedition Byrd encountered what he called an Unidentified Flying Object. It is stated that the UFO came out of the water at a 45% angel and the US vessels attacked the

[122] Tynnetta Muhammad, "Unveiling the Number 19: Understanding the Evolution of Time and Its Manifestation of Light In Our Physical Universe." *FinalCall.Com*, June 10, 2014. http://www.finalcall.com/artman/publish/Columns_4/article_101512.shtml

UFO. The UFO destroyed some of the US vessels, and Task Force 68 retreated. Skeptics believe that this was Nazi Germany technology, but Byrd believed differently. Byrd's diary on the incident is said to be locked and secure at the US Pentagon. On March 5, 1947 Byrd says in his diary, "We will have to face an enemy that can travel from pole to pole at incredible speeds." This wasn't Byrd's only discovery.

On another expedition while traveling 1,700 miles across the Arctic, he reported by radio that when he reached the North Pole he did not see ice below him, but land consisting of forest and mountains, vegetation, and strange animals.[123] Many have believed for centuries that the earth has a central sun at its core smaller than the sun in our solar system. Some say that this central sun in the earth is also responsible for the Aurora Borealis, the steam of lights that illuminate the Arctic sky at night. William Reed, author of **Phantom of the Poles** first thought of the idea that the North and South poles are not on the surface of the earth, but in mid-air since the true center of the earth is hollow.[124] Dr. Raymond Bernard, in his writing the **Hollow Earth** suggests,

> As the Earth spins on its axis, the motion is gyroscopic, like the spinning of a top. The outer gyroscopic pole is the magnetic circle of the rim of the polar opening. Beyond the rim the Earth flattens and slopes gradually towards its hollow interior. The true Pole is the exact center of the opening at the Poles, which consequently, do not really exist, and those who claim to have discovered them, did not tell the truth, even if they thought they did, having been misled by the irregular action of the compass at high latitudes.[125]

What lies beneath earth? This question has caused many people to enter into debate on whether there is an uncharted portion of the earth

---

[123] Dr. Raymond Bernard, **The Hollow Earth** (New York: Fieldcrest Publishing Co. Inc., 1996), 1.
[124] Bernard, **The Hollow Earth** 17.
[125] Ibid., 18.

that was occupied by people. Many have written on the subject, scientifically and in fiction. From John Uri Lloyd's *Etidorhpa*, 1895, Clement Fezandie's *Through the Earth* (1898), Charles Beale, *The Secrets of the Earth* (1899), William Alexander Taylor's *Intermere* (1901), Gabriel de Tarde's *Underground Man* (1896), and now many modern-day authors have researched and written on this subject. The fantasy tied to the theory has made most people skeptics. In ancient cultures though, this was a serious matter, and an integral part of their faith traditions. Mary Sutherland in her writing **In Search of Shambhala** concurs and in her research demonstrates how the Native American people believed that their ancestor came from the "womb" of the earth. In this history one of these passageways to the womb of the earth can be found in Sedona, Arizona at Montezuma's well. She also adds regarding the Hopi,

> ...The Hopi believe that the world we live in is the Fourth World and the other three are inside the earth. In stages, and through many hardships, they emerged from a hole called Sipapu. This emergence site, found at the bottom of the Canyon of the Little Colorado above its junction with the Colorado River, is a sacred place of pilgrimage for the Hopi. It lies in the Four Corners Area. Another Hopi legend tells of them also emerging from a world beneath the earth through a tunnel located at the base of the San Francisco Peaks near Flagstaff, Arizona. The Hopi legends say that their ancestors were driven to the surface by another faction of their own kind who turned on their own and was practicing sorcery. A clue to who that factor of their own kind was may be found in the Apache legends which state that the Two Hearts or the Children of the Lizard drove the Pueblos to the surface after they invaded their underground domain.[126]

---

[126] Mary Sutherland, "In Search of Shambhala," Living in the Light...Believe in the Magic, http://www.livinginthelightms.com/shambhala-read.html

Recently, by use of science and ongoing exploration efforts, many unknown underground caves and passage ways that lead deep into the earth's surface have been discovered. The Mammoth Cave in Kentucky, discovered in the early 1800's is an underground cave system of approximately 400 miles. Today it is a tourist attraction, and was first surveyed and mapped by a Black man who was a slave. The Er Wong Dong Cave in China starts at approximately 800 ft. in the earth's surface and is so big it has its own weather system. The Hang Son Doong Cave of Vietnam can hold one-half miles of 40 story high buildings. Ancient advanced civilizations, space travel, and communication are not new to the ancient people of the past. Crystal skulls, crystal balls, e.g. the *Atlantean Crystal Ball* (discovered by Raymond Brown in Bimini), pyramids, the use of water, and the power of thought, are examples of communication used by advanced civilizations of the past. Intergalactic communication continues to happen through telepathic powers. Tynnetta Muhammad relates,

> The story of TA HA begins with a frequency of sound and a prophetic message. This sound leads to the awakening of telepathy and the powers and ability to tune into the higher frequencies of sound emitted from the Divine world of thought forms. These thought forms vibrate at a certain frequency that materializes matter from paralleled worlds of intergalactic space-time. This frequency of sound generates from an ancient system known by scientists of our world, which measures space time through a mathematically coded and synchronized manifestation of all of our material forms that make up our physical universe. This total system of vibratory thought forms emanates from one Divine source identified with the Divine Creator and begins its ascension likened to a humming or ringing sound. [127]

---

[127] Tynnetta Muhammad, "Unveiling the Number 19: The Story of Ta Ha: A Struggle between the Forces of Darkness and Light," *FinalCall.Com*, November 8, 2005. http://www.finalcall.com/artman/publish/Columns_4/The_Story_of_TA_HA_by_Mother_Tynnetta_Muhammad_2266.shtml

As mentioned previously, this ringing sound resembles the ringing of the telephone or bell in the ear that the Honorable Elijah Muhammad said one would hear when being contacted by him or a divine being. The Prophet Jesus was a scientist and had the ability of telepathy (tuning in) and there is one out of every several hundred people in the East (Arabia) that can tune in on the people of the West (America) and tell them what they are thinking.[128] The people of Atlantis had a similar form of advanced communication. In the Bible and Holy Quran visions and dreams and other spiritual or psychic communication with the wheels are referenced often. These are viewed as experiences, rather than an occurrence separate from the participant. The Honorable Elijah Muhammad made mention on numerous occasions the natural abilities of the Black man to communicate telepathically,

> You can do it yourself if you will take time, clear your mind, and then go into some place where no one will disturb you, and concentrate on nothing but that Wheel or that Brother. After a while you can hear what the Brother is saying to himself. Maybe you can hear the motors going in one of the Wheels. It is not that we are people that have to wait and see everything happen before we know what's going to happen.[129]

The technology and means used to communicate with Minister Farrakhan in his experience is an ancient form of communication that is natural to the original people.

---

[128] Rassoull, *The Theology of Time*, 512
[129] Ibid., 513

Figure 7: Photo of Carlos Diaz and one of the smaller wheels that appear above him in Tepoztlan.

This Page Intentionally Left Blank

PART TWO

A <u>REAL</u> ~~Vision~~ Experience: "Whether in the Body or Out of the Body"

This Page Intentionally Left Blank

5 Elijah Muhammad, Farrakhan, and the Unseen World

5.1 *The Announcement: Fact or Fiction?*

Minister Farrakhan's testimony for the past 32 years, of his meeting with the Honorable Elijah Muhammad is real. His work, and his success, the duplication and continuation of the work of the Honorable Elijah Muhammad is a clear sign of the power of God to guide his servant. The vision experience and how it happened is important. It is not sufficient to only believe that it happened, but necessary that each student study the life of Minister Farrakhan that they come to know that it happened. This study must include a deeper review of the scriptures, mainly Bible and Holy Quran. Well how could Minister Farrakhan speak to a dead man? He did not. He spoke to a man that is alive. How did he speak to him; in a dream? No. It was real. To understand this phenomenal experience the reader must have respect for the knowledge of the subject to approach it properly. Hypocrites and disbelievers and even Satan himself will argue that the experience was a hoax, but cannot prove that the Honorable Elijah Muhammad is dead, nor will they engage the Nation of Islam on the subject. As with the Honorable Elijah Muhammad, Minister Farrakhan's success is a bearing of witness to the reality of his experience and the declaration of Elijah Muhammad as God incarnate.

> When you present a person with the true knowledge of how the Honorable Elijah Muhammad became the messenger of Allah – from Whom he received his infinite wisdom and the Source of his unique success – and when you provide a person with the proof of that truth, that person is going to react in one of two ways. He, or she, will either accept it or reject it. This rejection can take more than one form. Doubt

or uncertainty is one form. Disbelief, appearing as indifference or disbelief leading to actual opposition, is another form of rejection. Virulent hypocrisy, appearing first as acceptance, but later on becoming manifested for what it is, is another form of the rejection of the truth.[130]

The above quote by Jabril Muhammad speaks to what will happen with the continued work of the Honorable Elijah Muhammad, but in Minister Farrakhan. The vision experience of Minister Farrakhan will cause many to stumble because of their rejection of his testimony. The rejection of this truth sets the stage for betrayal and crucifixion. The parties involved in this betrayal do not recognize the unique source of the success of Minister Farrakhan, nor do they see that his success is rooted in his experience on the Wheel and what he received from the Honorable Elijah Muhammad. This misunderstanding will continue to exist in decent people who say they believe, love, and respect Minister Farrakhan, but do not study prophesies in the Bible and Holy Quran in its proper context. It is their ignorance and belief which keeps them stagnant, which will manifest overtime into hypocrisy because of their denial of the truth of the prophecies, which would help them to see Minister Farrakhan and his teacher correctly. Jabril Muhammad explains:

> There are many people who are still ignorant—sincere, good hearted— but ignorant of the minds of Allah and the Honorable Elijah Muhammad respecting Minister Farrakhan both before and since February 25th and the 26th, 1975. These good people are also ignorant of how to understand the prophetic word of God contained in the Bible and Holy Qur'an concerning the person, character, mission, message and work of Minister Farrakhan. Therefore, they have not accepted him as they might. Then, there are others who are not as good, at present. More about them another time. You know, dear readers, there is a point in time when after we accept the teachings of the Honorable Elijah

---

[130] Muhammad, *This is the One,* 53.

Muhammad, if we continue to refuse to accept prophecies that are being or are yet unfulfilled, we will then fall into hypocrisy. The Honorable Elijah Muhammad, with great insight, has said and written that if we understand the truth of the prophecies, from God, in the scriptures, we should not fall victim to misunderstanding, disbelief and hypocrisy. In other words, at a certain point in our development belief in the truth of the past and present truths is insufficient. There comes a time when our faith must involve God's words about events to come in the future. This is part of the practical value of the study of the Bible and Holy Qur'an.[131]

The "others who are not as good at present" mentioned by Jabril Muhammad in the above quote are those in whose hearts is a disease. These people have already fallen deep into hypocrisy and have almost no way out of their condition. The Honorable Elijah Muhammad says of this type of person:

They desire to make the Messenger think that they are true believers by saying that they believe that he is the Messenger of Allah, while in their hearts they do not believe that he is the Messenger, and Allah knows what is in their hearts – that they are liars. They come in believing and then disbelieve. After their disbelief, Allah seals their hearts so they cannot understand or believe. [132]

This type of scenario mentioned above has manifested itself in many towards Minister Farrakhan and the Nation of Islam. But, the continued work and success of Minister Farrakhan and the Nation of Islam bears witness to Bible and Holy Quran, as aspects of these two books are being fulfilled even as these words are being read.

Like the Apostle Peter, Minister Farrakhan's experience reflects what is written in the Bible,

---

[131] Muhammad, **This is the One,** 164-65.
[132] Muhammad, **Message to the Blackman**, 253.

> On the morrow, as they went on their journey, and drew nigh unto the city, Peter went up upon the housetop to pray about the sixth hour: And he became very hungry, and would have eaten: but while they made ready, he fell into a trance, And saw heaven opened, and a certain vessel descending upon him, as it had been a great sheet knit at the four corners, and let down to the earth.[133]

In Acts 10:10, Peter's trance resembles and foreshadows Paul's experience on the road to Damascus seen in Acts 22. In Paul's experience he heard the voice of Jesus, but in Acts 22:13-18 he received a message from a man who helped him see his mission and told him of a future meeting with the "Righteous One". Shortly after this talk with this man, Paul (named Saul at the time) had a vision experience where he saw the Lord speaking to him. Who is/was this righteous one? Paul in the Bible was being guided by Jesus from a secret place that is symbolically called heaven. The scholars say this ONE is Jesus, but the historical Paul never witnessed the Prophet Jesus in the flesh because the Prophet Jesus was physically dead. So how did this happen? This event foreshadows a future event that was to be fulfilled by Minister Farrakhan. Again, Minister Farrakhan's life has been in danger since the moment he began rebuilding the Nation of Islam and work of the Honorable Elijah Muhammad. The Christian, Islamic, and Jewish worlds, and their various schools of thought at some time or another have denounced, and distanced themselves from the Nation of Islam in America. Their move to distance themselves is based on their misunderstanding of the scriptures, and their erroneous view of the Nation of Islam in particular, but the darker people of America in general.

---

[133] See Acts 10:9-11 (KJV).

5.2   *The Testimony of Faithful Witnesses*

The value of the testimony of an eye witness is the most credible. Like any incident when there are multiple witnesses, what people see is based on their perception, which is formed by experience, knowledge, position of the witness in relation to the incident, and other factors.

A ***witness*** as described by Merriam-Webster Dictionary is,

> **1**: attestation of a fact or event: testimony
> **2**: one that gives evidence; specifically: one who testifies in a cause or before a judicial tribunal
> **3**: one asked to be present at a transaction so as to be able to testify to its having taken place
> **4**: one who has personal knowledge of something
> **5a**: something serving as evidence or proof: sign
> **b**: public affirmation by word or example of usually religious faith or conviction

There were many people who saw a body in a casket at a funeral in 1975. Most of them that witnessed this will say that they believed (or knew) they saw the body of the Honorable Elijah Muhammad in a casket, and this includes Minister Farrakhan. But, there are a small few who saw the same thing others saw (a body), and as witnesses saw it from a different perspective. Their view included God's view, which involves the escape from a wicked death plot on the life of the Honorable Elijah Muhammad. Regardless of a person's relationship, nearness and association to the Honorable Elijah Muhammad, each one was made by God to see his alleged death differently. Like Jesus of the Holy Quran and Bible, his life is the most misunderstood and his death is the most controversial. The Nation of Islam, America and the world is about to experience a similar trial once again, but through Minster

Farrakhan who is following in the footsteps of his teacher. The so-called death of the Honorable Elijah Muhammad must be understood and viewed from a divine perspective and through the scriptures. All the Prophets of God had witnesses of their work. The Prophets themselves were witness of God and his power. God always leaves witnesses to testify of his majesty. Jesus' disciples throughout the New Testament were his witnesses and testified of him. Their testimony was the most authentic, since they were his disciples and closes to him. People are witnesses onto themselves, and even Allah (God) himself is a witness of what is done.

> Say: What thing is the weightiest in testimony? Say: Allah is witness between you and me. And this Quran has been revealed to me that with it I may warn you and whomsoever it reaches. Do you really bear witness that there are other gods with Allah? Say: I bear not witness. Say: He is only One God, and surely I am innocent of that which you set up (with Him).[134]

According to Merriam-Webster Dictionary the word *testimony* means,

> **1a**: a solemn declaration usually made orally by a witness under oath in response to interrogation by a lawyer or authorized public official
> **b**: firsthand authentication of a fact: evidence
> **c**: an outward sign
> **2a**: an open acknowledgment
> **b**: a public profession of religious experience
> **3a** (1): the tablets inscribed with the Mosaic Law
> (2): the ark containing the tablets
> **b**: a divine decree attested in the Scriptures

In the Holy Quran the question is asked, "What is the weightiest testimony?" If a credible witness gives their testimony in a court of law,

---

[134] Holy Quran 6:19

this testimony is admissible. Below is an interview conducted by Jabril Muhammad with Joshua Farrakhan, son of Minister Farrakhan. The interview includes Brother Joshua's testimony as a witness of the activities surrounding the death plot and the alleged death of the Honorable Elijah Muhammad in February 1975. The interview is in its entirety as printed in three different news articles by Jabril Muhammad.

Jabril Muhammad (JM): Brother Joshua, three years ago, in 1991, you told your father and I, right after your fathers *Who Is God?* speech, something so fascinating to, that we just sat on the staircase for about thirty minutes, as you went into what you told us, was the first time you detailed the experience you and two other Brothers—had nineteen years and two months ago—when it was announced that the Honorable Elijah Muhammad died, in Mercy Hospital. One of the main things you said was that you and the other two brothers were in the hospital that night and through the next morning when he was pronounced dead. Will you run down that whole experience in the order in which you experienced it?

Joshua Farrakhan (JF): Well, as I recall it, about nineteen and a half years ago, as you call it, I was coming in from New York for Saviors' Day with my family, and I was staying with Alif Muhammad, who is the son of Herbert Muhammad. We were up playing games, or whatever, and it was rather late at night. We were very tired. Bro. Kamal was visiting and there were some other young brothers—

JM: Is that Bro. Kamal (Muhammad) who is the National Secretary?

JF: No sir. This is Bro. Kamal Karriem, whose father was the manager of Your Supermarket. We all were spending the evening there—

JM: What was the third brother's name?

JF: There was Bro. Kamal, there was myself, Hussein was there, and Alif. And Wallace (Mustafa Farrakhan) was there, my younger brother. And my older brother Louis (Farrakhan, Jr.) was there.

So we all were bunking in one room, so to speak, and we were very tired. So we had started to go to sleep, but for some reason, we were up talking late, but in and out of sleepiness, and consciousness. Then Alif had come into the room. It must have been 1:00 A.M. in the morning, or 1:30. It could have been a little later. He said that he needed two brothers to go with him on a detail. I said, what is the detail that we have to go on? He said, "I'll let you know, when I get you there, so get dressed." We hurried and got dressed. He had a very concerned look on his face so we knew he was serious.

JM: It was you and who else?

JF: Me and Brother Kamal. I, at that time, must have been, maybe 17.

JM: How old was he?

JF: Alif, himself, must have been about 19.

JM: The same Alif you're -

JF: Alif, right, who is my brother-in-law and Brother Kamal Karriem, was approximately the same age as me, or maybe one year older 18. We got dressed and we drove down to Mercy Hospital, which is off, I believe, King Drive, 35th Street, somewhere in that area. Alif told me that there was no one to stand post for the Most Honorable Elijah Muhammad, outside of his room. So, I said, what? I couldn't believe it! I said here we are in Chicago, at head-quarters, where there's thousands of Muslims gathering for the Saviors' Day convention, and the top brass so to speak was in town. Not only that, Elijah (Muhammad) Junior and Wali Baha—and there were Fruit here. So I said what would they be doing with just kids?

So instead of really questioning it, or having any disagreement to stand the post, I felt honored that I was chosen to stand this post. So we got up to the top floor. I believe it was the ninth or the tenth floor, maybe the tenth, and there was no brother up there. So shortly afterwards a brother come up off the elevator, a little old brother, maybe in his sixties. That puzzled me too. From an old man to a young man. In other words, people who weren't capable of doing the job, in case anyone came up to try to assassinate the Messenger, were there in the hospital guarding him. This is what I was thinking.

So, I looked at the old brother and he said he was—I asked him why wasn't he on post when we came up? He said he was down-stairs looking for the relief. So, we properly relieved him, and Alif had given us our instructions; he told us not to go into the room where his grandfather was, and just to every now and then walk down the corridor, and look in the room. You know, go by the room, and see if you see anything suspicious.[135]

JM: Was there a glass you could look through in the room?

JF: Yes there was.

JM: Could you see him in the room?

JF: Yeah, I looked in the room, anyway, even though Alif told me not to. I was hesitant to do it, but I did. Whenever Alif went to the other end of the hall I would look in at the Messenger. He was all hooked up. He was hooked up to some machines. He had tubes going up in his nose, in his mouth, intravenous in his wrist. So, I would look in and out. The strangest thing that struck me was there was like an old janitor with a bucket with a mop in it, you know, pushing the bucket with the mop and he went right into the room. So, I…well, basically before he got into the room, I had stopped him. I told him he couldn't go in. And Alif told me get out of the way and let the man do his job, you know, so I let him in. So, when he went in, I stood right on the inside of the door, with the door maybe twelve inches open. I was watching him mop the floor, because I had watched so many of those James Bond movies, you know, you see that this is how they just slip in to do something. They come in disguise. So, I watched the man and he mopped and everything, and he came out. Then Alif told me that he would sit in front of the door, and I could sit down at the other end of the hall with Brother Kamal, and when he got tired he would come and get us. So we were discussing some things about what if the Messenger died. And then I tried to excuse…

---

[135] Jabil Muhammad, "The Messenger, Minister Farrakhan and how Allah controls circumstances", *FinalCall.Com*, October 26, 2010. http://www.finalcall.com/artman/publish/Columns_4/article_7378.shtml

JM: You and Kamal talking?

JF: Me and Kamal. I tried to excuse that from my mind. After I brought up the question, I said, 'man I would just jump out the window. I would kill myself,' you know? So Kamal said, 'man, don't talk like that. The Messenger's not going to die. He's not going to go anywhere.' I trusted this brother's words, because he was one of these young men who could see in the water, who was a visionary, who could look into the future. So he walked out of the room, and I wanted to test his skills, so I was—

JM: Now where are you all now? Are you in a different room?

JF: There's a lobby at the end of the floor. And we both were in there, but Alif was down in front of the—

JM: Where you all were, could you see Alif?

JF: No, not unless we looked out the door. If we looked out the door, it was like looking down this hallway to the blue room. Brother Kamal had a very stern, bothered look on his face. And I guess, I did too if I could see myself, because the whole idea of me being on post was an honor, but it bothered me. So, I said I wanted to see if this brother really got these skills, you know, because he's telling me, don't worry, the Messenger's not going to die. So he went down the hall and I tried calling him mentally three times. And when he came back into the room, about ten minutes later, I said, 'man, you ain't got no powers,' cause I was trying to call you.' He said, 'I know, three times.' This shut me right up! (Laughter) So I said 'why didn't you answer me?' He said, 'man, there's something going on.' He sensed something. He said 'something ain't right.' So he told me, 'let's just keep our rounds even quicker, instead of fifteen minutes around the corridor; let's do them every five minutes.'

JM: Now what time is it now, would you estimate?

JF: It's around five in the morning. So there was a lot of snow. You know, the February 25th-look in Chicago, It was very cold, but it was a clear sky. You could see the dawn coming in.

JM: It was clear at that moment?

JF: It was clear, there was hardly any clouds, you know. It was just clear. Scattered, you know, a scattered cloud here, and there a scattered cloud—but they were white clouds.

JM: Now, all the night, did you get a chance to look at the clouds to see?

JF: Yeah, it was a little motion.

JM: Were there windows you could see through?

JF: Oh yes, there were big picture windows there in the sitting area.

JM: So all throughout the night, by reason of doing what you did, you were noticing the fact that it was not cloudy, or there were only a few clouds.

JF: Right. I was just looking around, saying, what kind of day is this? You know, the Messenger is sick. I'm a young kid up on the floor watching him on post. It's cold outside. No clouds, you know, that type of thing was going on in my mind. So, it started getting lighter and lighter. So I'm making more rounds, I open the door and I'm looking at the Messenger. I'm looking at the Messenger and he looked very hopeless, you know, eyes closed, his mouth was pretty much open. He looked wasted. It hurt me to see him in that condition. I would walk over to the bed, rub his feet. He was warm. And I said a prayer over him, you know, just praying, asking Allah to help him come out of this—they said it was a coma he was in.

JM: What did Kamal and Alif—did they do anything similar? What were they doing?

JF: Kamal did go in the room one time to say a prayer. I told him what I did, and he said that was a good idea and he wanted to go pray. But we did this without Alif's knowledge, because Alif would take a break and go sit in the lounge. We would have the front post, the front door post, or whatever you want to call that. We would slip in and say a prayer and ask Allah to strengthen him and bring him out of it. So this type of thing was going on through the night, or through the morning. We were still discussing the possibility of the Messenger dying. At that time, it seemed strange, but he said he got a funny feeling like something was going to happen. I don't know if someone was contacting him or not, but most of the time he seemed spaced. And if he could actually read what I was trying to tell him at one point, then I knew that if there was someone else that he could tune right into him. So I left him alone.

JM: Did it look like he was concentrating every now and then?
JF: Bro. Kamal?

JM: Yes.

JF: Yes, very much.

JM: Did he give any hint that he—looked like a person being contacted?

JF: That's what I thought it was. Because I asked him why couldn't he talk to me? He said he was busy doing something else and that sort of thing—'I didn't have time.' My thing was that he was just walking up and down the corridor, but why wouldn't he have time to speak back?

JM: He wasn't doing anything.

JF: He wasn't doing anything but patrolling the hallway. So it occurred to me that he might have been talking to someone else. Maybe, he could have been trying to reach the Messenger himself, because the Lord was in the next room.

JM: Either that or he was in communication, either sending or receiving, or both. Was that possibility or that thought in your mind? [136]

JF: So the time was going by, and the sun broke or came out.

---

[136] Jabil Muhammad, "Escape From a Death Plot: The Departure of the Honorable Elijah Muhammad", *FinalCall.Com*, November 2, 2010.
http://www.finalcall.com/artman/publish/Columns_4/article_7395.shtml

JM: It's still no clouds?

JF: No clouds to speak of. Sun came out.

JM: About five, six, something like that?

JF: Around seven, seven thirty, there was sunlight. And then I believe it was about 8:10 (AM) when they announced him dead. But the alarm went off and the doctors rushed into the room. I slipped into the room and watched them. They really didn't try to revive him, as far as I'm concerned. Whenever someone's heart failed, they would take these things with the electricity in it, cardiac machines, and give a charge to the chest. That didn't happen. They didn't do that. They pumped kind of a few times and pushed on his   chest with their hands and basically unplugged him from all of the machines. The doctor came out and told Alif, "Your grandfather's no longer with us." So Alif said, "What do you mean by that?" The doctor said "He's no longer with us." And he had a smile on his face. Alif couldn't understand, "What do you mean he's no longer with us?" He said, "In other words, he's dead," with a smile and a smirk on his face. Alif went straight to the phone and called Herbert.
I myself, I didn't feel nothing. I said a few hours ago, I said I'd jump out this window if the Messenger is dead. I'd kill myself. I couldn't live. And all of a sudden, they said he was dead, and I'm looking at him—

JM: Now you said that Alif went to the phone and called his father. What did you do?

JF: What I did was I wanted to—

JM: And after you tell me that, also talk to me about these clouds.
JF: I wanted to see the procedure that they were going to do to the Messenger, to see if they really were trying to revive him; to see if, even after they pronounced him dead, would they try to work on him longer. So I walked over to him and said —

JM: So you're still in the room?

JF: Yeah, I was in the room. I saw there were about four doctors, four white doctors, one white nurse, and a Black nurse. There's about five or six people. So I saw them, what they tried to do, and they unplugged the Messenger and when they finished unplugging him and all, his arms just fell to the side, in the shape of a cross. They just fell open. And his mouth was ...The doctor kept trying to shut his mouth and it wouldn't close. So they just kept shutting his mouth and it'd drop right back. So then it seem to me that he was trying to be smart, because he knew he had no control over the jaw, or whatever, and why just keep flapping it...

JM: Like mockery?

JF: Like mockery. That's basically, *exactly* what it was, really. So the Messenger just lay there. Then I went over to his feet and started rubbing his feet and I kissed his feet and said a prayer. I wanted Allah to take my life and give him my life so that he may live again because he was so much more important and great. But still I never had a feeling in my chest that he was dead. I never had that feeling.

Alif told me, "Don't call no one. Don't go to the phone. Don't do nothing." So, I took Alif's advice for a minute, until Dr. Charles came, the Messenger's doctor. I had gone out, and then I went back in. By this time there was about three doctors who came to officially announce him dead. Dr. Charles—who was the personal physician of the Messenger—came and officially pronounced the Messenger as legally dead. Once he did that, then Alif, I believe, called Herbert back again and said that Dr. Charles was there and he officially announced him dead.

JM: Did he call from within the same room?

JF: There's a phone outside maybe fifteen or twenty feet down from the room, a pay phone. So Alif went back and called again.

JM: Was there a phone in the room?

JF: No that was intensive care and it was about—the funny thing about it, the Messenger didn't have his own room. A man of that magnitude, was in a room with about six to eight people, other people, which one of the patients could have been faking, just laying up in there. All these things ran through my mind. [137]

Joshua Farrakhan's testimony serves as evidence of the death plot on the life of the Honorable Elijah Muhammad. As an eye witness and one of the few present at Mercy Hospital during the time of the departure of the Honorable Elijah Muhammad, his testimony should be carefully studied and considered. The following are the words and testimony of Mother Tynnetta Muhammad in an interview with Jabril Muhammad about her conversation with the Honorable Elijah Muhammad about the death plot on his life and his escape from that attempt by his enemies. The context in which she speaks is important, and as a witness, it is even more important. The following appeared in Jabril Muhammad's "Farrakhan the Traveler" column.

Brother Jabril Muhammad (JM): I don't think it's really public knowledge, except to the extent people know this about the Minister's public pronouncements, that there was a plot to murder the Honor-able Elijah Muhammad in 1975.

Certainly, many of us have deduced this from this and that. Then some of us—I have no idea how many, al-though I think the number is small—heard the Honorable Elijah Muhammad actually say that there would be such a plot—a specific plot—of such nature, magnitude and scope that, as he said to a few (including me) that only Allah could save him from it.

Now, did he ever speak to you, generally or specifically, about any kind of plot-ting against his life, at any point in time just prior to his departure February 1975?

---

[137] Jabil Muhammad, "The Honorable Elijah Muhammad's escape from a death plot", *FinalCall.Com*, November 8, 2010.
http://www.finalcall.com/artman/publish/Columns_4/article_7401.shtml

Mother Tynnetta Muhammad (MTM): Yes. He did. His first discussion with me of such a plot actually began in Mexico in 1974, around the latter part of 1974, because that was the last trip that we all took together in December. Actually it was Christmas Eve.

I recall that we had to refuel in Houston, or one part of Texas. I can't remember, right now, if it was Houston, but I believe it was. And from there, after the refueling, we landed in Mexico City.

JM: His and your arrival in Mexico, on Christmas Eve, is always fascinating to me, as I told you back in 1977, that was the day I was arrested for murder and what not. It was two days later, while I was still in jail, while reading a borrowed Bible, in Psalms, to comfort myself, when it came to me, that right then the Honorable Elijah Muhammad was in his "Gethsemane."

I can only say it came from Allah. I don't know how else to explain what came to me. Two days after that, when I got out, I telephoned Dr. Salaam, who was in Chicago, and told this to him.

Now, I'm skipping much now, to get Mother Tynnetta's next words.

MTM: Yes sir. I mean how I got this information is kind of mystifying to me because nobody seems to know about it. But I know the Honorable Elijah Muhammad requested not to leave on the 26th. And this man had something to do with it. I don't know how I know this, unless it was telepathically.

But I know that he requested not to leave and then sure enough, he did. He left on the 25th. So that was letting me know that this was a carefully designed departure. That only those whom God would reveal it to would know.

JM: Did you see this man at any other time?

MTM: Yes. Once after the hospital, after the announcement that he had passed, he came to the Palace, on either that day or the next day. And I remember again, he sat down in the living room.

He didn't talk to anybody. I don't know who he came to see, or who, he came to talk to. But I observed him again, and I said "My good-ness."

So that would make four times that I can recall clearly that I saw him, once at the dinner table, once at the hospital, and once at the Palace, and after the Honorable Elijah Muhammad was announced dead in the hospital.

JM: But you also saw him during Saviours' Day 1974?

MTM: Yes.[138]

5.3   We Want Farrakhan! How Do You Want Him? Dead!

Minister Farrakhan came to the realization that Honorable Elijah Muhammad was physically alive in December, 1980. He spoke of the Honorable Elijah Muhammad being alive publicly on February 22, 1981 to 3,000 people [139] at the Nation of Islam's annual Saviours' Day Convention. This was the first Saviours' Day Convention of this type since the alleged death of the Honorable Elijah Muhammad. Minister Farrakhan explains regarding his announcement,

No matter how much scorn, abuse or ridicule I would take; or how many friends I would lose by such announcement, I was convinced that I had to make that announcement and let the people start dealing with it— first by ridicule; then, as time progressed, they would gradually come to see the truth of that announcement. In February 1981 I made that announcement. I could say to the world, but I don't think that the world was listening. But to those who listened, particularly those who

---

[138] Jabil Muhammad, Farrakhan the Traveler. "The death plot against the Hon. Elijah Muhammad and his escape", FinalCall.Com, December 7, 2010.
http://www.finalcall.com/artman/publish/Columns_4/article_7481.shtml
[139] Jabril Muhammad, *Is It possible That The Honorable Elijah Muhammad Is Physically Alive???* (Phoenix, AZ: New Books Publication.,2006), 12.

had come to believe and hope in me, I said that Elijah Muhammad was not dead, but was in fact alive.[140]

Minister Farrakhan has fled from many cities in America for his life because of making bold statements like this. Back then he traveled from city to city teaching Black people and eluding those who would desire to kill him. On September 14, 1985 after a lecture at the Inglewood Forum in Inglewood, California, once again his life was in danger. He spoke to 19, 000 people as he put out a program of economic independence called P.O.W.E.R (People Organized and Working for Economic Rebirth). This threat for his life by the angry Jewish community led him to secretly travel with his wife, Mother Khadijah Farrakhan into Mexico where he had his experience on the Wheel. This experience has been the foundation of his work in America and throughout the world. The following is a portion of the transcript of the press conference by Minister Farrakhan and the Nation of Islam at the J.W. Marriott Hotel, Washington, DC. October 23, 1989. During this 'announcement' Minister Farrakhan revealed once again to the world his meeting with the Honorable Elijah Muhammad on the Mother Plane.

> … Ladies and Gentlemen of the Press, Brothers and Sisters, we are honored by your presence here this morning. I am a man who has great respect for the Press and the electronic media and I also have respect for myself and my mission. As you know, I do not readily submit to interviews, nor am I frequently seen on the television; for I am not before you of myself, nor do I do what I do to be seen of men. Therefore, I have never tried to abuse, or misuse the Press to seek advantage for myself, or the Nation of Islam. So, in calling this press conference, I am calling you because of the serious nature of the Announcement that I am about to make; an Announcement on which hangs the future of this nation, its leaders and the people of America. It is written in the book of Ezekiel,

---

[140] Muhammad, *Is It possible That The Honorable Elijah Muhammad Is Physically Alive???*, 35.

"When I say unto the wicked, You shall surely die; and you give him not warning, nor speak to warn the wicked from his wicked way, to save his life; the same wicked man shall die in his iniquity; but his blood will I require at your hand. "Yet if you warn the wicked and he turn not from his wickedness, nor from his wicked way, he shall die in his iniquity; but you have delivered your soul."

It is in this spirit that I make this announcement. In a tiny town in Mexico, called Tepotzlan, there is a mountain on the top of which are the ruins of a temple dedicated to Quetzalcoatl -the Christ- figure of Central and South America – a mountain which I have climbed several times. However, on the night of September 17, 1985, I was carried up on that mountain, in a vision, with a few friends of mine. As we reached the top of the mountain, a Wheel, or what you call an unidentified flying object (UFO), appeared at the side of the mountain and called to me to come up into the Wheel. Three metal legs appeared from the Wheel, giving me the impression that it was going to land, but it never came over the mountain.

Being somewhat afraid, I called to the members of my party to come with me, but a voice came from the Wheel saying, "Not them; just you." I was told to relax and a beam of light came from the Wheel and I was carried up on this beam of light into the Wheel. I sat next to the pilot; however, I could not see him. I could only feel his presence. As the Wheel lifted off from the side of the mountain, moving at a terrific speed, I knew I was being transported to the Mother Wheel, which is a human-built planet, a half-mile by a half-mile that the Honorable Elijah Muhammad had taught us of for nearly 60 years. The pilot, knowing that I was fearful of seeing this great, mechanical object in the sky, maneuvered his craft in such a way that I would not see the Mother Wheel (Plane) and then backed quickly into it and docked in a tunnel. I was escorted by the pilot to a door and admitted into a room.

I shall not bother you with a description of the room, but suffice it to say that at the center of the ceiling was a speaker and through this speaker I heard the voice of the Honorable Elijah Muhammad speaking to me as clearly as you are hearing my voice this morning. He spoke in short cryptic sentences and as he spoke a scroll full of cursive writing rolled down in front of my eyes, but it was a projection of what was being written in my mind. As I attempted to read the cursive writing, which was in English, the scroll disappeared and the Honorable Elijah Muhammad began to speak to me.

He said, *"President Reagan has met with the Joint Chiefs of Staff to plan a war. I want you to hold a press conference in Washington, D. C., and announce their plan and say to the world that you got the information from me, Elijah Muhammad, on the Wheel."*

He said to me that he would not permit me to see him at that time. However, he said that I had one more thing to do and when that one more thing was done that I could come again to the Wheel and I would be permitted to see him face to face.

He then dismissed me. I entered the small wheel and the pilot whom I still could not see, moved the craft out of the tunnel and took it up to a terrific height and maneuvered his craft that I might look down upon the Mother Wheel. I saw a city in the sky.

With great speed it brought me back to earth and dropped me off near Washington where I then proceeded into this city to make *The Announcement.* After I awakened from the vision, it seemed to vanish from my mind. However, on the morning of September 19, 1985, a great earthquake struck Mexico City and it was felt in the little town where I was staying. That earthquake brought the vision forcibly to my mind and I spoke it, later that morning for the first time to my wife, Khadijah Farrakhan, and Sister Tynnetta Muhammad, in the city of Cuernavaca.[141]

Figure 8: Nation of Islam, International Press Conference, J.W. Marriott Hotel, Washington, D.C., October 23, 1989.

---

[141] Louis Farrakhan, "International Press Conference, J.W. Marriott Hotel, Washington, D.C.," Official Nation of Islam Statements, http://www.noi.org/statements/.

Minister Farrakhan's powerful experience reveals Allah (God) and the Honorable Elijah Muhammad's direct role in the events of this world and more specifically their continued intervention in the lives of Black people through Minister Farrakhan. The value of his vision has affected the world.

Minister Farrakhan has been working from the guidance and instructions that he received in the above experience since September, 1985. Following this powerful experience, on October 7, 1985 Minister Farrakhan and the Nation of Islam hosted in New York City at Madison Square Garden a message that drew 20,000 people and another 3,000 to 5,000 in the Felt Forum watching via closed circuit television. Twelve days later on October 19, 1985, exactly one month after the staggering earthquake in Mexico; an earthquake struck the State of New York. In the early morning the earthquake struck north of New York City and shook parts of five states including southern Canada.[142] I think it is important for the reader to keep in mind that Minister Farrakhan is a *guided* man. Moses was given power by God over Aaron and controlled him, and this is the case with the Honorable Elijah Muhammad and Minister Farrakhan. The vision on the Wheel prompted Minister Farrakhan to take a specific course of action, endangering himself, his family, and his loved ones. How many would have done what he has done and continues to do? On January 7, 1986, President Reagan declared a national emergency after bombings at airports in Italy and Austria. He exercised his authorities under the International Emergency Economic Powers Act (IEEPA), and imposed economic sanctions against Libya. The State Department also declared all US Passports

---

[142] McFadden, Robert D. "Earthquake Shakes Parts of 5 Northeastern States." New York Times" 20 October 1985. http://www.nytimes.com/1985/10/20/nyregion/earthquake-shakes-parts-of-5-northeastern-states.html?pagewanted=all. (Accessed November 15, 2017).

invalid for travel in and out of Libya, unless authorized by the US.[143] On February 5, 1986, the same night he began his world tour, [144] Minister Farrakhan spoke out against President Reagan and the United States for imposing these sanctions. While traveling through Africa, he decided to go into Libya and warn the Libyan people. Prior to this, only a small group knew of his vision.

Minister Farrakhan elaborates,

> Ronald Reagan wanted to kill Qadaffi. When I found out the war was against Qadaffi, I was in Benin, and in Ghana, and Ouagadougou in Burkina Faso. And I sent all my family back, and I flew to Libya. And all of Qadaffi government was in my hotel, and I told them my Vision. They ran out of that room like Raid had been there. And the next thing I knew, Brother Qadaffi said he wanted me to speak and introduce him the next day; and 80 nations of the non-aligned movement were in Libya. And I stood in Tripoli, and repeated that Experience on the Wheel, and *told* Qadaffi what they were gonna do: They were gonna *bomb* the airport, destroy your water project. He listened. He got his airplanes out into the Sudan. The next thing I knew, an American plane was shot down, and one of those fine aircraft carriers that Mr. Trump brought over to Asia, was in the Gulf of Sirte. But something happened to it. By the time I got to Saudi Arabia, it came out in the Arab news that there was "an object over the Mediterranean." Just listen to me. I will die on what I am telling you. And I said to those with me, I said, 'The Wheel was there.' The electronic equipment on the aircraft carrier was messed up, so it had to go back to Florida. In the meantime, I was able to get *out* of Libya. I got into Saudi Arabia, and a few days later the bombs dropped on Libya. It was the greatest assassination attempt, most expensive in history. So they always wanted Qadaffi! But what I did not *know* was the war at that time was on two fronts: It was war with

---

Leagle, Inc. "FARRAKHAN v. REAGAN CIV. A. NO. 86-1783." Leagel.Com.
http://www.leagle.com/decision/19871175669FSupp506_11072.xml/FARRAKHAN%20v.%20RE AGAN (Accessed July 4, 2014).
[144] Muhammad, *Is It possible That The Honorable Elijah Muhammad Is Physically Alive???*, 4.

a Muslim country in Africa, but *war* on the *Nation of Islam, and Islam period*, in America.[145]

Tynnetta Muhammad questions the motive of Ronald Regan in her weekly column of the Final Call News,

> Why does Mr. Reagan want to destroy Muammar Qadhafi? Why does Mr. Reagan want to destroy the Libyan Jamahiriya? Africa is the prize. Neither the East, nor the West, can maintain white supremacy in the 21st Century without access to Africa. Since they cannot maintain their supremacy without Africa, they hate any leader who is concerned with the rise of Africa, with the liberation of Africa, with the decolonization of Africa, with the revolutionary struggle to unseat every puppet regime in Africa, and therefore, Muammar Qadhafi and the Libyian [sic] Jamahiriya are the Number One threat to Reagan's foreign policy with respect to Africa, Asia, Latin America and the struggling peoples around the world. [146]

The warning of Minister Farrakhan to the Libyan leader was revealed to him by God. On March 12, 1986 Minister Farrakhan traveled to Libya[147] risking everything valuable to him. He risked friendships; many of which he lost. Being committed to his teacher, he did as he was instructed to do in the vision and on March 16, 1986, he spoke of his experience to representatives of 86 nations around the world in his *Address to the World Conference on Racism - Zionism - Imperialism*, in Tripoli, Libya.[148] Jabril Muhammad explains in his book ***Is It Possible That The Honorable Elijah Muhammad Is Still Physically Alive???***,

---

[145] Farrakhan, Louis. "A Final Warning a Final Call." Press Conference, Watergate Hotel, Washington, DC, November 16, 2017. Accessed December 14, 2017. https://study.noi.org/documents,

[146] Tynnetta Muhammad, *The Comer by Night* (Chicago, IL: Honorable Elijah Muhammad Educational Foundation, Inc., 1994.) 40.

[147] Leagle, Inc. "FARRAKHAN v. REAGAN CIV. A. NO. 86-1783." Leagel.Com. http://www.leagle.com/decision/19871175669FSupp506_11072.xml/FARRAKHAN%20v.%20REAGAN (Accessed July 4, 2014).

[148] Muhammad, *The Comer by Night*, 39.

On the basis of that vision Minister Farrakhan delivered a powerful speech on March 16, 1986, in Tripoli, Libya. Before representatives of approximately 80 nations, he warned the then president, Mr. Ronald Reagan. At that time President Reagan was the Commander-in-Chief of the Armed Forces of the most powerful government of the Caucasian race, the United States of America. He warned President Reagan not to make war on Libya. He issued this warning from an authority superior to that which fueled the decision of Mr. Reagan and those with him to make war on Libya. At a certain point, in that 1986 speech, he stated, "On the night of September 17th, in a little village in Mexico, Allah gave me a vision, which involved Mr. Reagan sitting with the Joint-Chiefs-of-Staff to plan a war. I did not know where the war was, but it is clear to me that with the ships of the Sixth Fleet in the waters of the Gulf of Sidra, that Mr. Reagan, and the Joint-Chiefs-of-Staff have planned to make war on Libya to destroy the fruit of the El Fatiha Revolution." For the sake of His servant, Minister Farrakhan, and for the sake of an unwary general public, God Himself saw to it that the truth of the Minister's statement was confirmed in a powerful and public manner. Here, in brief, is part of how it happened. In 1987 the news that President Reagan and the Joint-Chiefs-of-Staff had secretly planned a war against Libya—a few weeks before the Minister received his vision—became public through The New York Times news services, the Washington Post and The Atlanta Journal. This news spread throughout America and the world, thus publicly verifying Minister Farrakhan's powerful experience.[149]

---

[149] Muhammad, *Is It possible That The Honorable Elijah Muhammad Is Physically Alive???*, 5.

The threat of Libya remained a thorn in the side of the United States and the vision of the U.S. under Ronald Reagan's administration and other Presidents was fulfilled by Barack Obama the 44th President of the United States and Secretary of State, Hillary Clinton. Twenty six years later, almost to the exact date of the New York earthquake on October 20, 2011  Libyan leader Muammar Gadhafi was murdered. During an interview on CBS News in America, Hillary Clinton boasted with joy when learning of the assassination of the foreign leader, "We came, we saw, he died". There were four major events that happened within a four month period that affected Minister Farrakhan and prompted him to deliver the 1989 press conference to the world.[150] One of those events was the death of Congressman, Mickey Leland of Texas[151] who died in a plane crash in Ethiopia on August 7, 1989 with 15 other people. The second event was what the American press called the "Beijing Massacre at Tiananmen Square" June 4, 1989, also called by the Chinese the "June 4th Incident".[152] The student led protests in Beijing ended with hundreds of people being killed by the Chinese government, after the protesters called for a more democratic China in the post-Mao China. The protests spread to over 400 cities and over 300,000 Chinese troops were deployed. The most chilling of these protests is the popular scene of the Chinese citizen standing in front of a military tank during the protest, a photograph taken by American photographer Jeff Widener.

---

[150] Jabril Muhammad, "More than a vision—bearing witness to the Minister's profound experience", *FinalCall.Com*, March 9, 2016.
http://www.finalcall.com/artman/publish/Columns_4/article_102953.shtml
[151] Ibid.
[152] Ibid.

On November 16, 2017, Minister Farrakhan would come once again to Washington, DC twenty-eight years after his 1989 press conference, and 32 years after his vision experience, to warn Donald J. Trump, the 45th President of the United States.

This warning was extended the government of America, as Minister Farrakhan revealed his knowledge of their unfolding plot to destroy black youth with their genocidal plans, and to wage war against the Nation of Islam in America. [153] He emphatically proclaimed that his message was being delivered from the Honorable Elijah Muhammad, on the Wheel, but through him. [154] Minister Farrakhan once again, as in 1989 restates some of his experience on the Mother Wheel,

> You may say, "Well, this is not the usual press conference." No, it isn't. No, this is far from that. I warned President Reagan, at that time, of the thinking that he had, not fully knowing it. But I knew enough to know that Ronald Reagan didn't have no love for Black people. The next year, 1985, after The Forum, I go down in Mexico. And on the night of the 17th of September, in a Vision I was carried up on the top of a mountain there, in a sacred valley in Tepoztlán. There is a temple at the top made like a pyramid, but it's a monument to the Christ figure of Mesoamerica, Quetzalcóatl. And there I was, at night, in a Vision-Like Experience, and one of these UFOs came over. I had people with me in the Vision. When we got to the top of that mountain this "wheel-like" Plane came over. Three legs came down from it. I thought it was going to land on the mountain. I said to Jabril, "Come on with me"—and a voice said,

[153] Farrakhan, Louis. "A Final Warning a Final Call." Press Conference, Watergate Hotel, Washington, DC, November 16, 2017. Accessed December 14, 2017. https://study.noi.org/documents.

[154] Farrakhan, Louis. "A Final Warning a Final Call." Press Conference, Watergate Hotel, Washington, DC., 2.

"Not them. Just you." So I walked forward. And as you have heard me say it many times—and I am not drunk, nor crazy, or a liar. See, when you have an experience, you say it the same way every time. And a beam of light came out of that Wheel, and drew me up into it; and I knew it was taking me to the Mother Wheel. I will not go into a lot of detail now, because the detail is in the packet; you can go and check it out. Because what I am saying to you, I want you intelligent ones, or not so intelligent, to do the research. And you will find that every word that I am saying to you [is] absolutely right. When I got inside the big Wheel, there was a scroll with cursive writing on it. I was trying to read it, Elijah Muhammad speaks, and the scroll rolled up. [To the technical team] You have his words? Put them up. Listen to what he said to me. He said, "President Reagan, in early September met with his joint chiefs of staff to plan a war. I want you to hold a press conference in Washington, D.C., and make known their plans. And tell them that you got it from me, Elijah Muhammad, on The Wheel." [Audience beginning to applaud] Listen! Just listen. Then he said: "You've got one more thing to do. And when you have done it, you may come again to The Wheel, and I will let you see me face-to-face." And he dismissed me.[155]

President, Donald Trump and the United States have been warned by Minister Farrakhan, as with previous presidents, going back to George HW Bush in 1989, and further back to Ronald Reagan. Minister Farrakhan has made specific mention to the "one more thing to do", which was told to him by the Honorable Elijah Muhammad on the wheel. This "one more thing" is directly related to the uplifting of black and brown people in America and humanity in general. It is also necessary for Minister Farrakhan to serve as an example and his life as a sacrifice for all to see and bear witness to the love of God for humanity, but through him and the Honorable Elijah Muhammad. This is an evident reality that is yet to be seen, but will soon be manifest to the

---

[155] Farrakhan, Louis. "A Final Warning a Final Call." Press Conference, Watergate Hotel, Washington, DC, November 16, 2017. Accessed December 14, 2017. https://study.noi.org/documents.

world as the prophecies unfold and are revealed in this time. The value of Minister Farrakhan is immeasurable, such as his very presence is keeping America and the world from the speedy chastisement of God that has befallen past nations in the scriptures, Holy Quran and Bible.

5.4   Testimony of the Vision Experience

As mentioned previously, with all significant men and women who have a divine impact on humanity in history, witnesses are present to observe, write, and speak of their character, goodness, divinity, and influence on the people. This is also the case with Minister Farrakhan's vision experience. These witnesses are companions, family, close friends, students, disciples, and even enemies. This was the case with the Prophets whose lives were a sign of things to come. The following is an interview with Mother Tynnetta Muhammad by Jabril Muhammad. They share intimate conversations with Minister Farrakhan about his vision experience only days after it happened. This interview appeared in Jabril Muhammad's weekly column, "Farrakhan the Traveler" in the Final Call News, August 20, 2014.

> **Jabril Muhammad (JM):** Now let's go all the way to the Honorable Minister Louis Farrakhan's vision. Let's go to 1985, in Mexico, when the Minister had the vision. There's an earthquake on the 19th day of September. The Minister comes with his wife, Mother Khadijah to your home and he talks to you and his wife, about his vision. As best as you can recollect, did he say it to you both something like 'Please come sit down I have something of importance to tell you.' How do you recall that experience?

> **Mother Tynnetta Muhammad (MTM):** How did he let me know that he had the vision?

> **JM:** Yes.

MTM: He came into my house. He was walking up the steps towards the kitchen, and then all of a sudden he got to the door and as he was greeting me, right at the door, he said "Oh." He says, "I just remembered that I had an experience."

JM: Now where was his wife Mother Khadijah at that moment?

MTM: I don't recall exactly. She sort of walked in, and maybe she was in the living room or just walked a little bit away from where he was, but not far away.

JM: That's when he began? Did he sit you both down?

MTM: No. He just said it kind of casually. And I said, "Really." I said, "What happened?" Then he went on to explain. Half standing and then I believe he sat down in the kitchen.

JM: And where is his wife, at that time? And did he tell you both what he did in the kitchen?

MTM: I believe she was by that time, in the kitchen.

JM: So he just said as a matter of fact and in that manner?

MTM: Yes. And I said, "Brother Minister," I said, "what you are saying is very important." That's what I remember you know, and he was like "Oh?" and "Huh?"

JM: He would be laughing if he was here right now.

MTM: Yes.

JM: How did his wife react?

MTM: I don't recall, because I was mostly concentrating on what he had said. He had dropped quite a bit. And I really don't recall her response or expression or anything like that very clearly, really.

JM: OK. Now of course I heard or learned of his vision from him when he came here a week or so later. Now to your best recollection, do you know if he said it to anybody else between the time he talked to you two and the time he talked to me?

MTM: Did he come immediately from here to Phoenix?

JM: Yes. From Mexico to here in Phoenix.

MTM: Did he? Well then he had to have. And then next time we heard it in a big manner was in New York when he was sitting with us up in that area.

JM: Then the next time he told it was on the plane. I wanted to get it on tape. I still have the tape somewhere and in the middle of talking, he broke down and started crying and said that it was like he had an inoculation and that now it's wearing off and he was beginning to sense something strange and significant had happened to him. It was a powerful experience with him on that plane, as we went to New York.

MTM: For many who don't want to hear the truth because the truth is very harsh, sometimes. It's harsh but we must hear it.

JM: You know, Mother Muhammad, I was reading in a book—it does have bearing on this because I cite this in the manuscript that so many people cannot accept the superiority of another person over themselves in certain areas. That's pitiful, and that's ridiculous.[156]

---

[156] Jabril Muhammad, Farrakhan the Traveler. "Prophecy is much more than a prediction", *FinalCall.Com*, August 20, 2014.
http://www.finalcall.com/artman/publish/Columns_4/article_101697.shtml

In the above interview Tynnetta Muhammad recalls her conversation with Minister Farrakhan about his experience on the Wheel. Despite opinions from detractors and critics, she and his wife Khadijah Farrakhan are witnesses of the events that have unfolded as a result of his experience and conversation on the wheel with the Honorable Elijah Muhammad and all that it has produced. These women are witnesses. They were the first to hear of his experience as he was recalling it, in the moment of recall. This is important and their testimony is relevant. Likewise with Jabril Muhammad, that heard of the magnificent vision only a week after Minister Farrakhan's experience. These words are printed below. The words that Minister Farrakhan shared with Jabril Muhammad about the outcome of his experience are profound. They demonstrate the sincerity, respect, humility, and the seriousness of the experience. All of what was said to Jabril Muhammad is a bearing of witness of the Honorable Elijah Muhammad being alive and Minister Farrakhan's work in America. Jabril Muhammad recalls the moment Minister Farrakhan dictated the vision to him,

> Then the next time he told it was on the plane. I wanted to get it on tape. I still have the tape somewhere and in the middle of talking, he broke down and started crying and said that it was like he had an inoculation and that now it's wearing off and he was beginning to sense something strange and significant had happened to him.[157]

---

[157] Jabril Muhammad, Farrakhan the Traveler. "Prophecy is much more than a prediction", Also see, Muhammad, *Closing the Gap*, 118-19, 375.

Muhammad also recalls in greater detail his conversation with Minister Farrakhan at the moment the vision experience was mentioned to him,

> Minister Farrakhan used Phoenix for most of the time he spent in preparation for his speech in Los Angeles. He now returned to Phoenix to prepare for his next speech, which was to come in New York City. Mother Tynnetta Muhammad and I were with Minister Farrakhan on the first day of his preparation for his New York speech. This discussion took place at a lake called Lake Pleasant, in Phoenix. Then as we were gathering our books and papers to return to Scottsdale (a city adjoining Phoenix) Minster Farrakhan informed me of his vision-like experience. I was at the same time both immensely gratified and profoundly moved by it and struck by what seemed to me to be the casual manner in which he told me what he did. I regarded what he told me as momentous, wondrous or spectacular, or even more than that. He did not seem to realize the weight and significance of what he was telling me. It was a few days later, while he and I were on a jet, our way on a route that would take us to New York City, that I asked him to please go over his vision-like experience again with me. I wanted him to put his experience on tape because I wanted his every word of his experience carefully preserved. To me, what he experienced was something that would powerfully reverberate around the earth. As he spoke into the tape recorder he began to break down. He said he was realizing that something very unusual had happened to him, which he could not explain. Tears began to roll down his cheeks as he spoke to me. It was evident to me that he was experiencing more fully the reality of his vision-like experience, even as he spoke. He said he felt as if he had been inoculated with something and now he was feeling the effects.[158]

Minister Farrakhan said that he felt inoculated[159] with something during his experience. What could this have been? And, does this have anything

---

[158] Jabril Muhammad, "More Than A Vision And A New Book For The Change Of Worlds", FinalCall.Com, October 4, 2016.
http://www.finalcall.com/artman/publish/Columns_4/article_103327.shtml
[159] Webster's New World College Dictionary defines inoculate as 1. a. to inject a serum, vaccine, etc. into (a living organism), esp. in order to create immunity
b. to communicate (a disease) in this way
2. to put or implant microorganisms into (soil, a culture medium, etc.) to develop a culture, stimulate growth, fix nitrogen, etc.

to do with the "book" that is mentioned in Revelation 5:1? Yes. It does, except this book is in English and is reserved for Minister Farrakhan.[160]

5.5   The Value of the Vision Experience: What is it?

I will say at this juncture and elaborate later, that the vision experience of Minister Farrakhan was what is called an out-of-body experience or astral projection. The Great Earthquake in Mexico City on September 19, 1985 allowed Minster Farrakhan to *recall* his vision experience and communicate it to others. Luis Minero explains the importance of recalling an experience like Minister Farrakhan's,

> We need to recall the experience, since a projection is not necessarily automatically recalled. The reason for this is that everything we perceive and experience outside the body is not automatically recorded in the brain and is not automatically accessible. On the contrary, this information accumulates in the nonphysical bodies, which are the ones that are active at the moment of the experience. In order to have this information accessible while in intraphysically awake, we need to recall the information while inside the body.[161]

Out-of Body Experience (OBE) – An experience where a person witnesses himself or herself floating or moving outside of their body. This is also called Astral Projection and is sometimes associated with and Lucid Dreaming.

The Holy Quran accurately describes what Minister Farrakhan experienced,

---

3. to introduce ideas, etc. into the mind of; imbue
Webster's New World College Dictionary, 4th Edition. (Houghton Mifflin Harcourt, 2010.)
[160] Read Revelation 5:1-14 for full context of this scripture.
[161] Luis Minero. **Demystifying the out-of-body Experience: A Practical Manual for Exploration and Personal Evolution**. (Woodbury, MN: Llewellyn Publications, 2012), 11.

By the star when it sets! Your companion errs not, nor does he deviate. Nor does he speak out of desire. It is naught but revelation that is revealed - One Mighty in power has taught him, The Lord of Strength. So he attained to perfection, And he is in the highest part of the horizon. Then he drew near, drew nearer yet, So he was the measure of two bows or closer still. So He revealed to His servant what He revealed. The heart was not untrue in seeing what he saw. Do you then dispute with him as to what he saw? And certainly he saw Him in another descent, At the farthest lote-tree. Near it is the Garden of Abode. When that which covers covered the lote-tree; The eye turned not aside, nor did it exceed the limit. Certainly he saw of the greatest signs of his Lord.[162]

What did Minister Farrakhan see? What are the greatest signs of his Lord? These signs are directly connected to the reality of the great Mother Wheel and the Honorable Elijah Muhammad's divinity as the exalted Christ. This is also connected to Black people in America's divine and beloved position with God. The *vision* of Minister Farrakhan continues to baffle even the serious student of the teachings of the Honorable Elijah Muhammad. His experience is more than a *religious experience* in the contemporary sense, but an actual communication with the Honorable Elijah Muhammad, from the Wheel or Mother Plane. As I have demonstrated in earlier chapters, the Wheel is real and these types of wheels have existed in ancient history. But, the 'Mother' Plane (wheel) built by Master W.F. Muhammad is the greatest and most powerful to ever exist. The Honorable Elijah Muhammad says of this Wheel:

> I have seen that plane. It's a powerful plane. It can dart in the sky just like what's called flying saucers. The plane measures one mile right through it. Allah showed me the plane. If you find me lying on what I tell you of what he said, I'll give you $10,000 out of my brothers vest pocket.[163]

---

[162] See Holy Quran 53:1-18.
[163] Muhammad, *Theology of Time*, 100.

Mr. Muhammad further elaborates on the Wheel and visions of the Wheel:

> …The drawings of the Wheel is found in the first and tenth chapter of Ezekiel. He said he saw in a vision of a wheel in a wheel. It didn't come down to Earth. He said he saw it rise up from Earth. I want you to listen to me good. I thought that it would have been best if I talked about this wheel. Ezekiel said that he saw in a vision of a wheel in wheel. Now you see, not only the outer part of the great wheel did he say he saw, but he said he saw a wheel in a wheel. Where is the other wheel Ezekiel? If Ezekiel saw any vision, he wasn't seeing visions of lies. Whenever they have a vision, it's the truth.[164]

Minister Farrakhan's vision experience is included in this type of experience. Why Farrakhan? Why should he have a vision and it be the basis of his declaration that his teacher is the exalted Christ of Almighty God? He is not lying! This reality is concealed in the true identity of the prophetic figure called Jesus.

> But Nay I call to witness the stars, That run their course (and) hide themselves, And the night when it departs, And the morning when it brightens, Most surely it the word of an honoured Apostle, The possessor of strength, having an honourable place with the Lord of Dominion, One (to be) obeyed and faithful in trust. And your companion is not gone mad. And of the truth he saw himself on the clear horizon. Nor of the unseen is he a tenacious concealer. Nor is it the word of the cursed devil.[165]

Jesus the Prophet of 2,000 years ago is no longer physically alive. Scholars have contended, and have confirmed that the Jesus spoken of in the Bible did not exist as the Bible depicts. The experience of Minister Farrakhan involves his communication with the Honorable Elijah

---

[164] Muhammad, *Theology of Time*, 113. See entire chapter of Ezekiel Chapter 1 and Chapter 10.
[165] See Holy Quran 81:15-25. This is the 1917 translation of Mualvi Muhammad Ali. This edition is the first translated edition given to the Honorable Elijah Muhammad by Master Fard Muhammad according to the Honorable Elijah Muhammad words, August 20, 1972.

Muhammad, who is not physically dead, but has been raised by God as Christ Almighty and more. It is the Supreme knowledge and wisdom of God Himself that has made this possible. If you are a believer in God, would you agree that God's power and ability to do what He pleases is infinite? I am not referring to an invisible God. If you agree, would not God have the ability to protect His servants from their enemies and His? The resurrection of the dead that the Bible speaks of is a spiritual death and resurrection. In another aspect, this also represents a physical death involving a death plot, but not with the Prophet Jesus. The Holy Quran makes reference to this death plot in 2:72,

> And when you (almost) killed a man, then you disagreed about it. And Allah was to bring forth that which you were going to hide. [166]

In this translation, Maulana Muhammad Ali explains,

> The very indefiniteness of the incident is an indication that it refers to some well-known event in history, and as almost all incidents of the stubbornness of the Jewish nation prior to the time of Jesus have been mentioned, it becomes almost certain that this incident refers to Jesus himself, as was with respect to his death that disagreement took place and many doubted his death. [167]

This death plot and attempted murder involved the Honorable Elijah Muhammad. The Holy Quran further states,

> When Allah said: O Jesus, I will cause thee to die and exalt thee in My presence and clear thee of those who disbelieve and make those who follow thee above those who disbelieve to the day of Resurrection. Then

---

[166] Holy Quran 2:72
[167] See foot note 110 for HQ 2:72-73.

to Me is your return, so I shall decide between you concerning that wherein you differ.[168]

What was it that they doubted? They doubted whether or not he was dead. The scholars suggest,

> Some commentators say that Jesus remained dead for three hours; others say for seven hours, and so on (Rz). But, the word is used here really to show that the Jewish plans to cause Jesus' death on the cross would be frustrated and he would afterwards die a natural death...[169]

This is one of the reasons why the man called Jesus is so misunderstood in religion. People expect his eminent return, and they expect a judgment that he (Jesus) will execute, but they do not know what he looks like. Some are even foolish to think that it does not matter what he looks like. This type of blind faith is not based on knowledge, but at its root it is based on a lie. The Holy Quran further states regarding Jesus' assumed death,

> And for their saying: We have killed the Messiah, Jesus, son of Mary, the messenger of Allah, and they killed him not, nor did they cause his death on the cross, but he was made to appear to them as such. And certainly those who differ therein are in doubt about it. They have no knowledge about it, but only follow a conjecture, and they killed him not for certain: Nay, Allah exalted him in His presence. And Allah is ever Mighty, Wise.[170]

The one who is called Jesus is a man, and this man was spiritually dead when he first spoke and was taught by God in person. The wicked sought to kill him for his preaching. This man loves God and his people

---

[168] Holy Quran 3:55.
[169] See foot note 436 for HQ 3:154.
[170] Holy Quran 4:157-158.

so much that he would suffer a second death. He would do this for the glory of God, and to fulfill the prophet's predictions. He was then raised from this dead state and taken to a safe place in the presence of God and away from his enemies. Here is a hint: Would not God have the ability to snatch his body from death and confuse his enemies? Keep in mind the words of Maulana Muhammad Ali in reference to Jesus,

"Some commentators say that Jesus remained dead for three hours; others say for seven hours, and so on…" "… [H]e would afterwards die a natural death…"

1Corinthians 15:12-26 (NIV) elaborates on the resurrection of Christ and the dead,

> But if it is preached that Christ has been raised from the dead, how can some of you say that there is no resurrection of the dead? If there is no resurrection of the dead, then not even Christ has been raised. And if Christ has not been raised, our preaching is useless and so is your faith. More than that, we are then found to be false witnesses about God, for we have testified about God that he raised Christ from the dead. But he did not raise him if in fact the dead are not raised. For if the dead are not raised, then Christ has not been raised either. And if Christ has not been raised, your faith is futile; you are still in your sins. Then those also who have fallen asleep in Christ are lost. If only for this life we have hope in Christ, we are to be pitied more than all men.

> But Christ has indeed been raised from the dead, the first fruits of those who have fallen asleep. For since death came through a man, the resurrection of the dead comes also through a man. For as in Adam all die, so in Christ all will be made alive. But each in his own turn: Christ, the first fruits; then, when he comes, those who belong to him. Then the end will come, when he hands over the kingdom to God the Father after he has destroyed all dominion, authority and power. ***For he must reign***

until he has put all his enemies under his feet. The last enemy to be destroyed is death. [emphasis added][171]

Minister Farrakhan publicly announced the Honorable Elijah Muhammad's divine exaltation and has maintained his position on this declaration. Despite the ridicule and slander of his enemies and doubt even by his friends, (even to this day) he continues to maintain his defense of his teacher's position as being *physically* alive.[172] He also continues to represent him as the first begotten of the mentally and spiritually dead, to enter into the 'elect' circle of the wise Gods (scientist), taught personally by Master Fard Muhammad. Master Fard Muhammad said He was God, the Supreme Being. He did not just say this to his followers in the 1930's, he also said this to the authorities in Detroit, Michigan.[173] Now, either he lied, or he told the truth. What is the base of the Honorable Elijah Muhammad's success in America among Black people? What follows is a statement from Minister Farrakhan to thousands at Saviours' Day 1981, almost 5 years before his vision experience:

> After his wife, Mother Clara, died in 1972, he said the end will come three years later. We thought he meant the Judgment of the world, but he meant the end of his first 40 years among us. *He had done his job and paid the price; and now he had to drink the bitter cup of death, but a Mighty God and a Mighty Saviour would save him from that death and confuse the enemy.* [emphasis added] I know you think Elijah is dead, but I'm here to tell you he is as alive as you sitting in that seat. Not only is he alive and well, he is in power now.
>
> The Honorable Elijah Muhammad told us, if Allah (God) had not shown him how he was going to escape, he would have no hope at all. One day,

---

[171] See 1Corinthians 15:12-26 (NIV).
[172] See, *Is it possible the Honorable Elijah Muhammad is Physically Alive* by Jabril Muhammad.
[173] True Islam, *Master Fard Muhammad: Who Is He? Who Is He Not?.* (Atlanta, GA: A Team Publishing, 2008), 24.

he was discussing the finality of death. His son was pressing him with questions, asking if when we die, can we ever be brought back. Finally, he replied, "If he's a real, great man and Allah (God) favors him much, if Allah (God) gets the body within 24 hours, He can revive it." We live in a world where you can die and have an *out-of-body experience*, [emphasis added] yet the White man, with his limited knowledge, can bring you back.[174]

Did the Honorable Elijah Muhammad escape a death plot? A failed death plot against the Messenger of Allah is baffling to the enemies of God. The ultimate aim of the enemies of God is to kill His Messenger. This is not new in our history. Many of the Prophets of God have been murdered throughout history. This escape from death is one of the most skillful plans that one could conceive. The Bible suggests,

But Christ has indeed been raised from the dead, the first fruits of those who have fallen asleep. For since death came through a man, the resurrection of the dead comes also through a man. For as in Adam all die, so in Christ all will be made alive. But each in turn: Christ, the first fruits; then, when he comes, those who belong to him. Then the end will come, when he hands over the kingdom to God the Father after he has destroyed all dominion, authority and power. For he must reign until he has put all his enemies under his feet. **The last enemy to be destroyed is death.**[175]

Death is a natural occurrence, but mental and spiritual death is an outrage. This is still yet another enemy to conquer; the mind of Yacub, the father of the white race. But, these verses are also related to Minister Farrakhan and what he too would be confronted with and have to conquer, or destroy. With the conquering of this mind and subsequent death, comes a renewed being. Eternal life becomes more than just a

---

[174] Louis Farrakhan, "A Saviour is Born for the Black Man and Woman of America" Keynote speech, Saviours Day from The Nation of Islam, Chicago, IL., February 22, 1981.
[175] 1 Corinthians 15:20-26.

saying, but a reality. A new growth takes place in the human being that transforms man and woman into God. This wisdom is what the Honorable Elijah Muhammad offered to Minister Farrakhan and what he taught him on the Wheel.

> When Allah said: O Jesus I will cause thee to die and exalt thee in my presence and clear thee of those who disbelieve and make those who follow thee above those who disbelieve. To the day of resurrection. Then to me is your return, so I shall decide between you concerning that wherein you differ.[176]

> Behold! Allah said: "O Jesus! I will take thee and raise thee to Myself and clear thee (of the falsehoods) of those who blaspheme; I will make those who follow thee superior to those who reject faith, to the Day of Resurrection: Then shall ye all return unto me, and I will judge between you of the matters wherein ye dispute.[177]

The confusion of many on the subject of Minister Farrakhan's experience, from my observation, is due to a misunderstanding of the how he is viewed in general, and specifically how he is viewed in relation to the events of the past and present, and even more specifically how he viewed in relation to Allah (God). Ezekiel chapters 2 and 3 speak specifically to Minister Farrakhan's experience.

> You must speak my words to them, whether they listen or fail to listen, for they are rebellious. But you, son of man, listen to what I say to you. Do not rebel like that rebellious house; open your mouth and eat what I give you." *Then I looked, and I saw a hand stretched out to me. In it was a scroll, which he unrolled before me. On both sides of it were written words of lament and mourning and woe.* [178] [emphasis added]

---

[176] See Holy Quran 3:55 Maulana Muhammad Ali translation.
[177] See Holy Quran- 3:55, Yusuf Ali.
[178] See Ezekiel 2:7-10.

And he said to me, *"Son of man, eat what is before you, eat this scroll;* *then go and speak to the house of Israel." So I opened my mouth, and* *he gave me the scroll to eat.* Then he said to me, *"Son of man, eat this* *scroll I am giving you and fill your stomach with it." So I ate it, and* *it tasted as sweet as honey in my mouth.* [emphasis added]"[179]

The Honorable Minister Louis Farrakhan's words at the press conference in 1989 mirrors the above scriptures.

> He spoke in short cryptic sentences and as he spoke a scroll full of cursive writing rolled down in front of my eyes, but it was a projection of what was being written in my mind. As I attempted to read the cursive writing, which was in English, the scroll disappeared and the Honorable Elijah Muhammad began to speak to me.[180]

Tynnetta Muhammad explains how she understood the vision experience when Minister Farrakhan first mentioned it to her September 19, 1985,

> I remember that I experienced great excitement, enthusiasm and palpitation of my heart and I said to him, Brother Minister, do you realize what you are saying? And he responded by asking me what did I see in this experience. I was so overwhelmed in my response that I could only think, my God, he literally had met with my husband. He has begun to communicate with him in his journey much like Ezekiel being taken up on a Wheel within a Wheel. As I began to piece this experience together, in later days, I recalled the scriptures from both Bible and Holy Quran that mentioned Moses mystical experience in the mountain, where he left the children of Israel below at that particular time, there were only a few elders or companions who were able to be present at the foot of the mountain. In the experience, the tablets were revealed and Moses was not able to see the face of his Lord, but was only able to see, according to the Bible, his hinder parts, his back parts, as he went

---

[179] See Ezekiel 3:1-3.
[180] Louis Farrakhan, *The Announcement: A final warning to the U.S. Government, (Chicago, IL:* FCN Publishing, Co., 1989, 1991) 6-7.

by him. And again, in each instance of his highly mystical contact with God, there was a great earthquake.[181]

Farrakhan's announcement revealed and uncovered the secret plans of the U.S. to plan a war on a small nation. Minister Farrakhan's announcement is a report and warning from Allah (God) and the Honorable Elijah Muhammad to the world, particularly to his enemies. The betrayal of Minister Farrakhan is rooted in the envy of God's enemies and their hatred of God's chosen people. This envy is also expressed by blacks who have a deep rooted self-hatred for themselves and their own people. Minister Farrakhan's announcement confirmed to the world that he (Farrakhan) is guided by a power greater than the power of this modern world.

---

[181]Jabril Muhammad, *Closing the Gap: Inner Views of the Heart, Mind and Soul of the Honorable Louis Farrakhan*, (Chicago, IL: FCN Publishing, Co., 2006) 379-80.

This Page Intentionally Left Blank

6 True Dreams, Visions and the Spirit of God

6.1 *Visions: Thought, Spirit and Mind*

Then I beheld, and lo a likeness as the appearance of fire: from the appearance of his loins even downward, fire; and from his loins even upward, as the appearance of brightness, as the colour of amber. *And he put forth the form of an hand, and took me by a lock of mine head; and the spirit lifted me up between the earth and the heaven, and brought me in the visions of God to Jerusalem,* [emphasis added] to the door of the inner gate that looketh toward the north; where was the seat of the image of jealousy, which provoketh to jealousy. And, behold, the glory of the God of Israel was there, according to the vision that I saw in the plain.[182]

In visions of God he took me to the land of Israel and set me on a very high mountain, on whose south side were some buildings that looked like a city. He took me there, and I saw a man whose appearance was like bronze; he was standing in the gateway with a linen cord and a measuring rod in his hand. The man said to me, "Son of man, look with your eyes and hear with your ears and pay attention to everything I am going to show you, for that is why you have been brought here. Tell the house of Israel everything you see".[183]

In my vision at night I looked, and there before me was one like a son of man, coming with the clouds of heaven. He approached the Ancient of Days and was led into his presence. He was given authority, glory and sovereign power; all peoples, nations and men of every language worshiped him. His dominion is an everlasting dominion that will not pass away, and his kingdom is one that will never be destroyed.[184]

When men are afraid of heights and of dangers in the streets; when the almond tree blossoms and the grasshopper drags himself along and desire no longer is stirred. Then man goes to his eternal home and mourners go about the streets Remember him—*before the silver cord*

---

[182] See Ezekiel 8:2-4.
[183] See Ezekiel 40: 2-4 (NIV).
[184] See Daniel 7:13-14 (NIV).

is severed, [emphasis added] or the golden bowl is broken; before the pitcher is shattered at the spring, or the wheel broken at the well, and the dust returns to the ground it came from, and the spirit returns to God who gave it.[185]

He hath said, which heard the words of God, which saw the vision of the Almighty, falling into a trance, but having his eyes open: How goodly are thy tents, O Jacob, and thy tabernacles, O Israel![186]

The vision experience of Minister Farrakhan and his meeting with the Honorable Elijah Muhammad can be referenced to similar experiences of Prophets of the past typologically. Minister Farrakhan and the Honorable Elijah Muhammad fulfill much of what is prophesied in the Bible and Holy Quran.[187] The vision also represents and fulfills prophecies spoken of and thus has a significant impact on America and the world. Many minor and major Prophets including common people have experienced visions. Visions have meaning, purpose and form, and represent a divine way that prophecy and revelation are communicated. In vision experiences, the visions are projected to the recipient in an *autobiography style* categorized in three parts; announcement, transition, and vision sequence. The announcement reports what is seen and can include descriptions of circumstances, events, and dates.[188] Burke O. Long in his writing, ***Reports of visions among the Prophets*** says,

---

[185] See Ecclesiastes 12:5-7 (NIV).
[186] See Numbers 24:4-5 (KJV).
[187] See, Elijah Muhammad, ***Theology of Time*** (Atlanta, GA: MEMPS, 1997), 318. "I'm a fulfiller; therefore, I have to go through that which prophets went through thousands of years ago, in order to make it worthless for you to have another prophet. That's right you don't need no prophets after me. I bring you face to face with God and the devil; therefore you don't need no more prophets. I'm fulfilling in your presence that which Moses, Aerial, Lot, Abraham and those before them. I fulfill all of them right before your face, but you don't know these things, because you never study scripture."
[188] Burke. O.Long, "Reports of Visions among the Prophets," ***Journal of Biblical Literature*** 95, no. 3 (1976): 355.

Regardless of the variety, the announcement almost invariably reports, rather like a technical formula, that the prophet "sees" or is "made to see."[189]

Maulana Muhammad Ali says of visions,

... [F]rom behind a veil, refers to *ru'ya* or dreams and *kashf* or visions, because a certain sight is shown in this case which has deeper meaning than that which appears on the surface... Hence God's speaking from behind a veil means His revealing certain truths in dreams and visions.[190]

If we observe Ali's statement, can it be concluded that Minister Farrakhan received truth from *behind a veil* in his vision? Is it possible that he did visit the Mother Wheel, spoke to the Honorable Elijah Muhammad and received instruction and revelation? What is the likelihood that this actually happened? Can we connect the vision to the prophetic writings in scripture through careful analysis and with the help of several simple scriptural rules? Yes! Through further study of Minister Farrakhan's vision and observation of the elements of his *Announcement*, we can gain understanding of its importance and typological relevance to scripture. The Honorable Elijah Muhammad had a similar vision experience [191] with his teacher Master Fard Muhammad, September 1971:

For nearly 40 years I have studied scripture and history, after Allah taught me for three years and four months. He gave me 104 books to study. He gave me the number of them and the place where I could find

---

[189] Burke. O.Long, "Reports of Visions among the Prophets," *Journal of Biblical Literature* 95, no. 3 (1976): 355.
[190] Maulana M. Ali, *The Religion of Islam*, (Columbus, OH: Ahmadiyya Anjuman Isha'at Islam, 1990), 17.
[191] On February 26, 2009 in Chicago, IL, I was present in a meeting with Minister Farrakhan where he elaborated on this "vision" of the Honorable Elijah Muhammad. Minster Farrakhan made mentioned that the book the Honorable Elijah Muhammad was shown "wasn't thick". He said that there was, "light coming from the depth of the letters". He called it a book of "Pure Light". He made specific reference to the Honorable Elijah Muhammad experiencing a "vision".

them. I studied, and he gave me a Holy Qur'an in Arabic, but I couldn't read it. So, He got me one in Arabic and English translated by Muhammad Ali of Pakistan. Later He found one translated by Yusuf Ali of Egypt; He brought me that one. Then He told me, "I will give you a Holy Qur'an when you learn how to read Arabic, then I will give you a Holy Quran in Arabic." He said, "I made it myself." *He showed me that Holy Quran in Arabic in September last, but I couldn't read it. I could only recognize one letter in it. I expect Him within a year to come back with that same book.*[192] [emphasis added]

How did the Honorable Elijah Muhammad experience his vision? In fact, Master Fard Muhammad communicated with the Honorable Elijah Muhammad every year, several times during each year while the Honorable Elijah Muhammad worked in America. This communication was important to the Honorable Elijah Muhammad's great success in America.[193] How did the communication happen?

Some critics have concluded that the Honorable Elijah Muhammad never mentioned or spoke specifically about dreams, or visions. Thus, this would nullify Minister Farrakhan's vision experience on the Wheel. I disagree. Obviously there are mixed feelings and controversy around this subject. Some of the controversy is due to sincere misunderstanding. The other controversy is rooted in an infectious hypocrisy stemming from jealousy and envy directed towards Minister Farrakhan. Nonetheless, the controversy exists.

My argument is that the Honorable Elijah Muhammad spoke on dreams and visions, in the public and in private on numerous occasions and experienced them. Also, keep in mind that at times these words, "visions" and "dreams" are used interchangeably by people, although they can be different. The Honorable Elijah Muhammad respected this form of communication by Allah. This is an ancient science. Between

---

[192] Muhammad, *Theology of Time*, 100.
[193] Muhammad, *This is the One,* 157-58.

April 17, 1970 and August 14, 1970 he permitted the "visions" of Brother Theodore 6X to be printed (in full) in the Muhammad Speaks Newspaper. Brother Theodore 6X says of his visions,

> In the year of 1965 Almighty God, whose proper name is Allah, who came to us in the Person of Master W. Fard Muhammad to who praises are due forever showed me a great vision that was in five parts. It was the first of three major visions; the second vision was in two parts. Those seven parts of the first two visions revealed to me many of the major tragic and disastrous things to come upon the Black race in particular: and America in general.[194]

On sharing his visions with the Honorable Elijah Muhammad, he agreed that it was a true vision from Allah and called Brother Theodore 6X a "minor" prophet. We cannot forget the fact that Master W. Fard Muhammad, Allah in Person, also had a "dream" when he was six years old. In his dream he was shown his future and purpose, not just for himself, but for all of humanity and more. How can a person who says that they believe in his teachings disregard "dreams" and "visions" as viable and authentic forms of communication from Allah (God), and not deny the dream of Master Fard Muhammad, Allah in Person? The Bible and Holy Quran bear witness to the visions and dreams of the Prophets and messengers of God in histories past. I cite below, two quotes that are deeply important to understanding the Divine mind of God in the Honorable Elijah Muhammad, and what was promised to him, by Master Fard Muhammad. These quotes are directly tied to Minister Farrakhan and what he experienced on the Wheel in his own vision. This is also found in the Bible, hidden in the experience of one of the most authentic and verifiable characters, and disciples of Jesus in the New Testament; Paul. Tynnetta Muhammad shares her testimony of what

---

[194] Theodore 6X, "The Prelude to My Visions", *Muhammad Speaks*, April 17, 1970, 15.

she heard the Honorable Elijah Muhammad say of his own dreams or visions,

> During one of the dinner settings of the Most Honorable Elijah Muhammad in the 1970's, he shared with a few of his followers a series of dreams in which he was stepping off of one revolving sphere onto another revolving sphere where the setting was all too surreal or of another world. He described seeing different colors greatly enhanced in tones and frequencies as in the green color for grass, trees and bushes. He described men dressed in apparel unlike the garments in today's society. They were like a type of uniform that I tried to imagine being worn by the actors in some kind of space odyssey such as Star Trek. He said that they appeared very focused, concentrating on their work assignment without conversation and they walked with a quick moving stride. He told us that this dream occurred twice within a year's time. He was also shown a book which had guilded [sic] or illumined Arabic Letters of which he could only recognize the letter "Lam." These dreams occurred in the month of September.[195]

Mother Tynnetta Muhammad is referring to an experience that happened in 1971, which is the highest form of revelation directly from God. The Honorable Elijah Muhammad was confident that he saw this book, and he was just as confident that Master Fard Muhammad would "come back" with that book again. He even confirmed it by saying *when* he expected to receive this book ("within a year"). Did he get it? Based on his own words, we can clearly see that Honorable Elijah Muhammad was in constant contact with Master Fard Muhammad. Read Revelation 5: 1-14 for what happened next to the Honorable Elijah Muhammad, but on the heels of a death plot. How does this relate to Minister Farrakhan and his vision experience?

---

[195] Tynnetta Muhammad, Unveiling the Number 19: City in the Sky, the New Jerusalem, *FinalCall.Com*, February 9, 2014.
http://www.finalcall.com/artman/publish/Columns_4/article_101213.shtml

Is it possible that the Honorable Elijah Muhammad from his exalted position communicates with Minister Farrakhan in a similar way that Master Fard Muhammad communicated with him? Absolutely. The Honorable Elijah Muhammad said he was to receive this NEW book from Allah, a NEW book written by ALLAH himself. This is the same book mentioned in Revelation that he took from God's hand. No one else could take it. It was made for him to build a NEW world with perfect WISDOM from God.

6.2   The exaltation of the Lamb of God

What Minister Farrakhan received on the Wheel in his experience was a portion of this book from Master Fard Muhammad, but given to him by the Honorable Elijah Muhammad in the form of a scroll, projected in his brain. This is the same scroll spoken of in Revelation 5:1-2. This is the same scroll mentioned in Ezekiel's vision experience on the Wheel when he was told to "eat the scroll".

> And he said to me, "Son of man, eat what is before you, eat this scroll; then go and speak to the people of Israel." So I opened my mouth, and he gave me the scroll to eat. Then he said to me, "Son of man, eat this scroll I am giving you and fill your stomach with it." So I ate it, and it tasted as sweet as honey in my mouth. He then said to me: "Son of man, go now to the people of Israel and speak my words to them.[196]

Once again the scroll is mentioned in Revelation and is given to one who was told eat it,

> But in the days when the seventh angel is about to sound his trumpet, the mystery of God will be accomplished, just as he announced to his servants the prophets." Then the voice that I had heard from heaven spoke to me once more: "Go, take the scroll that lies open in the

---

[196] Ezekiel 3:1-3

hand of the angel who is standing on the sea and on the land." So I went to the angel and asked him to give me the little scroll. He said to me, "Take it and eat it. It will turn your stomach sour, but 'in your mouth it will be as sweet as honey. I took the little scroll from the angel's hand and ate it. It tasted as sweet as honey in my mouth, but when I had eaten it, my stomach turned sour.[197]

This is a similar experience typologically that has been partially fulfilled by the Honorable Elijah Muhammad in September 1971. The Honorable Elijah Muhammad received the fullness of the wisdom of Master Fard Muhammad on his escape of a death plot to the Mother Plane or Wheel, February 25, 1975. This history is yet again to fulfill itself, but through Minister Farrakhan, who also fulfills aspects of the Lamb in revelation.

In Revelation, the Honorable Elijah Muhammad is called a "Lamb". The Lamb in the Bible is styled typologically as Christ. This is found throughout the New Testament, if we understand. He said he was the Jesus of the Bible and instructed his Ministers to "teach me through the volumes of the book". He always referenced the scriptures to himself and Allah, Master Fard Muhammad, in all of his teachings and writings. He said he was the Moses of the Bible and he even said he was the Muhammad of the Holy Quran. He did not say he was a prophet. He said he was the FULFILLMENT of the Prophets. There are many references by the Honorable Elijah Muhammad to himself in scripture; Bible and Holy Quran from his own mouth. But most important of all in the verifying of this great man's identity is the work that he performed among Black people in America. To understand him in the scriptures typologically is vitally important to understanding Minister Farrakhan and humanity, especially black and brown people in America.

---

[197] Revelation 10:1-9

| 144

When speaking of himself, the Honorable Elijah Muhammad taught,

> This is the true type of a man like Moses. If you study the prophecy concerning the last Messenger of God, according to the description given to the man by the Bible's prophecy in the Torah and Gospel, you will find that he is a man, according to Psalms, with the name of "Muhammad" and also you will find him in the Revelations under the symbolical name, "Lamb." He gets the name (Praised) from the honor of the "twenty-four elders" or Islamic Scientists. The position that he is shown under, the symbolical "Lamb" in Revelations, is like the Holy Qur-an's teaching one who is illiterate and whom the people will find written down in the Torah and the Gospel.[198]

He also says of himself in one of many references in the Bible as the Lamb, but this time he speaks of Jesus' (in Revelation) bearing of witness to the future of this Lamb,

> Moses' and Jesus' lives were examples of what would take place among the so-called Negro in America -- that lost and found people mentioned so much by Jesus in Revelations where it is shown that the Messenger becomes a lamb. In Revelations, the symbolic lamb is in the midst of four symbolic beasts. All of the scholars and scientists of the white race know this is not referring to Muhammad of 1,400 years ago.[199]

He also said June 4, 1972 during the Theology of Time lecture series,

> I am that One that He, Allah, took off aside. I call myself a "little fellow" because the Bible makes him little. It didn't make him a big sheep. I don't know how much is "Lamb" about me, but I know I am little.[200]

---

[198] Muhammad, **Message to the Blackman**, 158-59.
[199] Ibid., 188.
[200] Abass Rassoull, **The Theology of Time, by The Honorable Elijah Muhammad, Messenger of Allah**. (Hampton, VA: U.B. & U.S. Communications Systems, 1992)xxi-xxii.

He said of himself on June 18, 1972 during another Theology of Time lecture;

> I am risen up among you to condemn the white man's teaching and condemn him to death. This is what I am here for. I don't want you to think you're playing with no light boy at all. My size is very small, that's why they symbolically prophesied of me as being a little Lamb instead of a grown up Lamb.

He further acknowledges himself as the Lamb of God in relation to the 144,000 mentioned in the book of Revelation,

> Do not think that the 144,000 prophesied of, are the only ones who will be saved. The 144,000 refers to the first converts -- "the first ripe fruits to God and His Messenger, the first ripe fruits of God and the Lamb. [201]

What is spoken of in the Bible about the Lamb and the 144,000 converts in Revelation 14:1-5, happened in the LAST days. This is a prophecy that the Honorable Elijah Muhammad taught can be beaten, or does not have to pass. But, through Minister Farrakhan many more will be awaken. The Honorable Elijah Muhammad made it clear that the role and purpose of the Lamb (himself) is to establish a new civilization. *"Why he's called a Lamb further in the Revelation, is because he's the first that is born to bring about a new civilization, and he's the first of that new civilization."* This LAMB is the foundation of a NEW civilization that is also called by Christians today as the Kingdom of God. This lamb was seen in Revelation taking a book from God on the throne who sat with the twenty-four elders or scientist in the Bible. These are the same scientists we are taught about by the Honorable Elijah Muhammad. The Honorable Elijah Muhammad says of this new book and teaching:

---

[201] Muhammad, *The Fall of America*, 143.

You won't study the Bible in the Hereafter, nor will you study the present Qur'an, no. You will have a new book and that book will replace the present Bible and Qur'an... A new book is coming into being and that new book is the thing to which people should give ear. Now we're going the right way. These two former books, the Old Testament and the New Testament have served their purpose. Now we have to remove them and get a third and fourth book. They're (sic) two more to come. One is for you and the other is for the orthodox world. [202]

He taught that the Great Mahdi, Master W. F. Muhammad was and is the Supreme Being; the wisest of all the Gods that have ever lived. The Lamb of God did not die, but the Lamb was made into a GOD and the twenty-four elders around and about the throne shouted "worthy is the Lamb". Everything bowed to the Lamb except God Himself! This prophesy is progressive and has a three-fold reference[203] that applies to Minister Farrakhan directly. Jabril Muhammad mentions regarding this prophecy,

"There are some special prophecies that have a double reference, or they refer to, or cover time frames in which events occur and then re-occur. And there are still fewer very special prophetic events that are envisioned in a three-fold sense." In other words, there are some prophecies that come through visions that have single references; and there are even fewer that have double references. And there are even fewer still that have triple references. Visions, however, are not the only ways such information comes.

---

[202] Secretarius M.E.M.P.S, *The Theology of Time,* (Atlanta, GA: Secretarius MEMPS Publications 1997) 257-58.

[203] See Chapter 2; 2-2 "Laws and Rules of Interpretation". Theologian, Dwight Pentecost mentions about this type of reference, "The fact that the matter of prophecy is given in the form of intuition also furnishes the reason why it always sees the realization of that matter in particular events which are complete in themselves; i.e., a prophecy may appear as just one event, but in reality there may be a two-, three-, or four fold fulfillment." His mentioned of a possible four fold fulfillment; if we apply this in a modern context, the prophesy spoken of in Revelation chapters 4 and 5 not only make reference to Minister Farrakhan, but also an entire people who will be the beneficiaries of the new teachings, but through Minister Farrakhan.

If the One on the throne, in Revelation 4, refers to Master Fard Muhammad and the lion-lamb like man of Revelation 5 refers to the Honorable Elijah Muhammad, and if this scene is akin to, or if it is the same as the scene in Ezekiel, (chapters 1, 2, some of chapter 3 and chapter 10, and they are), then it is clear that these scenes were to have taken place in the great wheel-like plane, called the Mother Plane. Furthermore, all of this is connected to the Honorable Minister Louis Farrakhan and his work during these last 40 years; the rest of us and our future.[204]

Elijah Muhammad is all up into Allah's (God) mind. He represents the Blackman and woman; the spiritually dead in America and what God promised to us. He is the first begotten of the spiritually dead in the Bible. If Master Fard Muhammad was shown His future in a vision or dream, then why not the Honorable Elijah Muhammad? Even further why not Minister Farrakhan?

The late Malcolm X, in his autobiography spoke of an experience (vision) that he had with Allah, in the Person of Master Fard Muhammad. While his brother Reginald visited him, he learned that Reginald was suspended from the Nation of Islam. Malcolm prayed to Allah for intervention and relief for his brother and relief from his (Malcolm's) confusion. What Malcolm experienced the next night was an unexpected visit in his prison cell,

Reginald I learned, had been suspended from the Nation of Islam by Elijah Muhammad. He had not practiced moral restraint… When Reginald left, I was in torment. That night finally, I wrote to Mr. Muhammad, trying to defend my brother, appealing for him… Then the rest of the night, I prayed to Allah. I don't think anyone ever prayed more sincerely to Allah. I prayed for some kind of relief from my confusion. It was the next night as I lay on my bed, I suddenly, with a start, became aware of a man sitting beside me in my chair. He had on

[204] Jabril Muhammad, "Family And Unity In Bringing Hearts and Minds Together", FinalCall.Com, January 9, 2018. https://www.finalcall.com/artman/publish/Columns_4/article_103979.shtml

a dark suit. I remember. I could see him as plainly as I see anyone I look at. He wasn't black, and he wasn't white. He was light-brown skinned, an Asiatic cast of countenance, and he had oily black hair. I looked right into his face. I didn't get frightened. I knew I wasn't dreaming. I couldn't move, I didn't speak, and he didn't. I couldn't place him racially – other than I knew he was non-European. I had no idea whatsoever who he was. He just sat there. Then, suddenly as he had come, he was gone.[205]

Malcolm later learned who the man in his prison cell was and explains to the best of his understanding, the phenomenon that occurred that night in his jail cell,

It's impossible to dream, or to see, or to have a vision of someone whom you never have seen before-and to see him exactly as he is. To see someone, and to see him exactly as he looks, is to have a pre-vision. I would later come to believe that my pre-vision was of Master W.D. Fard, the Messiah, the one whom Elijah Muhammad said had appointed him – Elijah Muhammad – as His Last Messenger to black people of North America.[206]

How did these experiences occur? How did Allah show Himself to a person fully awake? Was this an act of a spirit, apparition, phantom, ghost or ethereal being? Was Malcolm X lying or was his experience a real encounter with Almighty Allah, who appeared in the Person of Master Fard Muhammad? Another spiritual experience by the former National Secretary of the Honorable Elijah Muhammad, Abass Rassoull, is further testimony. Not just testimony of the possibility of these experiences, but also testimony that the Honorable Elijah Muhammad is *physically* alive. Rassoull describes his experience where the Honorable Elijah Muhammad appeared to him at a very difficult time in his life,

---

[205] Alex Haley and Malcolm X, *The Autobiography of Malcolm X* (1964; repr., New York, NY: Ballantine Books, 1992), 214-15.
[206] Ibid,. 218.

...I laid on my bed and cried like a baby. It was then that I saw The Honorable Elijah Muhammad for the first time since his departure. I was lying on my back, wide awake and His head and shoulders appeared in a circle in front of me, about four feet above the bed. He did not have on His fez and He did not speak; He only smiled. He was there for two or three minutes. After He left, I got up, washed for prayer and said prayer. I have not missed a day of prayer since then, nor have I ever doubted again. Everything that I have done, of good, in the years since then have been based on the knowledge that **He is not dead, He did not lie, that He is The Christ and that we will see Him again.**[207]

Tynnetta Muhammad in her testimony explains,

Beginning on the evening of February 25th 1975, I dreamed that the Honorable Elijah Muhammad sat upright on the funeral bench where he had been laying with the sheet wrapped across his body in the style of the Ihram garments worn by the Pilgrims during Hajj. When I saw him sitting in this position, I exclaimed several times, he is not dead! A continual series of dreams have followed this one throughout the past 10 years to verify much information and evincing proof that the Honorable Elijah Muhammad lives. In one such dream I conversed with the Honorable Elijah Muhammad who explained to me some of the details of how he escaped the death-plot. He told me that they came and took him away to another place. Shortly after this, in the very next evening, I was shown a certain place where he was taken.[208]

6.3   *Debunking the Mystery God*

Visions and dreams have relevance as a viable form of communication for God to His servants and people. Before we go further into this subject, it is important to note that what is termed, *spirit* should be properly understood. This will remove ambiguity, vagueness or perceived *mystery ideas* surrounding the subject of Minister

---

[207] Rassoull, **The Theology of Time**, xxi-xxii.
[208] Tynnetta Muhammad, **The Comer by Night** (Chicago, IL: Honorable Elijah Muhammad Educational Foundation, Inc., 1994.) 84.

Farrakhan's vision experience. The Honorable Elijah Muhammad taught that man is God, but more specifically the Blackman, and brought clarity to the concept and idea of *spirit*. Mr. Muhammad explains,

> God is a man and we just cannot make Him other than man, lest we make him an inferior one; for man's intelligence has no equal in other than man. His wisdom is infinite; capable of accomplishing anything that his brain can conceive. A spirit is subjected to us and not we to the spirit.[209]

True Islam (Dr. Wesley Muhammad) mentions regarding this formless God,

> It is popularly assumed and even explicitly affirmed by Jewish and Christian theologians that God is an immaterial and formless spirit. Muslim theologians generally refrain from calling God a 'spirit', but nonetheless also affirm the He is immaterial and formless, possessing "neither body nor substance". Such an understanding of God derives from neither Bible nor the Quran nor Sunna, but instead derives from later interpretations of these texts. These later interpretations were influenced by Greek philosophy, particularly the ideas of the Greek philosophers Plato and Aristotle who are largely responsible for the development of the idea of an immaterial and formless deity.[210]

The Honorable Elijah Muhammad challenged the Yacub taught concept of *spirit* as a mystery, or something not known and further, its relationship to the material world. Mr. Muhammad continues,

> Are we living in a material universe or a "spirit" universe? We are material beings and live in a material universe. Would not we be making ourselves fools to be looking forward to see that which cannot be seen, only felt? Where is our proof for such a God (spirit) to teach that God is other than man? It is due to your ignorance of God, or you are one

---

[209] Muhammad, *Message to the Blackman*, 6.
[210] True Islam, *The Truth of God: The Bible, The Quran and Point Number 12*. (Atlanta, GA: All In All Publishing) 21.

deceived by the devil whose nature is to mislead you in the knowledge of God.[211]

The Honorable Elijah Muhammad is speaking about a fabricated idea of God. This fabrication was term *spirit* and was associated with a real God. God as **unknown or a mystery** has its origin with Yacub, but God as **other than a man** is an old belief that goes back millions of years, even trillions of years, long before the scientist Yacub. The Honorable Elijah Muhammad explains in what appears to be two contradictory statements,

> According to Allah, the origin of such teachings as a Mystery God is from the devils! It was taught to them by their father, Yakub, 6,000 years ago. They know today that God is not a mystery but will not teach it.[212]

He further elaborates on the worship of the unknown God:

> The belief in a God other than man (a spirit) Allah has taught me goes back into the millions of years--long before Yakub (the father of the devils) because the knowledge of God was kept as a secret from the public. This is the first time that it has ever been revealed, and we, the poor rejected and despised people, are blessed to be the first of all the people of earth to receive this secret knowledge of God.[213]

These statements do not contradict each other, but refer the two separate ideas about God,

1. The origin of a mystery (unknown) god.
2. The belief in God as other than man (spirit).

---

[211] Muhammad, **Message to the Blackman**, 6.
[212] Ibid., 2.
[213] Ibid., 9.

Both ideas suggest that the spirit (which is real) is the root of Gods existence only, but fail to acknowledge that man is indeed God. Here, falsehood has its root in the truth, i.e., spirit is real, but is a mystery or unknown to the ignorant or the deceived. The Honorable Elijah Muhammad questions this,

> Did God say that He was a Mystery God, or did someone say it of Him? Did God say that He was *only* [emphasis added] a Spirit, or did someone say it of Him?[214]

The word *only* is emphasized in the above quote because this statement implies that God has a spirit. But, he also said, *"A spirit is subjected to us and not we to the spirit."*

Spirit - A force that is directed or influenced by the conscious of a person; produced by thinking; often referred to as a feeling or intuitive thought. Spirit is often identified as being related to the Soul.

How can someone subdue something that does not exist? The Honorable Elijah Muhammad knew much more than what he taught to his followers. He asked the question "Is the spirit independent of material?"

> The word "mystery," according to the English dictionaries, is something that has not been or cannot be; something beyond human comprehension. The unintelligent, or rather ones without divine knowledge, seem to delight themselves in representing the God as something mysterious, Unknown.[215]

Based on the Honorable Elijah Muhammad's words, it appears that the words *mystery* and *God* together, as represented by the unintelligent, are

---

[214] Muhammad, *Message to the Blackman*, 4.
[215] Ibid., 2

oxymoronic and demonstrates a high level of ignorance. We are asked in the ***Supreme Wisdom Lessons*** given to the Nation of Islam by Master W. Fard Muhammad,

> Who is that Mystery God? The Son of Man has searched for that mystery God for Trillions of years and was unable to find a mystery God. So they have agreed that the only God is the Son of Man. So they lose no time searching for that that does not exist.[216]

The idea of a mystery God goes back millions of years. What does the Honorable Elijah Muhammad mean and how does this relate to what we know and term as *spirit* today? According to the definition of mystery as referenced by the Honorable Elijah Muhammad, mystery can be defined as,

1. Something that has not been or cannot be
2. Something that is beyond human comprehension

Something that *has not been* or *cannot be,* does not exist. Something that is *beyond human comprehension* does exist, but has not yet been perceived. It was not beyond the comprehension of the Honorable Elijah Muhammad, who said his teacher taught him Divine knowledge. What follows is an analysis of Minister Farrakhan's vision and not an explanation of *spirit* as taught by Yakub or believed by previous generations. Belief and knowledge are different. The belief in spirits and the knowledge of what spirit is; is different. The Honorable Elijah Muhammad asked the difficult question, "What is the basis of spirit?"[217] To attempt to answer this question would take more than just the few pages of this small book. The Honorable Elijah Muhammad said

---

[216] W. Fard Muhammad, *The Supreme Wisdom*, (Chicago, IL: Final Call Inc., 1995), 18.
[217] Muhammad, *Message to the Blackman*, 2.

that *spirit* is *thought* and to worship a spirit is like worshipping nothing at all.

The **Supreme Wisdom Lessons** of the Nation of Islam states regarding the mind of the Blackman,

> … [H]is mind travels twenty-four billion miles per second, which is considered the average speed of thought per second.[218]

Here, mind is associated with thought, as thought is associated with spirit. The fact that thought (spirit) travels implies that it has mass and occupies space. It (thought-spirit) has dimension and is influenced by another force that gives it momentum or velocity and direction. It also has the ability to influence other thought and matter. What do Muslims mean when they say a person has, *"returned to Allah"*? What is it that **returns** to Allah and how? The Honorable Elijah Muhammad taught against the idea of a mystery or unknown God. However, he does allude to the spirit as the *righteous mind,*

> There are many people who believe angels and Gods appear in the air some place, but if they're up there, we could see them. There is no such thing as formless spirits flying around in space, unless you want to declare such as the righteous mind. The righteous has a mind that wills certain things to be done and using certain things which are in space around, but it's not material.[219]

What follows is Tynnetta Muhammad elaboration on her talks with the Honorable Elijah Muhammad on the spirit and spirit world. She explains thought and its purpose in the lives of human beings, as taught to her by the Honorable Elijah Muhammad. She further teaches on the spirit or soul, telepathy and the electromagnetic field of man, and

---

[218] Muhammad, **The Supreme Wisdom**, 34.
[219] Muhammad, **Theology of Time**, 186.

parallel worlds or dimensions and how the thinking of the original people is multidimensional:

> He spoke a great deal about being in communication with the spirit world. I tried to comprehend in depth his explanation of that world, as he perceived it. Whatever one's approach to this subject may be, it comes down to one's definition and projection of the mind generated by thought and the complex beings of that thought world. Thought is consciousness and energy operating simultaneously in parallel or multi-dimensional worlds. Thought is the most important and precious commodity we possess. How we communicate or project our thoughts bring about the law of cause and effect that is set into motion in our everyday lives, because—*be* and *cause* is directly connected to God's divine law, which we had never been fully taught before…

Tynnetta Muhammad continues,

> On the other hand, the Honorable Elijah Muhammad has stated that what we call spirit or soul is the breath of life, the essence of our being. Our thoughts carry the image or images of what we think, which is ultimately made manifest in time. Rev. Moon stated that when I am in contact with that world (the spirit world), thoughts or information will be transmitted continually at all times.

> This sounds like the world of telepathy between thoughts sent and thoughts received. We are taught that the chosen servants of God see things that others do not see and hear things that others do not hear. They perceive what others perceive not depending upon their mental state of spiritual consciousness. Whatever mental state exists in the spirit world, it is consciousness directed by energy from a perpetual school of thought that surrounds us. It is a projection of our own knowingness. Whatever your thoughts can conceive it is known by spirit and transmitted by the living word, as we read in John Chapter 1: *"In the beginning there was the word and the word was God and the word is God and from God was everything made that was made."*

> This indicates that, surrounding us in the field of matter, thought form is the pervasive energy or electromagnetic sphere that brings matter into existence. This structure of thinking is multidimensional. Our brain

operates as the system or generator that brings our thoughts into reality. It is through our minds, housed in the brain, which taps into these parallel worlds of reality simultaneously. Thus, we can see, feel and hear things that are not yet manifested to our physical senses. That is the way God was in the beginning. He had the vision that none could comprehend but he himself.[220]

The Honorable Elijah Muhammad said in the 1970's that 30 years form then that some of his people would have the ability to "tune in". [221] This is specific to the use of telepathy which can only be attained by a person who has love in their heart.[222] There is a new knowledge and wisdom present in the world today. This new reality is happening as you read these words. The Honorable Elijah Muhammad said that all memory of this present world will be erased within 20 years of the deliverance of this new teaching, word, or wisdom.[223] This is happening and will be fully manifested through Minister Farrakhan.

6.4   The Physiology of Spirit and Soul throughout History

All things are made up of atoms, which are made up of sub-atomic particles.[224] These particles have a charge and either attract or repel each other. The most visible are the proton, electron and neutron, but there are smaller subatomic particles that are not as visible. A charge is defined as: the force inside a particle.[225] Charges can either attract or repel. So, what is the basis of Spirit? Do thoughts attract and repel? What is the Honorable Elijah Muhammad referring to when he says, *"but it's not material"*? What makes the brain's capacity infinite,

---

[220] Tynnetta Muhammad, Unveiling the Number 19: Journey to Korea - Meeting with the Rev. and Mrs. Sun Myung Moon, *FinalCall.Com*, September 1, 2003.
[221] Tynnetta Muhammad, Unveiling the Number 19: Entering into the World of the Telepath, *FinalCall.Com*, June 14, 2014.
[222] Ibid,.
[223] Tynnetta Muhammad, Unveiling the Number 19: Talking Crystals, Radio in the Head— Attuning to the Telepathic Voice Within, *FinalCall.Com*, June 26, 2013
[224] Cyndi Dale, **The Subtle Body: An Encyclopedia of your energy Anatomy**, (Boulder, CO: Sounds True. 2009),14.
[225] Ibid.

according to the Honorable Elijah Muhammad? Man and woman are electrical beings and the body is a conductor of the flow of electricity. For example, neurons are electrically charged nerve cells that transmit information throughout the brain.[226] (See Figure 9) Minister Farrakhan suggests that the activity of these nerves produce, "a continuous flow of electrochemical impulses that directs and drives human emotions."[227] These nerve cells are considered the foundation of the Central Nervous System. They are also associated with advance cognitive functions linked to the forebrain, i.e., cerebral cortex, hippocampus and amygdala.[228] This neural activity is linked to the subconscious mind.[229] An electrical current produces a magnetic field when flowing through a conductor.[230] The human body is the greatest conductor of electricity, more specifically the human brain and every human has an electromagnetic field:

> Electricity produces magnetism, but magnets can also make electricity: moving magnetic fields stimulate electron, which form electricity. Electricity and magnetism together form the *electromagnetic field,* which is defined as a field that asserts a force on particles that have electrical charge. In turn, this field is affected by the stimulated particles, and is the foundation of light.[231]

According to Dale, the Pituitary Gland is responsible for producing the electromagnetic field that surrounds the brain due to magnetite crystals associated with it.[232] (See Figure 10) Insects, fish and other forms of life have been known to generate light. What about man? Other

---

[226] Dale, *The Subtle Body*, 56.
[227] Louis Farrakhan, *Self Improvement The Basis of Community Development: Rising Above Emotions into the Thinking of God*, (Chicago, IL: Final Call, Inc.), 226
[228] Nelson Sprutson, "Pyramidal neurons: dendritic structure and synaptic integration," *Nature Reviews Neuroscience* 9 (March 2008): 206,
http://groups.nbp.northwestern.edu/spruston/Publications/pdfs/Spruston_NRN_2008.pdf
[229] Dale, *The Subtle Body*, 56.
[230] Ibid., 14.
[231] Ibid., 56.
[232] Dale, *The Subtle Body,* 61.

cultures have images of their sages, Prophets, and deities as illuminated beings. This is symbolic in their cultures, but alludes to what is real. Jesus and the angels have always been depicted with a "halo" above their heads. (See Figure 11) Even Lucifer (bearing light) was an illuminated entity. What does this mean?

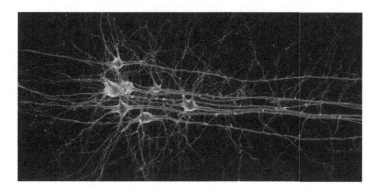

Figure 9: Neurons transmit messages throughout the brain with electrical and chemical signals. Photo: EPFL Human Brain Project

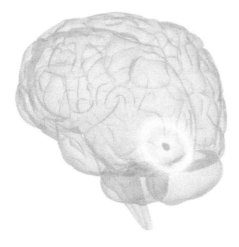

Figure 10: Pituitary Gland as shown as it is located in the brain.

Figure 11: Image of dark-skinned Illuminated Jesus with halo dated 530 CE, found in a Church of Rome.

Charles Fillmore in his book *Atom Smashing Powers of Mind* speaks of thought:

> Scientists have invented a machine that records the forces of thought. Every thought expressed by the mind radiates an energy as it passes through the brain cells, and this machine measures the force of these radiations.[233]

Modern technology surpasses what Fillmore mentions, but today understands energy as it pertains to electricity and the human anatomy. God is Spirit according to the Bible. It is the spirit of God that is the universal life that penetrates and sustains all life.[234] The Honorable Elijah Muhammad also suggests that the spirit comes from God,

---

[233] Charles Fillmore. *Atom Smashing Powers of Mind*, (Lee's Summit, MO: Unity School of Christianity, 1949), 14-15.
[234] Ibid.,10.

If there is nothing to produce the spirit, there is no spirit; nor can we know the truth without someone to teach the truth. Where there is man, there is the spirit. Where there is no man, there is no spirit, for the spirit cannot produce itself. We cannot expect to see that which cannot be seen. A spirit cannot be seen, only felt. It is like electricity. Electricity is a power produced by friction from a substance that has such power (electric) in it produced by the sun and moon upon the earth. It is not seen, but we know what makes it. So it is with God. We know that God exists and is All Wise, All Powerful, and that this quickening power called spirit is from Him. But who is this God? A spirit cannot think, but thinking can produce spirit.[235]

This spirit is the power of God in all living things and is tangible or real and is connected to *Soul.* This is considered the *Breath of Life.* True Islam (Dr. Wesley Muhammad) demonstrated in his research ***The Truth of God*** that before any life that we know, within darkness there existed a creative force called Spirit/Breath of God.[236] The soul is also present in the air.[237] Hubatz Men in his research on this subject explains but makes a different connection between soul and spirit,

The soul as defined by our Mayan ancestors, has material form due to the fact that everything has form. Soul was not confused with spirit, which was perceived as energy – solar energy. Spirit was named *k'inan,* derived from the word for the Sun – *k'in* – and the suffix *an* which is a conditional form of the verb "To be". Thus, k'inan is spirit or solar energy, and by inductive reasoning, soul is a manifested form of spirit. … [T]he Mayan understanding of the concept of Soul is a manifestation of spirit that is, of intelligent energy sublimated in the body, form and figure. So the soul was perceived by our Mayan ancestors as the object

[235] Elijah Muhammad. *Our Saviour has Arrived*, (Chicago, IL: Muhammad's Temple of Islam No.2, 1974), 65-66.

[236] Islam, *The Truth of God*, 237.

[237] Muhammad, *Theology of Time*, 19. "We can't see the air we are breathing unless we get a microscope, then we could see the very atom of life in the air. These atoms of life in the air are things that give us life and whenever the body gets to a point that it can't draw it in, then we say he's dead. The biggest soul we have is air. If you deprive someone air, then he's dead... That's the soul that they preach to you about; that's the real soul. It is your breath."

which is the conduit for spirit, the energy which permeates human intellectual manifestations. [238]

We can see here that *soul* and *spirit* are interrelated according to Hubatz Men and understood by the Maya as an integral part of human intelligence and its creation. Through study we come into awareness of the mind of God and are capable of manifesting the attributes of God to the point of spiritual perfection manifested consciously and eternally in the flesh.[239] The *Word* was made *Flesh* according to the Bible.[240]

Soul - The essence of a person, often referred to as the conscious, mind, or heart. A manifestation of the Life Force that exist in all living things. Soul is often identified as being related to the Spirit.

Life as we know it (in terms of matter) is based on interaction of electrical currents in the universe that only the developed man can understand.[241] Thought has an effect on matter and if directed and controlled will take form without space or distance being a barrier, thus the comment from the Honorable Elijah Muhammad, *"The righteous has a mind that wills certain things to be done and using certain things which are in space around, but it's not material."* Swami Panchadasi (William Walker Atkinson) in his writing **The Human Aura: Astral Colors and Thought Forms** describes thought forms,

A "thought form" is a peculiar manifestation of mental activity on the astral plane. It is more than a powerful disturbance in the body of the human aura, although this is the place of its embodiment or birth in the objective world... A thought-form is more than merely a strongly

[238] Men Hubatz, *Secrets of Mayan Science/Religion*, trans. Diana Gubiseh Ayala and James Jennings Dunlap II (Santa Fe, NM: Bear & Company, 1990), 24.
[239] Fillmore, *Atom Smashing Powers*, 150-51.
[240] See John 1: 1-14
[241] Fillmore, *Atom Smashing Powers*, 13.

manifested thought—it really is such a thought, but surrounded by a body of ethereal substance, charged with prana, and even carrying with it the vibration of the life energy of its creator.[242]

The "unseen" force of thought exists in every human being. Every human being has the ability to direct thought. From this unseen force, what is seen is manifested. This is a hint of the power of man to be like God, the creator. The ancient Egyptians respected the unseen so much that numerous deities were associated with the spirit. The most popular of deities was Osiris, God of the Underworld. Osiris after a brutal death perpetrated by his brother Seth was eventually raised after the discovery of his dismembered body by his wife Isis. The assembly of Osiris' dismembered body by Isis represented the first mummy. All desiring to be raised would have to pass by Osiris and be judged, thus the wrapping of the physical body as Osiris. (See Figure 12)

Figure 12: Osiris (left) Tutankhamun (middle) and Tut's spirit (right). Osiris is welcoming Tutankhamun into the Underworld while Tut's Spirit looks on.

---

[242] Swami Panchadasi, *The Human Aura: Astral Colors and Thought Forms*, (Yogi Publication Society, 1940), 47.

Osiris represented the Resurrection in the afterlife and the fertility of life.[243] This respect for the spirit is demonstrated throughout many religions and cultures, including Islam, Christianity and Judaism. In the Kundalini initiations of the ancient Egyptians, candidates would go through an intense 28-year study, consisting of fasting and prayer in anticipation of the challenge of releasing of the Kundalini.[244] After the candidate is prayed over, wrapped in linen like a mummy, and led to the King's chamber, they were placed in a sarcophagus in preparation for the trial. Bruyere illustrates,

> A 2,500 – pound lid was placed on the sarcophagus; the initiates would go into a kind of suspended animation and leave their bodies. While in this out-of-body state, they traveled to the four corners of Egypt. Nine days later, if the initiates were still alive, they would receive the privilege of taking the final test, which was to tell the presiding priest (who had already been informed by the four runners who had come from the four corners of Egypt) what had happened throughout the country over those nine days.[245]

In the above ritual the initiates are instructed to leave their bodies in an out of body state. This examination was one of the most difficult, since it was a life or death test. But, how did they leave the body? Was this an out-of-body experience involving the astral body? The ancient Egyptians viewed man as a being that was composed of multiple bodies and not limited to just the physical body or *khat*. They viewed the *khat* (physical body) as the form from which other spiritual bodies originated and grew. This idea was also held by Tibetan Buddhists of the 8th Century AD that incorporated in their philosophy the "Bardo body", or

---

[243] Ian Shaw and Paul Nicholson, *The Dictionary of Ancient Egypt*, 2nd ed. (New York, NY: Harry N. Abrams, Inc., 2003), s.v. "Osiris."
[244] In eastern philosophy the Kundalini represents the Serpent Fire that lay subtle and quite at the base of the spine, wrapped and nestled at the root chakra, to be released at the moment of enlightenment.
[245] Bruyere, *Wheels of Light*, 138.

the "invisible-matter" duplicate of the physical body. This body is also referenced as the astral body and resembles the *ka*; the life force, and *ba*; the soul of the Egyptians[246] The *ba* is represented by a human headed bird (See Figure 13) and is associated with the *ka* (life force) that dwells with it. The *ba* (soul) was also associated with the Jabiru stork and the Ram phonetically in Egyptian writing.

In order for the physical body to survive in the afterlife, it had to be united with the *ba* (soul).[247] The *ka* (life force) represents the cosmic spirit, essence or creative *life force* and was present with the human being as the *breath of life* or the Fire of Atum and even further; the emission of the *life force* in semen. The *ka* was represented by two human arms (See Figure 14) and since it came into existence with the human at birth, the *ka* (life force) was considered the double of the human being, whether alive or dead.[248] The *ka* here resembles the astral body. The *ba* would emerge when the *ka* left the physical body (khat) and remain with the khat in the tomb and united with the *ka* in the afterlife. This reunion transformed itself into the *akh* represented by the akh-bird.

Ka – Astral Body (Human Double)
Ba – Heart Soul
Sahu – Everlasting Ethereal Being
Khat – Physical Body

The body, symbolically, as the shell of spirit or soul can be traced back to the Egyptian Book of the Dead. Chinese Taoists viewed the physical body in a similar way. The symbolic reference to spirit and body has always existed along with the religion of a people, the

---

[246] Angus Haddow. "Out-of-body and near-death experiences: their impact on religious beliefs." *Journal of Religion and Psychical Research* 14, no. 2 (April 1984): 79-80.
[247] Shaw, Nicholson, *The Dictionary of Ancient Egypt*, s.v. "Ba."
[248] Ibid.

fundamental principle being that the body is just a vehicle to hold the life force or spirit; the self of man.[249] In the Egyptian teachings of the 19th Dynasty, *Atum* untied with the Sun God *Re or Ra* and was transformed to *Atum-Re,* also called *Atum-Ra.* Each night Atum-Re would pass through the underworld and unite with Osiris to form *Twin Souls* and emerge from darkness to the resurrection of a new day.[250] These Twin Souls, including the uniting of *Amun* and Ra (Amun-Ra) and the Egyptian *ka* are parallel to the twin astral and etheric bodies of man. Muhammad Ali says in his translations of the Holy Quran,

> The soul of man has in fact a mystic relation with the invisible Divine Spirit, which the materialist fails to realize.[251]

Muhammad Ali's statement regarding the relationship of the soul and spirit and the use of the words "mystic" and "invisible" in his analysis should not be taken to mean unreal. Angus Haddow in his article explains OBE as the Egyptians viewed it,

> There was the "ka" or double which was the energy-body possessing the form of the person to whom it belonged and closely associated with the khat in to which it came at birth and which it animated and preserved. There was the "ba" or the "heart-soul" which was the personality which lived in the khat, was preserved by the energy-giving "ka" and after death climbed the ladder of progress. They saw the "sahu" or "spiritual soul" as an everlasting ethereal being living in the "khat" and normally lived in the tomb where it could move around. The "ba" had the ability to leave the tomb and was able to go into the surrounding world, while some believed it lived in heaven. The "sahu" originated from the "khat" as wheat grows out of a seed providing a dwelling place for the "ka". The purpose of mummification was to preserve the body so that the sahu could emerge from the physical body after the ceremony and live eternally with the gods in heaven. <u>The</u>

---

[249] See Bruyere, *Wheels of Light*, 51.
[250] Claire Gibson. ***The Hidden Life of Ancient Egypt: Decoding the Secrets of a Lost World.*** (New York, NY: Fall River Press, 2009) 52.
[251] Holy Qu'ran 96:7 – MA See footnote.

Egyptian Book of the Dead (originally entitled The Chapters of Coming Forth by Day) contains prayers, hymns, petitions, and incantations to enable this to happen.[252]

Astral Projection should not be confused with Lucid Dreaming; a term coined by a Dutch psychiatrist and writer named Frederik Willems van Eeden toward the end of the 19th century. Both are quite different, but do have similarities. Astral projection is the traveling of the *astral body* while Lucid Dreaming is the state of consciousness and control, experienced while in a dream state. Lucid Dreams are sometimes characterized as being outside the body but partially aware, or in a state of semi-consciousness. While in the middle of the dream, we realize that we are dreaming.[253]

Figure 13: The *ba* (*soul*) depicted as a Hawk with a human head and hands.

---

[252] Haddow, "Out-of-body and near-death experiences: their impact on religious beliefs.", 79.
[253] Minero. *Demystifying the out-of-body Experience*, 12.

Figure 14: Ka Statue of King Awibra Hor of the 13 Dynasty, 17 BC.

Figure 15: The "ba" hovering of the mummified "khat'.

Lucid Dreaming was practiced in Tibetan Buddhism, Sufism and Indian Yoga. It was practiced as a type of yoga and called *dream yoga*. This form of yoga was used to exercise the maintenance of consciousness during sleep in the 18th century. The ultimate goal was to maintain consciousness so that the yogi would be able to consciously experience what they believed to be the afterlife.[254] Many have devoted their lives to the study of dreams. Brigetter Holzinger in her writing *Lucid Dreaming – Clarity of Dreams* makes reference to astral projection and lucid dreaming as viewed by another scholar:

> … [T]his phenomenon is a preliminary stage in recognizing the state of lucid dreams. The OBE that can occur in waking and in sleep is a dissociative phenomenon (the body appears separated from the soul), while the state of lucid dreaming could also be described as an associative phenomenon (complementation of sleep by the capacity of consciousness by added cognition).[255]

With lucid dreaming this type of consciousness happens while in dream. But with astral projection this consciousness is experienced with the projection of the astral body. Lucid dreams are not conscious astral projections. Although it is possible to control the dream, we are still in the dream state.[256] There are also instances when the recipient is placed in a *trance* state and experiences this phenomenon.

Lucid Dreaming – Process by which the person dreaming is aware that they are dreaming and have control of the dream experience.

---

[254] Brigitte Holzinger. "Lucid dreaming – dreams of clarity." *Contemporary Hypnosis* 26, no. 4 (December 2009): 217
[255] Holzinger, "Lucid dreaming" , 218
[256] Minero. *Demystifying the out-of-body Experience*, 13.

A *Trance* is a natural state of being; the state arrived when the physical body is sleeping and mind is awake and aware.[257] In the experiences of Peter and Paul, the trance was always a means by which God communicated to his servants. These trance experiences actually happened to them and "were not self-induced".[258]

Figure 16: The Mayan civilization demonstrated an understanding of the astral world through an attempt to call up their ancestors or the sacred being through the Serpent Vision that would appear through the mouth of the serpent in the form of an apparition.

[257] Robert Bruce, *Astral Dynamics: A NEW Approach to Out-of-Body Experience*. (Charlottesville, VA: Hampton Roads Publishing,1999), 220.
[258] See: Chad Brand, Charles Draper and Archie England, eds., *Holman Illustrated Bible Dictionary* (Nashville, TN: Holman Bible Publishers, 2003), s.v. "Trance."

This Page Intentionally Left Blank

7   What Really Happened?

7.1   *Farrakhan's Vision: How did it happen?*

> Now I lay me down to sleep,
> I pray the Lord *my soul to keep*,
> If I should die before I wake,
> I pray the Lord *my soul to take*.

The Honorable Minister Louis Farrakhan's vision experience cannot be understood without having a respectful approach toward his testimony and a serious analysis of this subject. How did his "vision-like" or "more than" a vision experience happen? The experience of Minister Farrakhan can be observed in context by what is called the Astral Body and the projection or traveling of this body called Astral Projection, Astral Traveling, and projection of consciousness, extracorporeal experience, mystic voyage, [259] or Out-of-Body Experience (OBE). This type of experience is also associated with multi-dimensional travel and also time travel.

> *Astral Projection* – The traveling of the astral body as it is projected from the physical body during sleep or a suspended conscious state.

A.E. Powell in describing the astral body explains,

> Briefly, the astral body of man is a vehicle, to clairvoyant sight not unlike the physical body, surrounded by an aura of flashing colours, composed of matter of an aura order of fineness higher than that of physical matter, in which feelings, passions, desires and emotions are expressed and which acts a bridge or medium of transmission between

---

[259] Minero. ***Demystifying the out-of-body Experience***, 3.

the physical brain and the mind, the latter operating in the still higher vehicle – the mind- body.[260]

Powell calls the astral body a *vehicle* in which the underdeveloped man lives a dreamy vague life, but the developed man is active and moves within the astral body at great speeds. The developed man's life becomes a continuous life of unbroken consciousness during the day and night.[261] Powell also suggests that the astral body is composed of astral matter that is finer than physical matter and interpenetrates it. According to Powell, every atom exists and functions in a world of astral matter. This astral matter is measured by its composition or grade, which ranges from solid astral to the finer astral; atomic astral and sub-atomic astral.[262] The astral body has been associated with the several chakras, which are body centers or vortices of man and represents the bridge between three-dimensional matter and spirit, and is a gateway to other dimensions not seen with the physical eye.

On the astral plane, this form of consciousness is considered the plane where ***transformation*** is made possible. Some associate the astral body with the fourth chakra (Heart), and consider it to be the first chakra beyond three-dimensional realities.[263] These chakras generate energy from the spine and appear as spinning wheels. (See Figure 17) Others associate the third chakra (Solar Plexus) with the astral body and the

[260] Arthur E. Powell, *The Astral Body and other Astral Phenomena*. (London, EN: The Theosophical Publishing House, 1929), 1.
[261] Ibid., 1-2.
[262] Ibid., 4.
[263] Rosalyn L. Bruyere, *Wheels of Light: Chakras, Auras, and the Healing Energy of the Body*, ed. Jeanne Farrens (New York, NY: Simon &Schuster, 1994), 46.

grounding of emotions and desires.[264] Although the astral is associated with at least three chakras, despite the theoretical differences, practitioners and occultist agree that the astral body is very real. C.W. Leadbeater's research, *The Astral Plane*, suggest that the existence of this plane is intermingled with matter and divided into seven sub-divisions.[265]

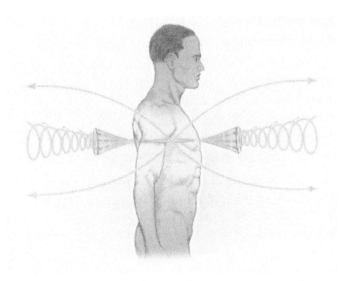

Figure 17: Position and rotation of the Heart Chakra in an adult male. (Image from "The Subtle Body")

---

[264] "Ether is also defined as Akasha, the astral light where all events, actions, thoughts and feelings that have occurred since the beginning of time are recorded…" It is this chakra and its association with the astral light that allows us to discover the inner–self and mission of self. We unleash the divine potential and draw from the infinite mind and memory of the originator. "We recognize that our inner worlds and subtle planes of being are as real as the material world; we are capable of absorbing and transmitting information from the subtler spheres and higher dimensions of reality." See Shalila Sharamon and Bodo J. Baginski, *The Chakra Handbook* (Wilmot, WI: Lotus Light Publications, 1988), 106-7.

[265] "First of all, then, it must be understood that the astral plane has seven sub-divisions, each of which has it corresponding degree of materiality and its corresponding condition of matter… we must not fall into the mistake of thinking of them (or indeed of the greater planes of which they are only sub-divisions) as separate localities in space- as lying above one another like the shelves on a book case or outside one another like the coats of an onion. It must be understood that the matter of each plane or sub-plane interpenetrates that of the plane or sub-plane below it, so that here at the surface of the earth all exist all exist together in the same space, although it is true that the higher varieties of matter extend further away from the physical earth than the lower." See Charles Webster Leadbeater, *The Astral Plane: Its Scenery, Inhabitants and Phenomena*, 3rd ed. (London: Theosophical Society, 1900), 17.

| 174

Chakra– Sanskrit word meaning turning or spinning. Vortices or body centers that conduct the flow of vital energy throughout the body.

The fifth chakra (Throat) is associated with the element ether which is known to have influence on astral material, i.e., astral light and plays a part in the harnessing of the collective memory of "ALL" or what some call the *Akashic Record, Record of the Astral Light*, etc...[266] Max Heindel in his writing **The Rosicrucian Mysteries** speaks to these ideas, but with regards to ether,

> The Reflecting Ether receives an impression of all that is, lives and moves. It also records each change, in a similar manner as the film upon a moving picture machine. In this record mediums and psychometrists may read the past, upon the same principle as, under proper conditions, moving pictures are reproduced time and again.[267]

What Heindel compares to the modern TV is a natural ability of man and woman. In fact, all that we see in the physical world has a metaphysical or unseen counterpart. But, how was Minister Farrakhan in a sleeping state taken from where he was, to the top of the mountain called Tepozte'catl in Tepotzlan, Mexico? How was he *carried up on that mountain, in a vision*? Was it an out-of-body experience? Powell explains regarding the astral body,

---

[266] "An account of the scenery of the astral plane would be incomplete without mention of what are commonly called the Records of the Astral Light, the photographic representation of all that has ever happened. These records are really and permanently impressed upon that higher medium called the Âkâsha, and are only reflected in a more or less spasmodic manner in the astral light, so that one whose power of vision does not rise above this plane will be likely to obtain only occasional and disconnected pictures of the past instead of a coherent narrative. But nevertheless pictures of all kinds of past events are constantly being reproduced on the astral plane, and form an important part of the surroundings of the investigator there." See Leadbeater, **The Astral Plane**, 28-29.

[267] Max Heindel. **The Rosicrucian Mysteries: An Elementary Exposition of Their Secret Teachings** (Oceanside, CA: Rosicrucian Fellowship), 32.

One of the first things a man learns to do in his astral body is travel in it, it being possible for the astral body to move, with great rapidity, and to great distances from the sleeping body. [268]

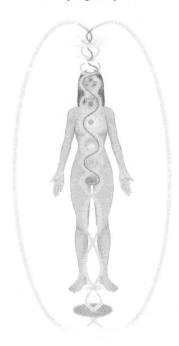

Figure 18: Twelve Chakra System and the illumination of three types of Kundalini. This illumination represents the radiance of a truly enlightened divine being. (Image from "The Subtle Body")

Minister Farrakhan in his vision experience was called or summoned to the Wheel for a magnificent meeting with the Honorable Elijah Muhammad. The manner in which he was called to this meeting demonstrates a greater Power that was in control of his astral faculties at the time of his experience and even up to this point. Luis Minero, a leading expert on out-of-body experiences explains the activity of astral body,

---

[268] Powell, *The Astral Body*, 2.

During an OBE our physical body remains at rest, usually in the sleep state, while we – the soul, spirit, or consciousness – distance ourselves from our physical body, exploring and experiencing other realities. We travel with a vehicle or body subtler than the physical one and with quite different and unique abilities from those of the physical body. We can venture far away from the body and gain access to realms and planes that are not necessarily similar to the physical reality.[269]

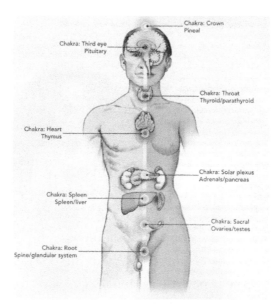

Figure 19: Chakra System in the male and female and the organs they are aligned to. (Image from "The Subtle Body")

Minero explains that every person has a natural *disconnection* from their bodies at night, but most people remain unaware of this disconnection from the physical body because they are unconscious throughout the entire process.[270] Separating from the body in most people is a "spontaneous projection" and only last for a view seconds. In other instances a person is able to view their resting sleeping body, which is termed, *self- bilocation.* [271] Many people have been reported to

---

[269] Minero, *Demystifying the out-of-body Experience*, 2.
[270] Ibid,. 4.
[271] Ibid., 7.

experience paralysis while sleeping; a state in which they are more conscious in the astral body (outside of the body) than in the physical body. This is termed *Projection Catalepsy* or *Astral Catalepsy*.

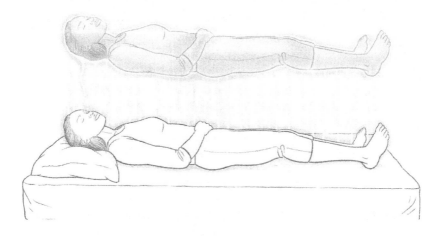

Figure 20: Astral Body separating from the sleeping physical body. Drawing from Luis Minero's *Demystifying out-of-body Experiences*.

This state is a normal sensation of the body during the disconnecting of the astral body from the physical body, and is harmless. This is not a new phenomenon. This is as natural to the human being as breathing. The soul of man is always at work, even when the physical body is asleep. In the religious context, the astral body has also been called the *soul*. There are many references to the word soul mentioned in Maulana Muhammad Ali's 1950 translation of the Holy Quran and numerous references to the word *spirit*. Certainly, the uses of the words soul and spirit have very relevant and important meanings in Islam.[272] Allah (God) says in verse 39:42,

> Allah takes (men's) souls at the time of their death, and those that die not, during their sleep. Then He withholds those on whom He has passed the decree of death and sends the others back till an appointed term. Surely there are signs in this for a people who reflect.[273]

Muhammad Ali further elaborates in the footnote associated with this verse,

> It is clear that it is not the animal soul that is taken away in sleep; it is the soul that stands for human consciousness. In death both are taken away. The statement further makes it clear that the word *tawaff a* is applied to the taking of the soul and not to the removal of the body from one place to another.

Can we assume that Minister Farrakhan's soul or conscious was taken while he slept? It is likely that his experience was an OBE. In Yusuf Ali's 1917 translation of the Holy Quran he states concerning the same above mentioned verse:

> This verse affords a conclusive proof that the Quran does not admit to the return to this life in this world of those who are actually dead. It states that the soul is taken away, either in sleep, in which case it is returned, or at death, in which case it is withheld and is not allowed to return. The soul can only be returned if death has not actually occurred.[274]

---

[272] The use of these words (soul and spirit) have important significance in Christianity as well. The soul is often used to reference the essence of the prophet or messenger. Like its use in the Holy Quran, it represents more than just thought, but the very being of the Prophet. The word spirit in the Bible is used in direct relationship to God, the devil ("evil spirits"), thoughts, and even significant contemplation. In the Bible, the spirit is like the soul in the Holy Quran; it travels and moves. The spirit has power and is more akin to "thought-spirit", meaning, the spirit has the ability to affect change and influence people. In the *New International Version Study Bible*, the word soul is mentioned in 95 verses and spirit is used 563 times.

[273] Holy Quran 39:42.

[274] Abdullah Yusuf Ali. *The Meaning of the Holy Quran* (Betsville, MD: Amana Publications, 1989.) 899. This is a revision of Ali's 1934 translation of the Holy Quran.

Astral Body – The spiritual body of man sometimes called the [A]etheric body or Soul; The non-physical counterpart of the human body that has the ability to separate and travel on the Astral Plane.

Haddow further illustrates how the astral body moves during the time of its travel:

> … OBE's are characterized by the sensation of being a spectator who looks down on his body; a lack of sensation of body weight, movement, and position sense; instantaneous movement from place to place without finding that physical objects present a barrier to movement; and increased acuteness to hearing and seeing.[275]

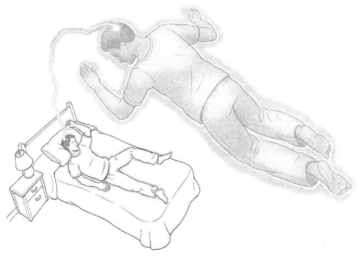

Figure 21: The Astral Body projecting from the Crown Chakra. Drawing from Luis Minero's Demystifying Out-of-Body Experiences.

Minister Farrakhan has mentioned in the past that he isn't certain whether he was awake or asleep when he had his experience on the night of September 17th. This very real experience is not unusual. Many

---

[275] Haddow, "Out-of-body and near-death experiences", 75-76.

people have OBE's and have thousands of case studies by parapsychologists and occultists on astral projection. There are many books on the subject by 100's of authors, many claiming to be the leading expert on Astral Traveling, Out of Body Experience, Astral Projection, etc… But, what's unique about Minister Farrakhan's experience, is that he did not only have the experience; he was called to the experience, then taught and sent back to his body with information about a secret meeting and planned war involving the United States and a small nation. In the experience he was given revelation beyond the comprehension of this world. All from a position that would appear to the wide awake man in a three dimensional space called "sleep". This requires a greater knowledge, force, and power to achieve. A.E. Powell describes the activity of the astral body in the sleeping state:

> When a man "goes to sleep", his higher principles in their astral vehicle withdraw from the physical body, the dense body and the etheric body remaining by themselves on the bed, the astral body floating in the air above them. In sleep, then, a man is simply using his astral body instead of his physical: it is only the physical body that is asleep, not necessarily the man himself. Usually the astral body, thus withdrawn from the physical, will retain the form of the physical body, so that the person is readily recognisable to anyone who knows him physically. This is due to the fact that the attraction between the astral and the physical particles, continued all through physical life, sets up a habit or momentum in the astral matter, which continues even while it is temporarily withdrawn from the sleeping physical body.[276]

Powell emphasizes that when the developed person sleeps the astral body slips out and the person comes into a fully conscious state of being outside the body. The astral body maintains a form that is clear to that person and is similar to the physical body. The person has the ability in

---

[276] Powell, *The Astral Body.*, 83

this developed state to move in the astral body with great speed, without disturbing the resting physical body.[277] The person in the astral body, if they are a student of a master, becomes active without interference from the resting physical body. [278] In Powell's other writings he calls these masters "invisible helpers".

7.2   Prophet Muhammad, Paul, and Out of Body Experiences

In Prophet Muhammad's magnificent vision-experience he was transported from one place to another and received great revelation from Allah (God). How does this relate, or does it relate to Minister Farrakhan's vision experience, September 17, 1985?

> Glory to him Who *carried His servant by night from the Sacred Mosque to the Remote Mosque*, [emphasis added] whose precincts We blessed, that We might show him of our signs! Surely He is the Hearing, the Seeing.[279]

> Glory to (Allah) Who did take His Servant For a Journey by night From the Sacred Mosque to the Farthest Mosque Who precincts We did Bless – in order that We Might show him some Of Our Signs: for He Is the One Who heareth And seeth (all things).[280]

Yusuf Ali in his translation of the Holy Quran says of the magnificent journey of Prophet Muhammad mentioned previously,

> The majority of Commentators take this Night Journey literally, but allow that there were other occasions on which a spiritual Journey or Vision occurred. Even on the supposition of a miraculous bodily journey, it is conceded that the body was almost transformed into a spiritual fineness... The Holy Prophet was first transported to the seat of the earlier revelations in Jerusalem, and then taken through the seven

---

[277] Powell, *The Astral Body*., 85-86
[278] Ibid., 89
[279] Holy Quran 17:1-Maulana Muhammad Ali.
[280] Holy Quran 17:1 – Yusuf Ali.

heavens even to the Sublime Throne, and initiated into spiritual mysteries of the human soul struggling in Space and Time.[281]

How was the body of Prophet Muhammad, *"transformed into a spiritual fineness"*? Was this too an astral experience? Abdullah Yusuf Ali further states that Prophet Muhammad was, *"initiated in spiritual mysteries of the human soul"*. This initiation is reflective of the Honorable Elijah Muhammad's vision in **September 1971** [282] and Minister Farrakhan's vision in **September 1985**. Both were introduced to higher forms of Wisdom by what they received and were taught. Paul in his letter to the Corinthians speaks of an experience that typologically and prophetically represents Minister Farrakhan's experience and testimony of the Honorable Elijah Muhammad.

It is not expedient for me doubtless to glory. I will come to visions and revelations of the Lord. I knew a man in Christ above *fourteen years ago, whether in the body, I cannot tell; or whether out of the body, I cannot tell: God knoweth;* [emphasis added] such a one caught up to the third heaven. And I knew such a man, *whether in the body, or out of the body, I cannot tell: God knoweth;* [emphasis added] How that he was caught up into paradise, and heard unspeakable words, which it is not lawful for a man to utter.[283]

---

[281] Yusuf Ali, *Holy Quran*, 671. Also see footnote 23.

[282] The following is an excerpt from The Theology of Time lectures series of the Hon. Elijah Muhammad, September 1972. "For nearly 40 years I have studied scripture and history, after Allah taught me for three years and four months. He gave me 104 books to study. He gave me the number of them and the place where I could find them. I studied, and he gave me a Holy Qur'an in Arabic, but I couldn't read it. So, He got me one in Arabic and English translated by Muhammad Ali of Pakistan. Later He found one translated by Yusuf Ali of Egypt; He brought me that one. Then He told me, "I will give you a Holy Qur'an when you learn how to read Arabic, then I will give you a Holy Quran in Arabic." He said, "I made it myself." *He showed me that Holy Quran in Arabic in September last, but I couldn't read it. I could only recognize one letter in it. I expect Him within a year to come back with that same book.*" Also see footnote 192. In the same meeting mentioned in footnote 192, Minister Farrakhan, while making reference to the Honorable Elijah's vision of the book shown to him by Master Fard Muhammad, he stated, "There was another book written in English from that book...When I was on the wheel the Honorable Elijah Muhammad showed it to me."

[283] See 2Corinthians 12:1-4.

| 183

Scholars assume that Paul was speaking in the third person, so it cannot be concluded whether the historical Paul spoke of himself or another person. Paul says, "…such a one was caught up in the third heaven." Paul then says in the following verses, "...but God knows – was caught up to paradise." This phrase **Caught up** in its Greek translation is *harpazo,*[284] and is a verb and also used in 1 Thessalonians 4:17.[285] 1 Thessalonians 4:17 [286] speaks of those that are **alive** being caught up in the clouds, and meeting with the Lord in the air. It is my view that in this instance Paul is speaking of another person who was caught up in the "third heaven" and was "caught up to paradise". But, whether he (Paul) saw him in the body or out of the body, he (Paul) could not tell. Also, whether Paul went to the third heaven in his body or out of his body or whether his soul "temporarily" left his body is not known by reading the text.[287] But, in his saying a second time, "And I knew such a man, whether in the body or out of the body, I cannot tell…" indicates that Paul *knew* this man while in his own experience. It is also generally accepted by some scholars that the "Lord" refers to Christ in verse (1) and not God. It is also accepted that Christ is the originator of Paul's experience, but Christ doesn't actually appear to Paul in this heavenly encounter.[288] However, in the *Apocalypse of Paul* the word "Lord" almost always makes specific reference to "God" not Christ. [289] It is understood though that the vision could have come from

---

[284] Grace To You. "Caught Up to the Third Heaven." GTY.ORG.
https://www.gty.org/library/bibleqnas-library/QA0088/caught-up-to-the-third-heaven.
[285] Ibid.
[286] See 1 Thessalonians 4:17 – "Then we who are alive and remain will be caught up together with them in the clouds to meet the Lord in the air, and so we shall always be with the Lord."
[287] Grace To You. "Caught Up to the Third Heaven."
[288] Margaret E, Thrall, Trevor J. Burke, and J. K. Elliott. *Paul and the Corinthians: studies on a community in conflict: essays in honour of Margaret Thrall.* Leiden: Brill, 2003, 328.
[289] The Apocalypse of Paul (also Visio Pauli or Ammonitio Pauli) is the account of the Apostle Paul's vision of Heaven and Hell and is a part of the New Testament Apocrypha. It was first written in Greek, possibly in third or fourth century. There is a version that exist in Latin, but there are original copies in Greek.

the Lord, and Christ was the agent who delivered it. [290] Paul's mention of the third heaven represents the place where the *one* he saw ascended. The NIV Study Bible states regarding the third heaven,

> The "third heaven" designates a place beyond immediate heaven of the earth's atmosphere and beyond the further heaven of outer space into the presence of God himself.[291]

Here, two other heavens are mentioned:

1. The earth's atmosphere
2. The universe containing the celestial bodies

Some scholars also call the third heaven the "dwelling place of God", but falsely assume that this is a place that the human spirit goes when a person physically dies. By Paul's reference to being *in the body* or *out of the body* [292]is not a reference to him dying physically. Paul says in his vision that he knew a man (14 years ago) in Christ. If we apply the Numerical Principle to the number 14, and view the antitypical reference, this *fourteen-year period* prophetically represents that period

---

[290] Margaret E, Thrall, Trevor J. Burke, and J. K. Elliott. *Paul and the Corinthians: studies on a community in conflict: essays in honour of Margaret Thrall*. Leiden: Brill, 2003, 329.

[291] *Zondervan NIV Study Bible*, (Grand Rapids, MI: Zondervan Publishing, 2002), 1816.

[292] The Expandable Bible says regarding Paul's experience in its translation; "I know a man in Christ [a believer] who was taken up [caught up; snatched away] to the third heaven [the presence of God] fourteen years…" The Voice Bible of the Ecclesia Bible Society translate this as; "Fourteen years ago, there was this man I knew—a believer in the Anointed who was caught up to the third heaven. (Whether this was an in- or out-of-body experience I don't know; only God knows.)…"The Worldwide English translation reads, "I know a Christian man. Fourteen years ago he was taken up into the place where God lives". Here the translation specifies that in Paul's experience he was taken to a place "…where God lives" The Expandable Bible translation says Paul was "snatched" away when referring to "caught up". This implies that something was taken suddenly, but by a force greater than the object being taken or snatched. The theologians never announce Paul's experience as a near death experience, but some suggest that he died and was taken to a place "heaven" like place after death. That is false. This experience of Paul is almost always overlooked by scholars when providing exegesis of this scripture (2Corinthians 12:1-4) while greater emphasis is placed on why he was not boastful, and the suffering from the thorn in his flesh (2Corinthians 12:5-8).

of time between the Honorable Elijah Muhammad's *September 1971* vision experience and the *September 1985* vision experience of Minister Farrakhan. In both experiences both men were shown wisdom from a book written by Master W. Fard Muhammad, Allah in person.[293] The scholars agree that Paul's experience probably occurred in the beginning of his ministry; which was in late 55 A.D. or early 56 A.D., sometime between Paul's return to Tarsus from Jerusalem (Acts 9:30) and his appointing by what is called in the Bible *Holy Spirit* (Acts 13:1–3).[294] Minister Farrakhan's experience happened almost eight years into the rebuilding efforts of the Nation of Islam, in absence of the Honorable Elijah Muhammad. If we apply the same principle, the 14th chapter of the Holy Quran says,

> I, Allah, am the Seer. A Book which We have revealed to thee that thou mayest bring forth men, by their Lord's permission, from darkness into light, to the way of the Mighty, the Praised One.[295]

The earthquake on September 19th in Mexico City vividly brought back to his memory that the Honorable Elijah Muhammad called him to this Great Mother Wheel. Minister Farrakhan is spiritually, a highly developed man. This is not a statement worth debating and is an absolute fact. When having an astral experience, in the developed man, who has developed his astral body, he has greater comprehension of his experiences and greater power to travel in the astral world with little

---

[293] See Revelation Chapter 5: 1-14. Also see Muhammad, Theology of Time, 62. "I am risen up among you to condemn the white man's teaching and condemn him to death. This is what I am here for. I don't want you to think you're playing with no light boy at all. My size is very small, that's why they symbolically prophesied of me as being a little Lamb instead of a grown up Lamb." (June 18, 1972). The fourteen years mentioned in 2Corinthians 12:1-4 could also be related to the departure of the Honorable Elijah Muhammad in February 1975, and the "Announcement" made by Minister Farrakhan of his exaltation on the Wheel in October 1989. This 14 year period is also relevant to the fulfillment of Paul's vision.
[294] Grace To You. "Caught Up to the Third Heaven." GTY.ORG.
https://www.gty.org/library/bibleqnas-library/QA0088/caught-up-to-the-third-heaven.
[295] Holy Quran 14:1-Maulana Muhammad Ali.

disturbance to the sleeping physical body.[296] In the astral world, where astral entities exist and communication with these entities takes place, the ability to receive instruction, as in the case of Minister Farrakhan is quite possible. Powell suggests such communication can be accomplished with the developed man while traveling in his astral body,

> ... He may meet and exchange ideas with friends, either incarnate or discarnate, who happen to be equally awake on the astral plane. He may meet people more evolved than himself, and receive instruction: or he may be able to confer benefits on those who know less than himself. [297]

Again, Minister Farrakhan's vision is a trial for many and will continue to become a trial for many more, especially when trying to understand how his experience happened.

> And when We said to thee: Surely thy Lord encompasses men. And We made not the vision which We showed thee but a trial for men, as also the tree cursed in the Quran. And We warn them, but it only adds to their great inordinacy.[298]

The Apostle Peter's experience was used to help Paul better understand his mission as it relates to the Jews and the Gentiles. Peter's experience is recorded as such,

---

[296] Powell, *The Astral Body*, 86.

[297] Ibid., 86.

[298] Holy Quran 17:60. Maulana Muhammad further elaborates regarding the same scripture: "The reference here is the vision of *Ascension* or the *Mi'raj* (B. 63:42), which was really a prophecy of the ultimate triumph of Islam." Muhammad continues, "In another report the words describing the condition in which he was at the time of *Ascension* are, *whilst I was in a state between that of one sleeping and one awake* (B59:6). In fact, it is quite true that he was not asleep – he was in a vision, but at the same time it was not a corporeal Ascension. He was actually carried to the Holy Presence, and he was shown great wonders, but it was in spirit that he was carried, and it was with the spiritual eye that he saw those wonders, not in body and with the physical eye, for things spiritual can only be seen with the spiritual eye. And this vision had an important significance." See HQ footnote 1441. This has a resemblance to the Hon. Minister Louis Farrakhan, in that his vision experience is the basis of the near triumph of Islam over Allah's enemies. The vision like experience is the basis of the faith of the Most Hon. Elijah Muhammad's divinity and escape from death and Master Fard Muhammad as Allah, to whom Praises are due forever. Muhammad mentions last in the same footnote; "His opponents as usual disbelieved in such visions and laughed at him."

Peter began and explained everything to them precisely as it had happened: "I was in the city of Joppa praying, and in a trance I saw a vision. I saw something like a large sheet being let down from heaven by its four corners, and it came down to where I was. I looked into it and saw four-footed animals of the earth, wild beasts, reptiles, and birds of the air. Then I heard a voice telling me, 'Get up, Peter. Kill and eat.[299]

What does this mean? Assuming Paul is a type of Minister Farrakhan (as well as Peter) how does this help him in his mission to fulfill and complete the first phase of the Honorable Elijah Muhammad's work? Paul had to be made to "see" Christ. Minister Farrakhan elaborates,

There were layers in the scales on Paul's eyes. The first scale was he had to see Jesus properly. Then he had to know that Jesus was in fact alive, so that he could declare that, "I know that my redeemer liveth and because he lives I too shall live and stand with him at the latter day." In the removal of the second scale, a third scale would [also] be removed, which was to take Paul out of the limited vision of Peter and the disciples, who were more nationalistic in their focus on the Jews and not on the Gentiles. Paul saw what Peter came to understand when he saw this cloth or sheet descend from heaven with all manner of meats on it. He said that he could not eat that which was unclean. Then he came to see that the vision was not talking about meat, but was talking about the different circumstances and condition of human beings beyond the children of Israel and that he could eat them. He could take the unclean and make them a part of the body of Christ.[300]

In the metaphysical sense, Professor Arthur McGriffert in his article *Mysticism in the Early Church* explains that Paul not only represents the oneness of the spirit, but also the *substance* of the spirit of Christ.

---

[299] See Acts 11:4-7 (NIV). Also see New International Version footnote. Here it explains that Peter's trance was a state of mind that God produced and used to communicate with. The scholars say that this was, "not merely imagination and dreams", but Peter's consciousness was affected and he was made to receive these visions from God. Also see Acts 22:17 on Saul's vision; Numbers 12:6-8 on Aaron and Moses; Galatians 1:11-12; Genesis 46:2; Ezekiel 1:1; 40:2; 43:3; Daniel 1:17; 4:10; 4:13; 7:1; 7:7; 7:13; Hosea 12:10; Joel 2:28; Acts 2:17.
[300] Muhammad, *Closing the Gap*, 136-137.

From a metaphysical perspective he speaks of Paul's unity with Christ as divine. He elaborates that the oneness,

> …enters into the believer and substitutes for his fleshly nature a spiritual and divine nature, so that he is a new creature altogether.[301]

He calls this mystical experience between Paul and Jesus a *divine indwelling* of the spirit, and also a *union*. But, takes it a step further and says that the experience was not just a union, but ***identity***.

It is evident that what Minister Farrakhan was told and taught by the Honorable Elijah Muhammad on the Wheel demonstrates the divine union between him and his teacher. This was also more than a union, but an identity, where the mind of Minister Farrakhan is being made one with his teacher. This is critical to the reformation of Blacks in America and all over the world. It is also the foundation in which the whole of humanity will begin to be raised to a higher understanding of God, Christ, and themselves. His life is an example of the Love that God has for his people and the mercy that he extends to all. His vision experience is a witness of God's love for the righteous all over the planet. How does Farrakhan, "take the unclean and make them a part of the body of Christ"? This is done through Minister Farrakhan's overwhelming love and expanded understanding of his teacher's mission to include all of humanity, and like Paul, through this wisdom he offers all to come into the presence of God, that they may see God as He is.[302]

His experience and mighty testimony also provokes betrayal. The betrayal is rooted in jealousy and envy, and the desire to take the credit and praise of Minister Farrakhan's position with God. This betrayal is

---

[301] Arthur C. McGiffert, "Mysticism in the Early Church." *The American Journal of Theology, Vol. 11, No. 3 (Jul., 1907)*, 407. Accessed: 08-08-2014 14:11 UTC
http://www.jstor.org/stable/3154512
[302] Muhammad, *Closing the Gap*, 137.

also related to the wickedness of this world, and as it pertains to those Blacks that are co-conspirators; the effects of slavery plays a part of this hatred for him. These Blacks who are envious and jealous of Minister Farrakhan represent in the modern context the Jews in the Book of Acts who fought against Paul, this includes those who say they are with the Honorable Elijah Muhammad, but reject Minister Farrakhan. This includes those who appear to be with Minister Farrakhan, but secretly reject him. This is the "Judas" factor of this drama that surrounds his work and it is all designed by Allah. The experience that Minister Farrakhan had on the wheel, *whether in the body, or out of the body*, is the cause of this betrayal. In previous chapters I try to lay a base to show the importance of Minister Farrakhan, and the reality of his vision on the Wheel, since what he received in his experience is the saving grace for all of humanity.

7.3   *The Transfiguration on the Mount*

The transformation of consciousness on the astral plane has a resemblance to the **transfiguration** or **transformation** of Jesus spoken of in the Bible. This Jesus not only represents a man, but also an entire people. In the Bible, the Gospels have similarities that have pinned on them the term *Synoptic,* and because of their nearness in content, they can be reviewed side by side (syn-optically), but this has caused a problem and is thus termed the Synoptic Problem.[303]

There are rules to reviewing and studying the scriptures. The Gospels of the Bible should be carefully analyzed and not taken on face value. Theologians suggests that because of the similarities of Matthew, Mark and Luke, a careful study and review of the written word, should

---

[303] Raymond Brown. *Introduction to the New Testament*, (New York, NY: Bantam, Doubleday, Dell Publishing, 1ed.1997), 111.

be priority over oral exegesis.[304] This review and study requires greater attention to the details of the Bible historically, prophetically. In the Synoptic Gospels; Matthew, Mark, and Luke, each describe the transfiguration of Jesus among while with his disciples,

Matthew 17:1-3- Six days later Jesus took with him Peter and James and his brother John and led them up a high mountain, by themselves. And he was transfigured before them, and his face shone like the sun, and his clothes became dazzling white. Suddenly their appeared to them Moses and Elijah, talking with him.

Mark 9:2-4- Six days later, Jesus took with him Peter and James and John and led them up high mountain apart, by themselves. And he was transfigured before them, and his clothes was dazzling white, such as no one on earth could bleach them. And there appeared to them Elijah with Moses, who were talking with Jesus.

Luke 9:28-30- Now about eight days after these sayings Jesus took with him Peter and John and James and went up on the mountain to pray. And while praying the, appearance of his face changed and his clothes became dazzling white. Suddenly they saw two men, Moses and Elijah, talking with him.

The transfiguration represented a change in the appearance of Jesus. The life of God in him was manifested from feeding on the eternal word of truth. This Jesus represents a man in the modern context. This change was witnessed in his countenance as his being was transformed. Mark does not reference a change in Jesus' face as does Matthew and Luke.

Minister Farrakhan explains this transfiguration,

On that day God was so please with your effort [referring to the Million Man March], that as the dove descended on Jesus his peace descended

---

[304] Brown. *Introduction to the New Testament*, 111-12.

on that multitude and you could almost hear the words, "These are my beloved sons, in whom I am well pleased." And just as on the mount Jesus was transfigured, meaning that the very impress and spirit and image of God came across his being, so that when from that day on when they saw him, they would see God. On that day black men were transformed. Some went away from the Million Man March never to return to the old mind and the old man that they were before that day.

In this instance Minister Farrakhan is making reference to the miracle of the Million Man March of 1995 held in Washington, DC. Nearly two million black men attended, and since then it has been the largest and most peaceful gathering in the history of America. But, while referring to Jesus Minister Farrakhan says,

> And just as on the mount Jesus was transfigured, meaning that the very impress and spirit and image of God came across his being, so that when from that day on when they saw him, they would see God.

How did this happen? How should we view the scriptures with regards to Minister Farrakhan and the Honorable Elijah Muhammad? How should we view Blacks in America today, Satan, and God? This is directly related to God's approval of Minister Farrakhan and his work.

The *Holman Illustrated Dictionary* suggests that the transfiguration was a visionary experience and explains its meaning:

> A mountain in the Bible is often a place of revelation. Moses and Elijah represented the Law and the prophets respectively, which testify to but must give way to Jesus... Moses and Elijah themselves were heralds of the Messiah (Duet. 18:15, Mal. 4:5-6). The three booths symbolize a new situation, a new age. Clouds represent divine presence. The close connection of the transfiguration with the confession and passion

prediction is significant. The Messiah must suffer, but glorification and enthronement, not suffering, are His ultimate fate.[305]

Minister Farrakhan saw several of his companions in his experience. These companions were affected by his vision experience when he shared his experience with them. Immediately they saw that this experience was *more* than just an ordinary dream, but a real experience. Many will give their testimony of the great event and bear witness of his ascension. Some will possibly see him as he ascends in the clouds of heaven for a second time. This is written in 2Peter 1:16- 18 and Acts 1:7-10. What follows are New International Version (NIV) and King James (KJ) versions of 2Peter and Acts 1,

> We did not follow cleverly invented stories when we told you about the power and coming of our Lord Jesus Christ, but we were eyewitnesses of his majesty. For he received honor and glory from God the Father when the voice came to him from the Majestic Glory, saying, "This is my Son, whom I love; with him I am well pleased." We ourselves heard this voice that came from heaven when we were with him on the sacred mountain. **(NIV 2 Peter 1: 16-18)**

> For we have not followed cunningly devised fables, when we made known unto you the power and coming of our Lord Jesus Christ, but were eyewitnesses of his majesty. For he received from God the Father honour and glory, when there came such a voice to him from the excellent glory, This is my beloved Son, in whom I am well pleased. And this voice, which came from heaven, we heard, when we were with him in the holy mount. **(KJ 2 Peter 1:16-18)**

> He said to them: "It is not for you to know the times or dates the Father has set by his own authority. But you will receive power when the Holy Spirit comes on you; and you will be my witnesses in Jerusalem, and in all Judea and Samaria, and to the ends of the earth." After he said this, he was taken up before their very eyes, and a cloud hid him from their

---

[305] See: Chad Brand, Charles Draper and Archie England, eds., *Holman Illustrated Bible Dictionary* (Nashville, TN: Holman Bible Publishers, 2003), s.v. "Transfiguration."

sight. They were looking intently up into the sky as he was going, when suddenly two men dressed in white stood beside them. "Men of Galilee," they said, "why do you stand here looking into the sky? This same Jesus, who has been taken from you into heaven, will come back in the same way you have seen him go into heaven." **(NIV Acts 1:7-10)**

And he said unto them, It is not for you to know the times or the seasons, which the Father hath put in his own power. But ye shall receive power, after that the Holy Ghost is come upon you: and ye shall be witnesses unto me both in Jerusalem, and in all Judaea, and in Samaria, and unto the uttermost part of the earth. And when he had spoken these things, while they beheld, he was taken up; and a cloud received him out of their sight. And while they looked steadfastly toward heaven as he went up, behold, two men stood by them in white apparel; Which also said, Ye men of Galilee, why stand ye gazing up into heaven? this same Jesus, which is taken up from you into heaven, shall so come in like manner as ye have seen him go into heaven. **(KJ Acts 1:7-10)**

What follows is an excerpt from Minister Farrakhan's Announcement and the strikingly similar events of his vision that typologically mirror events mentioned in scripture. Minister Farrakhan describes his experience,

> However, on the night of September 17, 1985, I was carried up on that mountain, in a vision, with a few friends of mine. As we reached the top of the mountain, a Wheel, or what you call an unidentified flying object (UFO), appeared at the side of the mountain and called to me to come up into the Wheel.[306]

By comparison we can observe,

Matthew 17:1 - Six days later Jesus took with him Peter and James and his brother John and led them up a high mountain, by themselves.

---

[306] Farrakhan, *The Announcement: A final warning to the U.S. Government,* 5-6.

Mark 9:2 - Six days later, Jesus took with him Peter and James and John and led them up a high mountain apart, by themselves.

Luke 9:28 - Now about eight days after these sayings Jesus took with him Peter and John and James and went up on the mountain to pray.

Minister Louis Farrakhan (MLF) - However, on the night of September 17, 1985, I was carried up on that mountain, in a vision, with a few friends of mine.[307]

Here we see by comparison the vision, as an experience is relevant when we apply the scriptural rules of typology. In Prophet Muhammad's experience, Allah (God) took his soul and he traveled by way of the soul and received knowledge through his *soul vehicle*. But, still there is a greater meaning and the point again is that this was representative of a future event and an anti-typical figure that I believe is Minister Farrakhan.

The comparison of Minister Farrakhan's vision experience in relation to the transfiguration of Jesus, and the Night Journey of Prophet Muhammad is not an allegorical reference.

> Surely We revealed it on the Night of Majesty. And what will make thee comprehend what the Night of Majesty is? The Night of Majesty is better than a thousand months. The angels and the Spirit descend in it by the permission of their Lord —for every affair —Peace! it is till the rising of the morning.[308]

While speaking of Prophet Muhammad, Muhammad Ali's introductory comments in the Holy Quran parallel what Minister

---

[307] Minister Louis Farrakhan has been to Tepotzlan several times for the purpose of pray and meditation, but was taken back to this mountain in his vision experience.
[308] Holy Quran 97.1-5 – Maulana Muhammad Ali.

Farrakhan received and the majesty of the revelation of the wisdom and its benefit to humanity.

> It was the *Night of Majesty* (one of the last ten nights of the month of Ramadan), which first witnessed the shining of that light which was destined to illumine the whole world. And the coming of the first revelation on the Night of *Majesty*, which gives its name to this chapter, contained a clear indication that the most majestic of all revelations was now being granted to the world, and that the majesty of this revelation, as well as of its recipient, would be established in the world.[309]

Minister Farrakhan's experience (as the Honorable Elijah Muhammad) has striking similarity to Moses experience on the mountain in Exodus 24:15-24. This is also reflective of Jesus' experience on the Mountain in Matthew 4:1-11.

> When Moses went up on the mountain, the cloud covered it, and the glory of the LORD settled on Mount Sinai. For six days the cloud covered the mountain, and on the seventh day the LORD called to Moses from within the cloud. To the Israelites the glory of the LORD looked like a consuming fire on top of the mountain. Then Moses entered the cloud as he went on up the mountain. And he stayed on the mountain forty days and forty nights.[310]

In Exodus 24:15-24 Moses had an experience where he is taken up into a cloud. Moses stayed in this mountain for 40 days and forty nights. We know for certain that the historical Moses never spent forty years in Egypt fighting a Pharaoh who enslaved whites. This is a prophecy that speaks of a people who would anti-typically resemble this.

> And We appointed for Moses thirty nights, and completed them with ten, so the appointed time of his Lord was complete forty nights. And

---

[309] See Introduction to Chapter 97 of the Holy Quran by Maulana Muhammad Ali.
[310] Exodus 24: 15-24.

Moses said to his brother Aaron: Take my place among my people, and act well and follow not the way of the mischief-makers.[311]

As I mentioned early, in Minister Farrakhan's experience he admits that he felt that he was *inoculated* with something that he could not explain.[312] He also acknowledges that when he was taken up on the Wheel and saw the scroll roll down in cursive writing, it was indicative of what was being written on his heart or inside of his head.[313] This testimony of his experience and what was put in his head/heart was at the command of Allah, but imparted by the Honorable Elijah Muhammad, who is giving Minister Farrakhan this knowledge directly. Minister Farrakhan explains what he received in his experience,

> After 1985, and my experience with him [his more-than-a-vision experience] I even more clearly understood why I didn't have to study. Because this that I am going to (if it is the will of Allah) back from my next meeting with him, is that of which it is written, "no eye that has seen, no ear has heard," so no book contains it. So there's nothing for me to study. That's revelation. When he reveals it to me, if I'm worthy, I'll reveal it to others; but there's nothing for me to study. It's just for me to get it in me and I believe a portion of it is already in me from my first visit with him. That's what I think the scroll was that came down that I saw--well something was being written in me, so that even right now, although I'm not a great student of Bible and Qur'an, but I stand and speak and the Bible comes up. The Qur'an comes up. Things come up. They come out of me in a very fantastic order.[314]

As Moses was a guardian, (in some translations even a God) over Aaron, and was given control over Aaron, so it is with the Honorable Elijah Muhammad and Minister Farrakhan. Minister Farrakhan is being fed wisdom and revelation and is controlled by God and the Honorable

---

[311] Holy Quran 7:142.
[312] Muhammad, *Closing the Gap*, 381-82. Also see footnote 159.
[313] Ibid., 375.
[314] Ibid., 118-19.

Elijah Muhammad. This creates a very hostile environment for Minister Farrakhan, similar to the hostility that surrounded the messengers, and Prophets of the past. This nearness to God and truth that transforms the life of everyone that hears it, is a threat to the wicked of this world. His warning to the governments of the world is a threat to the wicked, if they do not turn from there wicked ways. This sets the stage for betrayal, which leads to crucifixion. This is the price that Jesus had to pay in order to be raised. This is the price that some of the Prophets had to pay in order to be raised. The Honorable Elijah Muhammad paid the same price, and was raised, which fulfilled prophecy.

This Page Intentionally Left Blank

PART THREE

They Planned, and God Planned

8 Betrayal and Crucifixion

8.1 *And they said, "Kill Him!"*

"Et tu, Brute?" (You too Brutus?)

In William Shakespeare's play *Julius Caesar*, these are Julius Caesar's final words to his beloved soldier and companion Brutus, when rushed by Brutus and a devious group of conspirators who stabbed him to death. This phrase has been considered to represent the epitome of betrayal. The stories leading up to Jesus' crucifixion in the Gospels read like the great stories of love, betrayal and conspiracy. Like Othello, betrayed by his jealous and envious ensign, Judas is seen as one who conspires against Jesus for no reason except, envy.

> Now as Jesus was going up to Jerusalem, he took the twelve disciples aside and said to them, "We are going up to Jerusalem, and the Son of Man will be *betrayed* [emphasis added] to the chief priests and the teachers of the law. They will condemn him to death and will turn him over to the Gentiles to be mocked and flogged and *crucified* [emphasis added].[315]

There is an ongoing dispute that the events leading up to the crucifixion of Jesus did not happen two thousand years ago. The Honorable Elijah Muhammad taught that this was a prophecy and that the Jesus of two thousand years ago was not the one to bring in the New Kingdom. Scholars of religion suggests that the writings of Flavius Josephus also Yosef Ben Matityahu (Joseph son of Matthias), a Jewish historian of the first-century, justifies the existence of the passion events

---

[315] See Matthew 20:17-19.

as described in the Bible. This is questionable by some theologians. But if this is true, what relevance does it have in the modern context? These parables are mixed with scenes of fear, miracles, suspense, betrayal, honor, conspiracy, loyalty, faithfulness, trust and doubt, jealous and envy and even murder. All of this leads to the tragic death of the beloved of God. The characters of the Bible are reflective of people whom we have all seen and may perhaps know.

There are religious leaders, politicians, soldiers, slaves, educated people, uneducated people, poor people, rich people, blind people, crazy people, believers, and even prostitutes. The list continues. These people represent the present day world and this includes Jesus. But, were Jesus' enemies in control of his fate? Or, was this a Divine plan by God to try his servant, only to raise him in the presence of the same enemy? Let us also consider that Jesus was aware of his enemies' plans. Let us consider that all involved, including Jesus, were a part of a drama that God was the producer of. J Duncan Derrett questions in his writing **The Iscariot, Mesîrâ, and the Redemption**, whether Jesus was aware of his betrayer in relation to God's plan,

> One who comes to the New Testament with a fresh mind is struck by the intellectual and moral difficulties apparently needlessly aroused by such a sentence as Mark 14:21: that the Son of man goes as it has been written about him, but woe to that man through whom the Son of man is *given up* (or handed over: παραδυδοταυ): it would have been better for that man if he had never been born! The whole story is impregnated with an apparently implausible paradox: Jesus was *given up,* yet he gave himself (Mark 10:45, Barn 5:1-2). God gave Jesus up (Rom 8:32: παρέδωκεν), yet Jesus himself insists repeatedly that Judas is his 'giver-up' (Mark 14:42 ὁ παραδυδο με). The twelve were chosen, almost appointed by Jesus (Mark 3:14, 16), and Judas is not only 'one of the Twelve, a phrase that recurs as a refrain, but he is described, in a passage which has often puzzled readers (Mark 14:10), as 'the One of the Twelve. The impression given by the synoptics is that Jesus knew the

identity of him who would *give* him up; St John rubs the point in melodramatically.[316]

This quote suggests that Jesus knew his betrayer. Was this historic or prophetic? The accounts of the Old and New Testaments are all questionable historically. The Honorable Elijah Muhammad said that 75% of the Bible is prophetic. So, this does not negate the truth of the Bible theologically and mathematically when we consider the *God Factor* and His plan prophetically. Michael Baigent in his writing *The Jesus Papers* suggests regarding the New Testament's history,

> Certainly the New Testament is bad history. This is impossible to deny. The texts are inconsistent, incomplete, garbled, and biased. It is impossible to deconstruct the New Testament to the point where nothing remains but heavily biased, dogmatic Christian mythology... ...the pagan historians themselves, in particular Tacitus and Pliny the Younger, while sparse in their information, do report – and by so do confirming that a Jewish messiah was crucified during the period when Pontius Pilate was the prefect of Judaea, and further, that a religious movement, centered upon and named after this particular messiah, was in existence by the end of the first century A.D. Consequently, we must admit that there is some real history in the Gospels, but how much of it is there?[317]

So how much of the gospels writings on Judas are historical? Whether historical or prophetic, the question must be asked, what was the root of Judas' betrayal of Jesus? What would cause a friend and close companion to be disloyal? What would cause the disciples to turn a deaf ear to their Lord, Jesus, in his time of suffering? If we figuratively put Minister Farrakhan in the place of Jesus, we can assume that he also has a betrayer, maybe several. This association is not based on trying to mix

---

[316] J Duncan M. Derrett. "The Iscariot, Mesîrâ, and the Redemption." *Journal for the Study of the New Testament* no. 8 (July 1, 1980): 2.
[317] Michael Baigent, *The Jesus Papers: Exposing the Greatest Cover-Up in History* (New York, NY: Harper Collins. 2006) 123-124.

and match scripture so that Minister Farrakhan fits, just to make a point. The reference is sound enough, based on the Minister's work, the time, and what has been revealed in scripture, to make the comparison. If we apply the principle of *Double Reference*, we can apply the reference of Jesus to Minister Farrakhan, in addition to several other figures in scripture, including the instances where others referenced Jesus as the Son of Man, Son of God, Master, etc…[318] We can also assume, because of this double reference as the Son of Man; that he will be betrayed. Why?

It is Minister Farrakhan's work and representation of the Honorable Elijah Muhammad as *the* Messiah and exalted Christ that upsets the enemy's plans to hold the ex-slaves captive. Because of this, the truth is upsetting their wicked rule over the people of God. To allow him to live is to end their world and rule. At the root of their hatred for Minister Farrakhan and the Nation of Islam, is envy. Minister Farrakhan says of this point in **Self Improvement the Basis of Community Development**,

> At the root of the lies and murder plots against Jesus, Paul, Peter, Muhammad, was Envy. Envy arose in the hearts of the political and spiritual leadership because one was coming to replace their rule; one more favoured in the sight of Allah (God); one more pleasing and acceptable in the public eye. …Since the Envier cannot climb up to heaven to the Grantor of gifts and benefits, his or her anger is focused on the recipient of Divine Favour. Though their efforts (lies, murder) are directed at the recipient, their actions are in fact a challenge against Allah (God) Himself to warfare.[319]

The enemies of God are hateful of the position that their ex-slaves have with God and His promise to the Original people, more specifically the Blacks in America. This was the same idea that surrounded the plot

---

[318] We can also apply the Principle of Agreement, Three Fold Principle, and Context Principle.
[319] Louis Farrakhan, **Self Improvement the Basis for Community Development**: *Study Guide 17, Hypocrisy and Conspiracy Part 2* (Chicago, IL: Final Call Inc., n.d.),2.

to kill Jesus.[320] Judas is a *type* of person who is susceptible to the wiles of Satan because of a diseased heart. Envy has no redeemable qualities and it is a form of the deepest hatred that one could possess, and it will lead to murder. To this point, there is a person or persons who will play into the conspiracy to kill Minister Farrakhan. Why? They are disappointed in an idea and expectation that they have of Minister Farrakhan and this expectation will lead them to being used. This disappointment will lead to treachery and envy and they will become tools in a conspiracy.

It was not thirty pieces of silver that caused Judas to conspire against his master.[321] It was hatred against Jesus and God, for what Judas thought he deserved for his faithful service. This of course grew over time as Judas began to see himself as more knowledgeable and better than his master. The enemies of God desired to kill the Messenger. As Jesus rose in power and influence among the people, the Jewish Sanhedrin became concerned over how he would upset their plans to rule over the people. This is symbolic to today's Supreme Court Judges and/or members of Congress. The plan was hatched! Caiaphas the high priest initiated a plot to kill Jesus. The plot thickens; the plan to kill Farrakhan has been hatched. The enemies of the Honorable Elijah Muhammad are the enemies of Minister Farrakhan and the righteous all over the earth.

These enemies are the "rich slave-makers of the poor", who are found in positions of influence throughout America and the world. Many of them are government officials, private and public corporate figures, heads of religious and educational institutions, heads of entertainment and banking conglomerates. These are the ones who

---

[320] See: **Study Guide 17, Hypocrisy and Conspiracy**: "The Jews, during the time of Jesus, felt that spirit of exclusivity as the "chosen of God". Jesus represented the ultimate threat to their exclusivity both in this condemnation of them by identifying them as the children of Satan and his declaration that God was his Father". 2.
[321] Farrakhan, **Self Improvement**, 4.

control every area of human endeavor and there are others. These are the warmongers, the secret councils, and wicked rulers in high places. These are those controlled by Satan. Who launched this plan? Who is Caiaphas?

> Then the chief priests and the Pharisees called a meeting of the Sanhedrin. "What are we accomplishing?" they asked. "Here is this man performing many miraculous signs. If we let him go on like this, everyone will believe in him, and then the Romans will come and take away both our place and our nation." Then one of them, named Caiaphas, who was high priest that year, spoke up, "You know nothing at all! You do not realize that it is better for you that one man die for the people than that the whole nation perish." He did not say this on his own, but as high priest that year he prophesied that Jesus would die for the Jewish nation, and not only for that nation but also for the scattered children of God, to bring them together and make them one. So from that day on they plotted to take his life.[322]
>
> As you know, the Passover is two days away—and the Son of Man will be handed over to be crucified." Then the chief priests and the elders of the people assembled in the palace of the high priest, whose name was Caiaphas, and they plotted to arrest Jesus in some sly way and kill him. "But not during the Feast," they said, "or there may be a riot among the people.[323]

Who are the players in this drama today? Certainly, Judas Iscariot, but he was not the only one. There were others, namely Pontius Pilate, Herod Antipas, the Sanhedrin (Pharisees and Sadducees), Israel and numerous Gentiles among the population. All of these groups played some part in the betrayal or crucifixion of Jesus and all will play a part typologically in the deliverance of Minister Farrakhan into the hands of God's enemies. God and Christ have a plan too. The prayers of the believers in Acts testify of the plot,

---

[322] See John 11:47-53.
[323] See Mathew 26:2-5.

On their release, Peter and John went back to their own people and reported all that the chief priests and elders had said to them. When they heard this, they raised their voices together in prayer to God. "Sovereign Lord," they said, "you made the heaven and the earth and the sea, and everything in them. You spoke by the Holy Spirit through the mouth of your servant, our father David: "Why do the nations rage and the peoples plot in vain? The kings of the earth take their stand and the rulers gather together against the Lord and against his Anointed One. Indeed Herod and Pontius Pilate met together with the Gentiles and the people of Israel in this city to conspire against your holy servant Jesus, whom you anointed.[324]

The Holy Quran speaks to this conspiracy:

And for their saying: We have killed the Messiah, Jesus son of Mary, the Messenger of Allah, and they killed him not, nor did they cause his death on the cross, but he was made to appear to them as such. And certainly those who differ therein are in doubt about it, but only follow conjecture, and they killed him not for certain. "Nay, Allah exalted him in His presence. And Allah is ever Mighty, Wise.[325]

This reference to Jesus makes mention of a plot to kill the messenger, more specifically the Honorable Elijah Muhammad. He represents the anti-typical figure in the above-mentioned verse, but escaped the plot in February 1975. How do we know this to be the case? Historically, scholars know that there is no archeological evidence that proves that a man named Jesus died on a cross. The Holy Quran bears witness that he did not die on a cross, but he was made to appear as such and the Honorable Elijah Muhammad taught that Jesus did not die on a cross. It clearly makes reference to his escape from death. According to the Bible Jesus was hung on a tree,

---

[324] See Acts 4:23-27 (NIV).
[325] Holy Quran 4:157- 158.

You know what has happened throughout Judea, beginning in Galilee after the baptism that John preached how God anointed Jesus of Nazareth with the Holy Spirit and power, and how he went around doing good and healing all who were under the power of the devil, because God was with him. "We are witnesses of everything he did in the country of the Jews and in Jerusalem. They killed him by hanging him on a tree, but God raised him from the dead on the third day and caused him to be seen.[326]

Peter and the other apostles replied: "We must obey God rather than men! The God of our fathers raised Jesus from the dead—whom you had killed by hanging him on a tree. God exalted him to his own right hand as Prince and Savior that he might give repentance and forgiveness of sins to Israel.[327]

How could Peter and the other apostles see Jesus carried off to be crucified on the cross, yet bear witness that he was lynched from a tree? Why would the scripture writers say; *"We are witnesses of everything he did in the country of the Jews and in Jerusalem"*, yet say he was hung and raised from a hanging in three days, but make no reference to crucifixion on the cross? These are several points out of many that confirm that the Jesus spoken of in scripture is misunderstood, and misrepresented. This figure Jesus typologically has more relevance to Black people in America, than white people in Jerusalem two thousand years ago. In fact there are several Jesus *types* mentioned in the Bible and Holy Quran. The Jesus, *"**whom you had killed by hanging him on a tree**"* does not represent a man from two thousand years ago. This Jesus, prophetically, represents the countless slaves who were lynched at the hands of the slave master for over 310 years while in slavery and still today.

Each of the Gospels gives a different account to the betrayal and crucifixion of Jesus. This is largely due to the time in which the

[326] See Acts 10:37-40 (NIV).
[327] See Acts 5:29-31 (NIV).

scriptures were written; including the fact that a large percentage of the early Christian population was illiterate and could not read nor write. The early Christians lived in an oral culture and only 10 percent of their population could read.[328] So, there are a lot of inconsistencies in the history of the Passion Narratives, as mentioned previously. The synoptic gospels borrow from one another, but mainly Mark; this theory is called Markan Priority. Mark has priority over the other Gospels for being more authentic and is credited as an earlier source.

Markan Priority – A theory that implies that the Gospel of Mark was the first and most authentic of the synoptic gospels. This theory claims that the other gospels borrow its text from Mark.

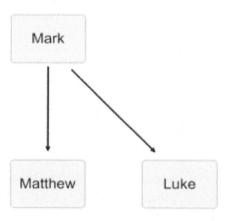

Figure 22: Markan Priority

---

[328] Bart D. Ehrman. *The Lost Gospels of Judas*, (New York, NY: Oxford University Press, Inc. 2006) 35.

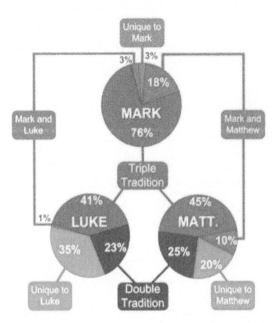

Figure 23: Shows the relationship of the Synoptic Gospels and the Double and Triple Tradition hypothesis. These hypotheses suggest that Luke and Matthew have similar scripture and borrow from each other (Double Tradition), while all three have similar scriptures and relate to each other (Triple Tradition). There are also other hypotheses that are called, "source hypotheses".

Contemporary scholars do not think that the evangelists were eyewitnesses of Jesus' ministry and this is what attributes to the differences of the arrangements of the Gospels.[329] Matthew and Luke take and borrow from Mark. The Bible as a historical document continues to be questioned and scholars have concluded that they are not literal accounts of Jesus' ministry. According to Raymond Brown in *Introduction to the New Testament,*

> The Gospels are not literal records of the ministry of Jesus. Decades of developing and adapting the Jesus tradition had intervened. How much

---

[329] Brown, *Introduction to the New Testament,*109; According to Brown, the arrangement of events in the Gospels differ based on the account of the evangelist. If the evangelist was not an eyewitness to the ministry of Jesus then he could not know the sequence of the events. So for each Gospel the writer arranged the scripture according to the spiritual need of his community and what seemed logical to them.

development? That has to be determined by the painstaking scholarship which most often produces judgments ranging from possibility to probability, but rarely certainty.[330]

Here, Brown concludes that there is rarely certainty among scholars as to the historical authenticity of the gospels and Jesus' ministry. Brown however introduces the idea that the historical inaccuracy does not negate the theological importance and that what may be reported as untrue historically can be adapted to bring a person to faith.[331] It is also noted by Brown that Matthew and Luke were probably written 10 to 20 years after Mark.[332] To conclude this point, the Bible is a book that has significant importance to humanity today, but it needs to be interpreted properly. The Honorable Elijah Muhammad taught in the Muslim Program,

> **Point #2-** We Believe in the Holy Quran and the Scriptures of all the Prophets of God.

> **Point #3-** We Believe in the truth of the Bible, but we believe that it has been tampered with and must be reinterpreted so that mankind will not be snared by the falsehoods that have been added to it.[333]

This falsehood mentioned has deceived the world about Jesus' true identity, betrayal and crucifixion. Minister Farrakhan explains regarding the death plot of Jesus,

> It is important that we understand the word "plan" in the context of the statement, "And the Jews planned...". The Arabic word "makara" signifies something underhanded. The Jews did what they did, not openly, but in secret. This is also demonstrated in the biblical account: "Then said Pilate unto them, Take ye him and judge him according to

---

[330] Ibid., 10.
[331] Brown, *Introduction to the New Testament*, 109.
[332] Ibid., 7.
[333] Muhammad, *Message to the Blackman*, 163.

your law. The Jews therefore said unto him, 'It is not lawful for us to put any man to death." Thus, not only did they plan the murder of Jesus, but they set up Pontius Pilate, the Roman Governor, as a front for their plan that they might escape detection. Compare the relationship between Pontius Pilate and the Jews in the New Testament, to the relationship between the Executive Branch (President and Staff) of the U.S. Government and the Jews today. The term "Jew" is not exclusively limited to describing a people who call themselves "Jews". This term also describes a certain orientation of the mind and spirit. While the person may not be a "Jew" in the religious sense, a person may be that by definition of his or her thinking and planned action (s) against the Apostle of God.[334]

There were numerous attempts to kill Jesus. The same is true with Farrakhan. Minister Farrakhan has been able to elude his enemies as Jesus eluded his. (Luke 4:14-30) These things upset the rulers. Minister Farrakhan's bearing of witness of the Honorable Elijah Muhammad and his tireless work to expose Satan, the enemy of God, is what prompts them to murder him. (John 5:16-18) According to the Bible, during the time of Jesus, Caiaphas, who was a Sadducee controlled the temple among those who were aristocrats. They were normally in opposition to the Pharisees, (like Democrats and Republicans) but for the purpose of killing Jesus, they would join together. Both groups often worked to damage the reputation of Jesus and the idea of Christ's existence. This caused them to band together like hypocrites. The death of Jesus was a common interest among those who he offended. The death of Farrakhan is an interest of those with similar desires. Minister Farrakhan's vision experience and his declaration of faith that the Honorable Elijah Muhammad is the exalted Christ, and will destroy the power of Satan, is the most controversial subject of the world. This is written in the scriptures; Bible and Holy Quran. The secret counsels of the wicked that plot daily; their plans will fail,

---

[334] Farrakhan, *Self Improvement*, 1.

Know they not that Allah knows their hidden thoughts and their secret counsels, and that Allah is the great Knower of the unseen things?[335]

Seest thou not those who are forbidden secret counsels, then they return to that which they are forbidden, and hold secret counsels for sin and revolt and disobedience to the Messenger. And when they come to thee they greet thee with a greeting with which Allah greets thee not, and say within themselves: Why does not Allah punish us for what we say? Hell is enough for them; they will burn in it, and evil is the resort![336]

Secret counsels are only of the devil that he may cause to grieve those who believe, and he can hurt them naught except with Allah's permission. And on Allah let the believers rely.[337]

Their plotting was on the account that Jesus was not popular among the aristocratic community and often challenged them and their belief and actions against the people and God. Minister Farrakhan represents this to the American public and the world. His representation of the Honorable Elijah Muhammad is extremely unorthodox and is almost enigmatic to the unlearned. John MacArthur writes regarding Jesus in a modern context,

Consider the account of Jesus' public ministry given in the New Testament. The first word of his first sermon was "Repent!"--a theme that was no more welcome and no less strident-sounding than it is today. The first act of his public ministry touched off a small riot. He made a whip of cords and chased money-changers and animal merchants off the Temple grounds. That initiated a three-year-long conflict with society's most distinguished religious leaders. They ultimately handed him over to Roman authorities for crucifixion while crowds of lay people cheered them on. Jesus was pointedly, deliberately, and dogmatically counter-cultural in almost every way. No wonder the religious and academic

---

[335] Holy Quran 9:78.
[336] Holy Quran 58:8.
[337] Holy Quran 58:10, Also see Acts 13:42-26,17:1-7, 23:1-14, Holy Quran 6:124, 14:46-47.

aristocracy of his generation were so hostile to him. Would Jesus receive a warmer welcome from world religious leaders, the media elite, or the political gentry today? Anyone who has seriously considered the New Testament knows very well that he would not.[338]

The United States government is envious of the growth and rise of the Nation of Islam, whom Minister Farrakhan represents.[339] As it was with Paul and his teaching to the Gentiles and his meeting with the Sanhedrin Council, so will it be with Minister Farrakhan. Christianity did not exist until the end of the 1st Century. Paul did not disagree with Christianity since it did not exist. Paul disagreed with how one becomes Jewish. Therefore all of Paul's converts were not converts to Christianity, they were converts to Judaism and Jesus was hailed as King of the Jews. But, Jesus was a Righteous Muslim.

Paul never saw or read any of the Gospels. Paul's meeting with God's enemies in the scripture "Acts" has remarkable similarities to Jesus' day in court among the Sanhedrin and Caiaphas, the High Priest. Prophetically, the similarities are all too familiar to the likeness of Minister Farrakhan. He, like Paul, is testifying of the arisen Christ, and he, like Paul is being criticized and persecuted because of it. Minister Farrakhan, like Paul, is considered insane and a lunatic because of his bearing of witness to Jesus Christ. Paul is and was a sign of Minister Farrakhan. Acts 23:1-15 in its entirety reads,

> Paul looked straight at the Sanhedrin and said, "My brothers, I have fulfilled my duty to God in all good conscience to this day." At this the high priest Ananias ordered those standing near Paul to strike him on the mouth. Then Paul said to him, "God will strike you, you whitewashed wall! You sit there to judge me according to the law, yet you yourself violate the law by commanding that I be struck!"

---

[338] John MacArthur, On Faith: Read the Gospels: Jesus Christ is not Politically Correct, *The Washington Post*, August 14, 2009.
[339] Farrakhan, *Self Improvement*, 5.

Those who were standing near Paul said, "You dare to insult God's high priest?"

Paul replied, "Brothers, I did not realize that he was the high priest; for it is written: 'Do not speak evil about the ruler of your people. Then Paul, knowing that some of them were Sadducees and the others Pharisees, called out in the Sanhedrin, "My brothers, I am a Pharisee, the son of a Pharisee. I stand on trial because of my hope in the resurrection of the dead." When he said this, a dispute broke out between the Pharisees and the Sadducees, and the assembly was divided. (The Sadducees say that there is no resurrection, and that there are neither angels nor spirits, but the Pharisees acknowledge them all.)

There was a great uproar, and some of the teachers of the law who were Pharisees stood up and argued vigorously. "We find nothing wrong with this man," they said. "What if a spirit or an angel has spoken to him?" The dispute became so violent that the commander was afraid Paul would be torn to pieces by them. He ordered the troops to go down and take him away from them by force and bring him into the barracks. The following night the Lord stood near Paul and said, "Take courage! As you have testified about me in Jerusalem, so you must also testify in Rome." The next morning the Jews formed a conspiracy and bound themselves with an oath not to eat or drink until they had killed Paul. More than forty men were involved in this plot. They went to the chief priests and elders and said, "We have taken a solemn oath not to eat anything until we have killed Paul. Now then, you and the Sanhedrin petition the commander to bring him before you on the pretext of wanting more accurate information about his case. We are ready to kill him before he gets here."

The plot launched to take the life of Paul in Acts was diabolical.[340] It was a conspiracy of more than 40 people who agreed to bring him in and question him on the basis that they wanted more information about his ministry. Paul was rescued from his accusers. This chapter reads like an exciting drama of truth over falsehood, a story of conspiracy and betrayal, but it is an actual real account of the life of Minister Farrakhan.

---

[340] See Acts 23:12.

He is a man loved and hated by many and like Paul; he is a man condemned without just cause.

8.2   *Judas: The Dissatisfied Laborer*

Judas is a type that represents the person who desires to betray his brother or sister. Judas as a symbol represents the lower self that is in constant competition with the higher self. Judas is portrayed in Christian thought in a negative light. David Bartlett in his writing **John 13:21-30** explains,

> Judas is a far more threatening figure than Pilate or the Jewish leaders to those of us Christians who read John's Gospel. Judas is the reminder that every day is judgment day and that on any day some faithful follower, like Judas—or like you or me—might turn tail on the light and stumble out into the darkness, caught up in evil or caught up by evil's prince.[341]

Bart D. Ehrman suggests that the earliest mention of betrayal of Jesus is in Mark, but it does not mention Judas as the betrayer, except to say that it would be "better that one not to have been born."[342] Ehrman also describes Judas according to the gospels and from the Christian perspective as a money grabber and one encouraged by the Devil. He also suggests that Judas may have been the Devil himself.[343]   For centuries the figure Judas is the antithesis of all that is good. Why? What follows is Matthew's account of the arrest of Jesus. The arrest took place shortly after Jesus met with his disciples in the Garden of Gethsemane.[344] He met with his disciples there and prayed in the Mount of Olives. They were confronted by Jesus in Matthew's account three

---

[341] David L. Bartlett, *"John 13:21-30." Interpretation* **43**, no. 4 (October 1, 1989): 393.
[342] Ehrman, *The Lost Gospel*, 138.
[343] Ibid.
[344] See Matthew 26:36-46.

times, because they fell asleep on their posts. What does this mean? Minister Farrakhan explains,

> That very dark hour of Jesus, when he was in a certain and delightful spot that he loved so well, called the Garden of Gethsemane, in the Mount of Olives, there they say he prayed until the sweat was dropping from his brow. In the same hour when he was praying, (for he was conscious of the hour) his disciples were in a state of sleep or suspended consciousness. They were not aware of the hour. It appears that there were aspects of what he said and taught that they didn't agree with and did not necessarily believe: not because they were disbelievers, but they could not bear the pain of the thought of him leaving them.
>
> Nor could they bear the pain of the thought that they might not see him again for a while. In that dark hour of their suspended consciousness, when they awaken to the reality of that hour of their suspended consciousness, when they awaken to the reality of that hour, the soldiers were already upon him and them and took him.[345]

Matthew's account of the arrest of Jesus shows,

> While he was still speaking, Judas, one of the Twelve, arrived. With him was a large crowd armed with swords and clubs, sent from the chief priests and the elders of the people. Now the betrayer had arranged a signal with them: "The one I kiss is the man; arrest him." Going at once to Jesus, Judas said, "Greetings, Rabbi!" and kissed him. Jesus replied, "Friend, do what you came for." Then the men stepped forward, seized Jesus and arrested him. With that, one of Jesus' companions reached for his sword, drew it out and struck the servant of the high priest, cutting off his ear. "Put your sword back in its place," Jesus said to him, "for all who draw the sword will die by the sword.
>
> Do you think I cannot call on my Father, and he will at once put at my disposal more than twelve legions of angels? But how then would the Scriptures be fulfilled that say it must happen in this way?" At that time Jesus said to the crowd, "Am I leading a rebellion, that you have come out with swords and clubs to capture me? Every day I sat in the temple courts teaching, and you did not arrest me. But this has all taken

---

[345] Muhammad, *Closing the Gap*, 217.

place that the writings of the prophets might be fulfilled." Then all the disciples deserted him and fled.[346]

The disciples in this instance were no different than Judas. They all fled and abandoned his teachings. What is the responsibility of the disciple to the master? What manifested this state of suspended consciousness among the disciples? The disciples were faced with a great trial, to bear witness and testify of Jesus. This was a trial for all of those who walked with Jesus and it is a trial for all of those who walk with Minister Farrakhan.[347]

> *Judas Iscariot* - According to the New Testament, one of the twelve original apostles of Jesus Christ. He is notoriously known as the "betrayer" of Jesus, and represents in Christian tradition the disillusioned disciple.

The media machine will attack Minister Farrakhan with slander and propaganda. The enemy will continue to insert his agents and hypocrites among the faithful believers. Satan will continue to offer worldly possessions and idols to worship, all the while, challenging Allah (God) by secretly plotting against the Nation of Islam and the baited trap; Louis Farrakhan.

But, still the trial exists for the believers in God. Some will fall victim to their own ideas of God and their unwillingness to accept Minister Farrakhan and his vision experience and testimony of the Honorable Elijah Muhammad. What about Judas? According to the Bible, Judas was a laborer and disciple of Jesus. Historically, there are few certifiable facts about whether Judas existed. The earliest authentic Christian writings are considered to be the writings of Paul, and in none

---

[346] See Matthew 26:47-56.
[347] Muhammad, *Closing the Gap*, 217.

of his writings does he mention Judas or any of the companions of Jesus by name.[348] As mentioned previously, there is an ongoing debate with scholars of religion, of whether or not Jesus and his disciples existed as they are depicted in the Bible. Master Fard Muhammad taught the Honorable Elijah Muhammad the true history of Jesus. If the Holy Quran verifies the truths of the Bible, why doesn't it say anything about Judas?

The biblical accounts of Judas place him as a very intelligent and respected person between Jesus and the other disciples, but with different expectations. One of the first instances of the betrayal and disillusion of Judas was when Mary anointed Jesus with perfume/oil as a sign of honor for his soon to be deliverance and crucifixion. Judas exposes himself as many have and will continue to expose themselves with how they view Minister Farrakhan and his position with God and Christ. The position Judas held allowed him to conceal his motives. Van Dyke-Plant and Hall in an article *Betrayal and healing: the aftermath of Judas' kiss*, explains the position of Judas:

> Judas is represented as the controller of the purse strings for the disciples; money is always a symbolic as well as an actual means of power. His desire for revolution as one of the Iscarii apparently had led Judas to join the disciples hoping that Jesus was the Messiah who would restore the freedom of the Jews. He was not a Galilean, and therefore was an isolated fringe member of the disciples with different expectations of Jesus.[349]

Everett Falconer Harrison in his writing *The Son of God among the Sons of Men* suggests regarding Judas' role among the others,

---

[348] Ehrman, *The Lost Gospel*, 14.
[349] Nancy van Dyke Platt and Richard H. Hall, "Betrayal and healing: the aftermath of Judas' kiss.," *Journal of Pastoral Care and Counseling* 59, no. 4 (December 1, 2005): 361-62 This reference is to point out that the person(s) who is to betray Minister Farrakhan has influence and authority. In the larger sense, this reference is to any person with a mind of betrayal that fits the type.

... [We] gain the information that Judas was treasurer of the group about Jesus and that he was a thief—a bad combination. John alone gives him this label, speaking with that directness that characterizes his writings on moral and ethical themes. Judas must have been a clever scoundrel, managing to hide his peculations and retain his post. In such company, however, it would occur to no one to keep a watchful eye on him. The atmosphere was one of trust, and Judas evidently made the most of it.[350]

Because of his role and post, none of the disciples spoke out against Judas. Envy is a characteristic that cannot be easily detected. The disciples were not innocent at all and followed along with Judas in his rebellion. Judas manifested his disapproval of the master while the others concealed theirs.

But one of his disciples, Judas Iscariot, who was later to betray him, objected, "Why wasn't this perfume sold and the money given to the poor? It was worth a year's wages." He did not say this because he cared about the poor but because he was a thief; as keeper of the money bag, he used to help himself to what was put into it. "Leave her alone," Jesus replied. "It was intended that she should save this perfume for the day of my burial. You will always have the poor among you, but you will not always have me." Meanwhile a large crowd of Jews found out that Jesus was there and came, not only because of him but also to see Lazarus, whom he had raised from the dead. So the chief priests made plans to kill Lazarus as well.[351]

In Mark's account of this event, although it does not mention the names of those present, we can infer that they were disciples and they also questioned Jesus about this act of kindness towards him. This is an indication that other disciples and companions doubted this act of the kind woman. This is reflected in how the some judge Minister Farrakhan today, with doubt and suspicion.

---

[350] Everett Falconer Harrison. "The Son of God among the sons of men." *Bibliotheca sacra* 105, no. 418 (April 1, 1948): 173-174.
[351] See John 12:4-10 NIV.

While he was in Bethany, reclining at the table in the home of a man known as Simon the Leper, a woman came with an alabaster jar of very expensive perfume, made of pure nard. She broke the jar and poured the perfume on his head. Some of those present were saying indignantly to one another, "Why this waste of perfume? It could have been sold for more than a year's wages and the money given to the poor." And they rebuked her harshly. "Leave her alone," said Jesus. "Why are you bothering her? She has done a beautiful thing to me. The poor you will always have with you, and you can help them any time you want. But you will not always have me. She did what she could. She poured perfume on my body beforehand to prepare for my burial. I tell you the truth, wherever the gospel is preached throughout the world, what she has done will also be told, in memory of her."[352]

What prompted the companions of Jesus to respond this way? Why would they speak harshly to someone performing an act of kindness to Jesus? Is it that the disciple's saw exclusivity to Jesus? The woman in this pericope is reflective of the kindness of Black people towards Minister Farrakhan and also countless others who are his friends. These are those who desire to help Minister Farrakhan and the Nation of Islam. Judas and the disciples understood the value of the perfume, but they did not understand why Jesus permitted it to be used the way that it was used. There are many people and organizations that will help the Nation of Islam, but how will the Nation of Islam accept their help and assistance? Will the Nation of Islam and its followers respond like Judas and the foolish ones who rebuked the woman for her kind act towards Jesus? Will these kind acts be the precursor to a great *falling away*? This is a trial for many. Minister Farrakhan said in a National Student Laborer's meeting in Chicago, IL. May 8, 2010:

Teachers are going to come from all over the world to teach us all that we need, down to the most useful and non-useful parts of the atom.[353]

---

[352] See Mark 14:1-9.
[353] Farrakhan, Louis. "National Student Laborers Meeting." Muhammad University of Islam Auditorium, Chicago. May 8, 2010. Lecture.

This is necessary in order for the Nation of Islam to assume its rightful place. But the woman who poured oil or perfume on Jesus was only doing her duty. The oil represents knowledge. In the last hour, many of the disciples lost faith. Minister Farrakhan explains while making reference to the crucifixion of Jesus,

> Now they were called upon to be a witness for him. In that hour of the cry of "crucify him" it appeared that there were no witnesses of him… So at his crucifixion, none of them, according to scriptures, none of them were present, except John and these women. The six women and the one man represented an untold number that were growing into belief in him *but were not present*. The events of the hour were making a whole new cadre of believers. Regardless to their lapse the disciples could have been raised *in the next instance*, or they could have been replaced by those who bore resemblance to them, in terms of faith. But under a new reality, they became renewed in the knowledge that he was in fact alive. Some of the old can be made new but most of the old will be gone; unworthy, unfit to be with him in that next dispensation.[354]

The desire for influence and power and nearness to Jesus could cause this type of response in the disciples toward anyone who desires to help him. All of the disciples according to Mark had a desire for power and nearness to Jesus and even argued with each other over who was the greatest among them.[355] But, Jesus had developed a following and those that heard his word listened and performed miracles like the twelve disciples. This concerned the disciples. Why? They attempted to stop the believers in Jesus, so he had to instruct them to leave the people alone.[356]

Mark shows a more intimate relationship with the disciples than the other Gospels. Judas was not the only disciple to blame for the betrayal,

---

[354] Muhammad, *Closing the Gap*, 217-218.
[355] See Mark 9:33-37.
[356] See Mark 9:38-41.

although he was the one who led them to the place of his arrest. The other disciples fled, what does that mean? They could not handle his meeting with destiny, and they could not drink from his bitter cup. James and John confronted Jesus in a pericope in Mark that revealed their lusts for authority, but they claimed to want nearness to him. They desired his position among the people and even thought that they could lead the people better. Mark's account of this is as follows:

> Then James and John, the sons of Zebedee, came to him. "Teacher," they said, "we want you to do for us whatever we ask." "What do you want me to do for you?" he asked. They replied, "Let one of us sit at your right and the other at your left in your glory." "You don't know what you are asking," Jesus said. "Can you drink the cup I drink or be baptized with the baptism I am baptized with?" "We can," they answered. Jesus said to them, "You will drink the cup I drink and be baptized with the baptism I am baptized with, but to sit at my right or left is not for me to grant. These places belong to those for whom they have been prepared." When the ten heard about this, they became indignant with James and John.
>
> Jesus called them together and said, "You know that those who are regarded as rulers of the Gentiles lord it over them, and their high officials exercise authority over them. Not so with you. Instead, whoever wants to become great among you must be your servant, and whoever wants to be first must be slave of all. For even the Son of Man did not come to be served, but to serve, and to give his life as a ransom for many."[357]

The minds of James and John are symbolic of those around Minister Farrakhan who have similar thoughts. This attitude is a form of jealousy, and shows a high level of disregard for the work of Minister Farrakhan and to a larger degree a disregard for God's choice for His people. In essence this type of mind is arrogant and evil.[358] Judas played a significant role leading up to the crucifixion and because of his

---

[357] See Mark 10:35-45.
[358] See Holy Quran 7:11-13, The Devils Opposition to Adam.

influence; he was able to conceal his motives. John MacArthur confirms in the *Murder of Jesus*, Judas' role and the disciples view of him,

> It is significant that Judas was the group's treasurer. This reveals how trusted he was. And in fact that others followed his lead in this instance reveals that he had gained not only their trust but also to a very large degree, their respect. Evidently, none of the other disciples ever suspected he would become a traitor, because even when Jesus prophesied that He would be betrayed by one of them, not one person pointed the finger at Judas. They all seemed to doubt themselves more than they doubted Judas. (Mark 14:19)[359]

The disciples did not suspect Judas because of his closeness to Jesus and his position among them. Even in the circle of Jesus, among the disciples, existed politics and bureaucracy. Judas was a thief, and stole from the treasury of the believers and followers of Jesus. He was not a man of integrity and his questioning of the perfume used to anoint Jesus was a sign of his misunderstanding. This type of person exists today and has no regard for the community; the poor. Judas eventually became disappointed over Jesus and his disappointment caused him to rebel and view Jesus improperly. Judas' hidden desire in the present-day community is lust for power and influence. Vandyke-Plant and Hall describe the heart of the Judas type:

> Behind the behavior of the betrayer exists a passion for power; an inability to accept limits or boundaries, and a position with authority such as that of bishop or priest that permits them to imprint their own understanding on the community. They imitate those qualities that they so dearly desire. They con the community with their dishonesty and wear one face for some and another face for others, They play the members of community with masterful skill, granting power to others who are useful and capriciously withholding it when they are opposed

---

[359] MacArthur. *The Murder of Jesus* (Nashville, TN: Thomas Nelson Inc. 1984) 17.

or cannot profitably use individuals or groups in the achievement of their own power initiatives.[360]

Let us consider that the Honorable Elijah Muhammad is correct about the life of Jesus and that the historical Jesus was a prophet and died over two thousand years ago. Let us consider that the Jesus whom the world expects to come, the one who was resurrected, is not a matter of history, but prophecy. If we consider this; then who is Judas? This person(s) represents an anti-typical figure(s) that will do what has been written of thousands of years ago, and that is to betray and deliver the Son of Man! According to the Gospels, Jesus knew his betrayer. Jesus was aware of his crucifixion and accepted it as a part of the salvation of the people. He was aware of the New Kingdom that was to be established by God, but through him. Matthew's account of the matter reads,

> When evening came, Jesus was reclining at the table with the Twelve. And while they were eating, he said, "I tell you the truth, one of you will betray me." They were very sad and began to say to him one after the other, "Surely not I, Lord?" Jesus replied, "The one who has dipped his hand into the bowl with me will betray me. The Son of Man will go just as it is written about him. But woe to that man who betrays the Son of Man! It would be better for him if he had not been born." Then Judas, the one who would betray him, said, "Surely not I, Rabbi?" Jesus answered, "Yes, it is you."[361]

Betrayal is not exclusive to one person. Betrayal can be committed by a group of people and this is like conspiracy. The conspirators gain nothing from their attempts to murder Minister Farrakhan. Judas' plan

---

[360] Platt, Hall. "Betrayal and Healing", 364.
[361] Matt. 26:20-25.

to deliver Jesus was not a secret to Jesus,[362] but more importantly, it was the direct will of Allah. But, so was Jesus' ascension.

> In my former book, Theophilus, I wrote about all that Jesus began to do and to teach until the day he was taken up to heaven, after giving instructions through the Holy Spirit to the apostles he had chosen. After his suffering, he showed himself to these men and gave many convincing proofs that he was alive. He appeared to them over a period of forty days and spoke about the kingdom of God. On one occasion, while he was eating with them, he gave them this command: "Do not leave Jerusalem, but wait for the gift my Father promised, which you have heard me speak about. For John baptized with water, but in a few days you will be baptized with the Holy Spirit."[363]

The spirit of Satan moved Judas. In the Gospels, only Luke notes that after the temptation of Jesus by Satan that he (Satan) would depart until "an opportune time"[364] only to reappear at the moment of Judas' betrayal of Jesus.[365]

> Now the Feast of Unleavened Bread, called the Passover, was approaching, and the chief priests and the teachers of the law were looking for some way to get rid of Jesus, for they were afraid of the people. Then Satan entered Judas, called Iscariot, one of the Twelve. And Judas went to the chief priests and the officers of the temple guard and discussed with them how he might betray Jesus. They were delighted and agreed to give him money. He consented, and watched for an opportunity to hand Jesus over to them when no crowd was present.[366]

---

[362] Matthew 26:45-49 "Then he returned to the disciples and said to them, "Are you still sleeping and resting? Look, the hour is near, and the Son of Man is betrayed into the hands of sinners. Rise, let us go! Here comes my betrayer!"

[363] Acts 1:1. Also see Luke 24:50-53, "When he had led them out to the vicinity of Bethany, he lifted up his hands and blessed them. While he was blessing them, he left them and was taken up into heaven. Then they worshiped him and returned to Jerusalem with great joy. And they stayed continually at the temple, praising God." Also see New International Version Study Bible, 1684.

[364] See Luke 4:13, also see, Mark 1:12; Matthew 4:8-11.

[365] Kim Paffenroth. *Judas: Images of the lost disciple* (Louisville, KT: Westminster John Knox Press. 2001) 19.

[366] Luke 22:1-6.

John's account of this matter reads differently. Judas was not suspected by anyone, but Jesus.

> After he had said this, Jesus was troubled in spirit and testified, "I tell you the truth, one of you is going to betray me." His disciples stared at one another, at a loss to know which of them he meant. One of them, the disciple whom Jesus loved, was reclining next to him. Simon Peter motioned to this disciple and said, "Ask him which one he means." Leaning back against Jesus, he asked him, "Lord, who is it?" Jesus answered, "It is the one to whom I will give this piece of bread when I have dipped it in the dish." Then, dipping the piece of bread, he gave it to Judas Iscariot, son of Simon. As soon as Judas took the bread, Satan entered into him. "What you are about to do, do quickly," Jesus told him, but no one at the meal understood why Jesus said this to him. Since Judas had charge of the money, some thought Jesus was telling him to buy what was needed for the Feast, or to give something to the poor. As soon as Judas had taken the bread, he went out. And it was night.[367]

Satan makes a declaration in the Holy Quran, when he says to Allah, "Respite me till the day when they are raised".[368] Satan arose in Judas' heart towards his teacher at a moment of weakness in Judas. Judas was no different than the other disciples, except that Satan used him. Judas was a victim to his own low desires. This is the satanic force of self that sees itself as better than everyone else. The other disciples demonstrated weakness, too. Judas had been afforded the same authority as the others that labored with Jesus. It is important to note that Judas was no lightweight man. Judas was considered a figure of authority and Judas was considered a *heavyweight*, among the disciples or a disciple of great knowledge and influence. He performed miracles and was taught the same wisdom as the other disciples. He also

---

[367] John 13:21-30.
[368] Holy Quran 7:11-18.

benefited from the same nearness or access to Jesus as any other laborer.[369]

In the Gospels of Judas, he was looked at far differently and was considered to be extremely near to Jesus, so much that Jesus revealed to him the mysteries of the kingdom and considered him the thirteenth disciple, because he stood outside of the twelve and was the only one who understood him.[370] But, did he really understand his beloved master? Ehrman in his writing, *Peter, Paul and Mary Magdalene*, argues that in the early days of the Christianity, there were women apostles. He further argues that Mary was the first Apostle of Jesus.[371] If this is possible, would it have anything to do with the six women who were with Jesus at the time of his crucifixion? It was two women named Mary that came to see Jesus in the tomb. It was Mary that he revealed himself to after his resurrection and it was Mary who was the first to bear witness to the resurrection. So, it is with Minister Farrakhan.

8.3   *Post-Betrayal*

Let's review the scenes of Jesus' interactions with his enemy's post-betrayal. Jesus was first taken to Annas, who was the Father –In-Law of Caiaphas.[372] Annas still had influence, but had been removed by the Romans as high priest and was still quite influential among the Jews. It was Annas who first questioned Jesus.[373] Peter and another disciple accompanied Jesus. The other disciple was known among the aristocracy and Peter was asked to stay outside. As the meeting began, a woman on duty asked Peter if he was with Jesus and Peter denied.[374]

---

[369] Luke 9:1-6.
[370] Ehrman, *The Lost Gospel*, 136.
[371] Bart D. Ehrman. *Peter, Paul, and Mary Magdalene: The Followers of Jesus in History and Legend* (New York, NY: Oxford University Press Inc., 2006) 251-53.
[372] John 18:12-13.
[373] John 18:19-23.
[374] John. 18:15-18; Matthew 26:57-58, 26:69-75.

This was his first denial of his Master. During Jesus' questioning, which was unlawful, Peter was asked two additional times, one of those times by a relative of the man whose ear he cut off. Peter denied Jesus again. Who will represent Annas today, anti-typically? Who are those who will represent Peter? Jesus defends his innocence and he is bound and sent off to Caiaphas.

Matthew 26 reads differently as Jesus was taken directly to Caiaphas, questioned, then beaten and spat upon.[375] Mark does not make specific reference to Caiaphas or Annas by name, but gives details of the incident.[376] It was here where they sought false witness against Jesus. Caiaphas questioned Jesus about whom he said he represented and who he said he was. It is the same with Minister Farrakhan and his mighty testimony of the Honorable Elijah Muhammad as the exalted Christ of the Christians and Jews. But, there will also be wicked ones who consider themselves Muslims who will be involved in this plan. They hate that Master Fard Muhammad is considered the long awaited Mahdi and they hate that Allah is seen as a Man! Jesus was condemned for saying he was the Son of God and Minister Farrakhan is condemned for saying he is the Son of Man, Son of God, and the Vicar of Christ; the Honorable Elijah Muhammad. The next morning, Jesus was taken to Pilate.[377]

Mark's account also mentions that Jesus was condemned and the trial reconvened the next morning. But, who is Pilate? The Synoptic Gospels read differently, Matthew mentions the names of those in authority, Mark does not, while Luke mentions very little about the actual arrest. Pilate questioned Jesus and found no wrong with Jesus' claims. Although Jesus had taught in Judea[378] where Pilate was the

---

[375] Matthew 26:57-67.
[376] See Mark 14:53-65.
[377] See Matthew 27:1-2, Mark 15:1, Luke 23:1, John 18:28-29.
[378] Luke 4:42-44.

presiding Governor, Pilate did not want to handle the case of Jesus and when he learned that Jesus had taught in Galilee, he found reason to turn him over to Herod, who had jurisdiction there.[379] Although, Pilate and Herod were enemies, Herod was happy to see Jesus. Herod heard great things about Jesus[380] and desired to kill him, but he sent him back to Pilate. From this point on Pilate and Herod became friends.[381] All hypocrites band together and this was the case with Pilate and Herod. Will this be the case with Minister Farrakhan? Will those influential politicians, clergy and even disciples band together as did Pilate and Herod to falsely accuse Minister Farrakhan, because of their own cowardice and greed? Pilate knew that Jesus was handed over because of envy.

Pilate's wife pleaded with him, to have nothing to do with the crucifixion of Jesus, since she had dreams that troubled her much.[382] Who is she? Could she represent the pleading sympathizers of the Church, or maybe the wife of some world-renowned politician or influential clergy or leader? Pilate wanted to please the people. There was an effort from the Roman and Jewish authorities to kill Jesus. Scholars have wrestled with the Jewish involvement in the matter of Jesus, but it has not been completely ruled out and continues to be debated. During the time of Jesus, Sadducee priest dominated the Sanhedrin and great influence there.

From a religious perspective, they were bitterly angry with Jesus and his claims as the Son of God, but had no just reason to kill him. Pilate's attempts, as with others to get Jesus to admit wrong did not work. In all of this drama around Jesus, where were his disciples?

---

[379] Luke 23:5-6.
[380] "Now Herod the tetrarch heard about all that was going on. And he was perplexed, because some were saying that John had been raised from the dead, others that Elijah had appeared, and still others that one of the prophets of long ago had come back to life. But Herod said, "I beheaded John. Who, then, is this I hear such things about?" And he tried to see him." Luke 9:7-9.
[381] Luke 23:8-12.
[382] Matthew 27:18-19.

Edward Falconer Harrison suggests that this same drama written of thousands of years ago will repeat itself in the end:

> Terrible as the crime of Judas is, another is due to arise at the end-time whose kinship to the traitor is marked by his bearing the same cognomen—'the son of perdition' (John 17:12, II Thessalonians 2:3). He, too, will make common cause with Satan, but he will aspire to something never dreamed of by Judas, for he will seek to exalt himself to the place of deity and try to command the worship of other men. Only then will the full capacity for wickedness possessed by the human heart be revealed.[383]

Could this be the time that Falconer is referring to? This *person* is the ruler of darkness and the underworld and is often called the anti-Christ. This person is also an agent of Satan. Satan is the person Minister Farrakhan is calling to a battle with Allah (God) and his Christ. Minister Farrakhan's lecture, *Who are the real Children of Israel*, delivered in Atlanta, Georgia, June 26, 2010, was a dare to the satanic forces that attempt to come against God and Christ. In this most profound and enlightening message, Minister Farrakhan exposes the Jewish connection in the Trans-Atlantic slave trade and exposes their involvement in the dreadful economic and social condition of Blacks in America. Once again he pledged his life to save Black people and humanity from the evil forces that seek to destroy life itself. These are those who say they are Jews, but are not, but are the *Synagogue of Satan* and are Zionists with influences that impinge on the masses of people totaling almost 7 billion. Minister Farrakhan's letter to Abraham Foxman was a courageous warning and challenge. [384] The Anti-Defamation League in response to Minister Farrakhan showed their

---

[383] Harrison. "The Son of God among the sons of men.", 179.
[384] Louis Farrakhan, "The Honorable Minister Louis Farrakhan's June 24, 2010 letter to the National Director of the Anti-Defamation League, Abraham Foxman," NOI.ORG, http://www.noi.org/statements/letter_06-24-2010.html (accessed July 4, 2010)

disregard for the truth that was presented.[385] This letter and others, written by Minister Farrakhan to the Presidents of America are warnings that resemble the Letters of Paul in the Bible. Read them! In the *Report on Anti-Semitism in Argentina 2006*, sponsored by the Centre for Social Studies of the Argentine Jewish Associations Delegation (DAIA), says in its report that the Honorable Minister Louis Farrakhan is "considered one of the most important anti-Semitic forces in the United States".[386] This report in its criticism of the book, *The Secret Relations between Blacks and Jews* says,

> ... [T]he Nation of Islam is responsible for the edition of the pseudo-academic book The Secret relations between Blacks and Jews which falsely argues that Jews have joined in a coalition of kidnappers and slave proprietors and have played a disproportionate role in the development of slavery. Such work, condemned by renown personalities of the Institute of African-American Studies of Harvard University for being considered the Bible of new anti-Semitism and has been widely distributed for the followers of Farrakhan, and has acted as the most effective anti-Jewish instrument in the United States since Henry Ford published the International Jew in the 1920s.[387]

Satan is the man of sin. Minister Farrakhan will be empowered to end the wicked machinations of Satan on his return from Wheel in the very near future.[388] On his return, Minister Farrakhan *will be* as the Exalted Christ, the *Crusher of the Wicked*, ushering in a new reality based on universal wisdom from God that is infinite. This has been witnessed by the writers of the scriptures thousands of years ago, and foretold by the

---

[385] The Anti-Defamation League, "ADL Slams Farrakhan For Blaming Jews For Financial Ruin Of Blacks.' ADL: Fighting Anti-Semitism, Bigotry and Extremism.," NOI.ORG, http://www.noi.org/statements/letter_06-24-2010.html (accessed July 4, 2010)
[386] Marisa Braylan, "Report on Anti-Semitism," (June 2007): 234, http://www.adl.org/Anti_Semitism/as_argentina_report_2006.pdf (accessed July 14, 2010).
[387] Marisa Braylan, "Report on Anti-Semitism," (June 2007): 234-35. http://www.adl.org/Anti_Semitism/as_argentina_report_2006.pdf (accessed July 14, 2010).

[388] See, 2Thessalonians 2:1-12 on the Man of Sin. Also see, 1John 2:18-27; 1John 4:2-4, 2John 1:7-8.

Prophets. The fulfillment of the "end of days" for which the Prophets spoke of, is now. This is not allegorical. The scientists and theologians of religion know this to be true, and all eyes are on the Honorable Minister Louis Farrakhan and the Nation of Islam in the West.

This Page Intentionally Left Blank

9 Letters of Warning and Guidance to America and the World

9.1 *Open Letter to the President George W. Bush*

Summary:

On December 1, 2001, the Honorable Minister Louis Farrakhan sent a letter to President George W. Bush to address the 9/11 World Trade Center attacks in New York City and at the Pentagon. Minister Farrakhan offered guidance and wisdom to President Bush (43) that he may use to make the right decisions about going into war in pursuit of the alleged attackers of the World Trade Center bombings. He furthers shared with the President his vision experience, when he spoke to the Honorable Elijah Muhammad in 1985.

December 1, 2001

George W. Bush, President of the
United States of America
The White House
1600 Pennsylvania Avenue N. W.

Washington, DC 20500

As-Salaam Alaikum.
(Peace Be Unto You)

Dear President Bush,

May this letter find you, your family and staff in the best of health and spirit in spite of the prevailing circumstances.

I am Minister Louis Farrakhan, National Representative of the Honorable Elijah Muhammad, whom I believe Allah (God) raised among the Black people of America to teach us Islam as a means of our reformation and resurrection. He was also raised by Allah (God) as a Warner to the government and people of the United States of America. I sit in His seat by Allah's (God's) and His permission, therefore, His Mission is my Mission, and, it is out of my sense of mission and duty that I write.

I am deeply concerned for our country, and, I am deeply concerned for you.

I used the possessive pronoun our, because the blood of my ancestors soaks this soil and their blood has been shed on every foreign battlefield for the preservation of this nation. Therefore, we as a people feel a deep sense of ownership of America as much as any American. It is also out of this deep sense of concern and ownership that I write to you. I write you from my prison. A prison without bars that has been made for me because of the passion for truth and justice out of which I speak, and, the propaganda that makes me appear to many as anti-White, anti-Christian, anti-Semitic, and anti-Gay. None of these names accurately describe who I am. I hope that you will open your heart to what I am writing notwithstanding the prison from which I am writing.

George W. Bush

Since Adam, there has not been one person or nation with power and dominion over the whole earth. This is the awesome position that America holds by Allah's (God's) permission. This indeed is a great trial for you and for America, because, when Allah (God) allows anyone of us to rule over His servants and a great part of His creation, He does so to see how we act. If we act well, He will not replace our rule; however, if we allow the power, wealth, and wisdom that we possess over Allah's

(God's) servants and creation to blind us so that we act other than as Allah (God) would desire us to act, then, He acts through the forces of nature and through people to overturn our rule.

This is a very dangerous Hour, but, it is an Hour filled with great opportunity. What is needed in this Hour is Right or Divine Guidance. This Guidance must be in accord with the Time and what this Time demands.

It is written in the Book of Revelation "The nations were angry, and thy wrath is come, and the time of the dead, that they should be judged, and that thou shouldest give reward unto thy servants the prophets and to the saints, and them that fear thy name, small and great, and shouldest destroy them which destroy the earth. " (Chapter 11 verse 18)

The Honorable Elijah Muhammad said, "We are living in the Day of Judgment." This is what is producing the anger of the nations and the Wrath of Allah (God). This is the time that those who have been deprived of justice must receive justice, for, it is only our acting on the principle of justice that will ease the anger of the nations and take away the Wrath of Allah (God). There can be no Justice without Truth, and, there can be no Peace in the world without Justice.

As a nation, America is blessed with wealth, wisdom, science, technology, and, abundance. America is also blessed with the awesome power to destroy nations of people. In order for you and America to receive the greatest of Allah's (God's) Blessings, which is the longevity and perpetuity that former great nations and empires have not enjoyed, you must rule according to the Will and the Way of Allah (God).

Mr. President, you and this nation stand in the position of the Vicegerent of Allah (God). (The person or nation that rules the earth in the place of Allah (God)). This is why America must rule the world as Allah (God) Himself would rule, for, she is now standing in His place by His permission.

Allah (God) also has awesome power to destroy. He is called The Possessor of Power over all things, and, He is also called The Destroyer, The Avenger. However, none of these attributes are His principle attributes. All of His attributes of might and power to avenge and destroy are balanced by His major attributes, which are Beneficence, Mercy, The Nurturer - of all things making them attain stage after stage until they reach perfection, and, King or Judge - who judges with justice. These are the four greatest attributes of Allah (God).

If America is to be truly triumphant in this Hour, these four great attributes must give balance and direction to America's awesome power to destroy and her desire to avenge the horrible act of September 11th.

When I heard you say that this act against America on September 11th has given purpose to your administration and that you feel that it is your mission to destroy the terrorists, their networks, those who harbor them, and, that the awesome power of America will be used toward this end. This, you hope will be the legacy that you leave to future generations; you also hope that the children and the American people will live without the fear of such evil as we experienced on September 11th. However, within these statements are my reasons for deep concern.

You have risen to the challenge of this Hour and this Hour has given you the support of the American people and the support of most of the nations of the earth. In my humble judgment, what you see as the purpose of your administration must not hinder or blind you from seeing the possibility of an even greater purpose and potential legacy.

It is out of this desire to see you fulfill that which will give you the greatest legacy that I write to you as a humble servant appealing to a great and powerful nation and ruler. I respectfully say to you that I believe if you continue this effort in the way that you presently have in mind, it will not end terrorism, but unfortunately may increase it.

On September 17, 1985, I had a vision-like experience where I was told of the secret plan of President Ronald Reagan who had met with his Joint Chiefs of Staff in early September 1985 to plan a war. I was not told whom that war was against, but, within a few months it became clear to me that the war was against Libya and its Leader, Muammar Gadhafi. President Reagan on coming into office had as one of his aims the desire to get rid of Muammar Gadhafi, and to place in the leadership of Libya a regime more favorable to America's foreign policy interests.

The desire of President Reagan also concerned the planning of a war involving young Black men here on the soil of America. This is what inspired me to tour the country talking to Black men urging them to stop the killing of one another, and, this is what eventually led to the Million Man March on October 16, 1995. Another of President Reagan's desires was to make null and void the treaty that was signed by his predecessor, President Jimmy Carter, returning the Panama Canal to the Panamanian people by the year 2000.

President Manuel Noriega of Panama was demonized by the press, tried in absentia and found guilty of drug dealing. This was used as the justification for a violent action that was taken against Panama using the armed forces of America. However, the real aim was to place in Panama a government of America's choosing, and, to nullify the treaty signed by President Carter that gave the Panama Canal back to the Panamanian people.

During President Reagan's administration, Muammar Gadhafi was demonized in the American press. The bombing of a discotheque in Germany was used by President Reagan to justify the most expensive assassination attempt in the history of this nation.

I need not bore you with the details of this because you have access to information that will verify the truth of what I am writing.

I am writing this to show a consistent pattern of behavior of America's Presidents, administrations, and the press with respect to those Muslim leaders and other leaders that America has chosen to denounce as rogues, and to use as a justification for military action to cover their real purposes.

President Richard Nixon wrote that the enemy of democracy was not communism, but, fundamentalist Islam. Every President since the Nixon/Ford administration has taken some military action against a Muslim nation. President Jimmy Carter felt that the overthrow of the Shah of Iran, Mohammed Reza Pahlavi, and his replacement with the Islamist regime of Ayatollah Khomeini was a threat to America's vital interests. So, Saddam Hussein was given 80 billion dollars with America's approval by the Saudi government and the rulers of the

United Arab Emirates to make Saddam Hussein a strong military power to use him against the rise of the so-called fundamentalist regime in Iran. During President Carter's administration, the American Embassy in Iran was taken and the hostage crisis began.

The effort of Jimmy Carter to free the hostages through military action after the fall of the Shah of Iran was a failure. In the negotiations between our government and the government of Imam Khomeini, it was agreed that the hostages would be released, but not during the administration of President Carter. The hostages were released in the early days of President Reagan's administration. President Reagan also saw Imam Khomeini and his desire that the Iranian people return to the purity of the faith of Islam as a threat to America's vital interests in that area of the world.

Your father fulfilled President Reagan's desire concerning the Panama Canal. Your father also had a problem that involved Saddam Hussein and Iraq. At the same time that he was prosecuting the war against Saddam Hussein, a part of that conflict also involved young Black men, gangs and drugs in America. Although the Gulf War was won by the allied forces, Saddam Hussein remains in power and has become a fixation with every succeeding President.

Mr. President, you have now inherited that which Presidents Reagan, Carter, your father, and President Clinton were not able to complete. What I have been shown is that you have decided to fulfill their unrealized expectations.

Afghanistan is only a preliminary to a much wider war which is already planned, and this war also has a home front aspect as well. Should you persist in this, you will do what no Islamic Leader is able to do. No leader of any Muslim nation can call for Jihad or Holy War and cause the Muslim world to obey that call. The only one who can call for such is one who sits in the position of Khalifah or successor of the Prophet Muhammad (Peace Be Upon Him).

Since the destruction of the Caliphate of Islam by corruption within the ranks of Islam, and European machinations; the rise of nationalism among Muslim nations has made it difficult and nearly impossible to unify the Arab and Muslim world on the question of Jihad. However, Mr. President, if you follow what you have in your mind, which many of those around you are encouraging you to do, then, you will do what Osama Bin Ladin and no Muslim extremist could ever do.

You will unite the Muslim world in hostility against America and Great Britain, and, you will use your great position of power inadvertently to call for a Holy War against the West.

You will force the more moderate Islamic regimes either not to side with you, or to side with you at the risk of being overthrown by growing Islamist forces within their countries.

The coalition that you are gathering will fall away from you and you will have to pursue this war alone. I am afraid that this extended war may take a turn that you and your advisors least expect, and involve America in the greatest of all wars, the War of Armageddon, in which no nation will be left out, including Russia and China.

I believe there is a better way to win. A way that may appear more difficult, but, you will be assured of the Help of Allah (God).

The world is with you to pursue those who perpetrated this act of war against America, and, your pursuit of the guilty parties is right and proper. However, Mr. President, it will take great courage on your part to look at America's policies with a critical eye, and, it will take even greater courage to break from the policies of the past and make a new beginning for this nation and the world.

You have sent a strong signal to the world in your statement that the Palestinians should have an independent, sovereign state. If you pursue this course with firmness and justice, the hot bed of terror in the Middle East will subside. The more fair, just and equitable the solution to the Palestinian/Israeli conflict, the more the anger of those on both sides will subside, and, America will get the credit of settling this 53 year old problem with justice, thereby justifying America's position as the Vicegerent of Allah (God). Mr. President, with the backing of the American people and the leaders of the world, if you reexamined policies that are unfair and changed them, this signal to the world would bring the world and those so-called enemies and rogue states into your and America's sphere of influence.

Since America is peopled by the people of the entire world, and, all have contributed to America's greatness, then, America as the world ruler has an obligation to the entire world.

There is no need for a clash of civilizations. The Muslim World has much to learn from the West and the West has much to learn from the Religion of Islam.

Creating the climate for dialogue will make a great future for America, and, under her rule a peaceful world can come into existence. There is no nation on this earth that I know of where I would have the freedom to speak as I do or write the Head of State as I am writing, and, I truly appreciate this freedom.

There is no nation on this earth that offers more in the way of freedom than this nation, however, unrighteousness is what we all should work to overcome, because in the final analysis, it is righteousness, that will make this nation truly great. I am appealing to you and imploring you Mr. President to orchestrate an end to policies that are unjust.

I appreciate the privilege that I have to live in America, and, with all her faults there is no nation on this earth where I would rather live. However, this freedom that I enjoy under the constitution lays on me a heavy responsibility. That is, to protect the best of this nation and to work to overcome those weaknesses of the nation that are causing her fall.

I have traveled to many countries and have spoken to most of the Heads of State and Government, and, not one of them has ever said to me that they hate the American people, but, they have said that they are displeased with America's foreign policies.

I believe that I can be of service to you, our nation, and to all of those whom you believe are America's enemies. I believe that all of them can be made the friends of America. The whole world would like to have America as a true friend, but, America can never be a true friend of the people of the earth until and unless she rules with the Wisdom and Spirit of Allah (God) which reflects itself in our love for humanity, our love for truth, and our exercise of the principle of justice.

The nations would be willing to share their resources with America with joy if they believed that they would get a fair price for what they produce that would allow them to raise the standard of living of their people. There is nothing that the earth possesses that America could not have easy access to, if America determined to rule the nations of the earth with the principle of justice.

If America turns away from this principle and does what she is doing because she has the power to do it, then, Allah (God) who grants power will take it from America and bring another people in her place. This does not have to be, but it will be based on how America conducts herself in this Hour of her greatest trial and her greatest potential triumph.

Mr. President, please think and pray over what I have written, and, speak to your advisors and close friends concerning it. I pray that Allah (God) will grant you the wisdom to see that what I am saying to you is good and is the way to triumph over the evil and hatred that is in the world against the United States of America.

May Allah (God) grant you the wisdom to see deeply into the Prophets' utterances concerning this Hour.

I pray that we will be triumphant over terror and become the Friend of Allah (God) in so doing.

Best wishes for your success.

Thank you for taking the time to read these words. I Am Your Servant in the war against evil,

Honorable Minister Louis Farrakhan
Servant to the Lost-Found Nation of Islam in the West[389]

---

[389] Louis Farrakhan, "Letter of warning to President George Bush: December 1, 2001." NOI.ORG. https://www.noi.org/letter-to-president-bush-12-01-2001/

Summary:

Below is the Second letter to George W. Bush in its entirety, October 2, 2002. This is the second letter to George W. Bush and is an appeal from Minister Farrakhan. Here we see almost 13 months later, President Bush is warned of America's plans to make war with the Muslim world. Minister Farrakhan makes reference to his previous prophetical letter and cautions the President to stay his hand on America's effort to go into Iraq.

National Representative of the Honorable Elijah Muhammad and the Nation of Islam

In the Name of Allah the Beneficent the Merciful.

October 30, 2002

George W. Bush, President of the United States of America

The White House
1600 Pennsylvania Avenue, N.W.
Washington, D.C. 20500

As-Salaam Alaikum.
(Peace Be Unto You)

Dear President Bush,

May this letter find you and your family well.

I am writing this letter to once again appeal to you in the strongest way that you might heed my humble counsel and sincere warning to you. I am not your enemy, nor am I an enemy to this country, but, I do believe that the course that you are guiding the nation on will increase many enemies for you and the nation at home and abroad.

In my last letter, I respectfully called your attention to U.S. Presidents and their dealings with Islamic nations and leaders over the last several years, and, I warned that should you pursue what I know is in your mind and heart concerning Saddam Hussein and Iraq that you would lose the great advantage that you gained after September 11, 2001, and, that the coalition would fall apart and you might be forced to go it alone. Also, I opined that if you did such, you might run into something that your advisors had not thought of or perceived. This is already happening. Nations are becoming afraid of you and the tremendous power of America. In this state of fear, they will not stop trying to attain weapons of mass destruction because they believe that is the only thing that you will respect.

There is a rising chorus of anti-war demonstrations in the nation and throughout the world and it will intensify as you move toward war with the thought of occupying Iraq. The anti-war demonstrators will blame every death of an American service person and every death of an Iraqi citizen on you and this will produce a crisis for your administration within the United States, as well as in countries throughout the world.

I am writing to plead with you that there is a better way. However, the more you talk and the stronger you talk about regime change, you paint yourself into a corner from which it becomes increasingly difficult to extricate yourself.

There are times in history when men of conviction go against the tide of world thought and opinion, bringing suffering upon themselves to establish a new truth or a new idea. However, this is not that time for you. In my judgment, this is a time when the President of the United States must not only listen to his advisors and study their agendas, but, he must listen to world opinion. If the President of the United States seems to show no respect for world opinion or for the thoughts of the members of the Security Council of the United Nations, then, your actions will turn the nations of the world against you and against America.

Your actions will also render the United Nations an ineffective institution for future peacekeeping.

Ancient Babylon was a city that caused all who traded with her to wax strong, but, at a certain point, the neighboring nations turned against Babylon and she was destroyed and left as a sign. The Book of Revelation speaks of a mystery Babylon that ancient Babylon was a sign of. The Honorable Elijah Muhammad, my teacher and guide, said that America is the fulfillment of that mystery Babylon.

Mr. President, you must study prophecy in order to beat it.

Look at the nations to the north and south of you. Are they pleased with you, your administration and your polices? Look at your friends in the Middle East. Are they really pleased with you, your administration and policies? Look at your European friends and your African and Asian friends. The prophecy teaches that, they will take your money and whatever you offer, but they will hate you and ultimately make you desolate.

We are headed into a terrible time. I am writing this letter as a final witness of my deep concern for you and for the nation, believing, however, that you are bent on doing what is in your heart with respect to Iraq and Saddam Hussein.

Mr. President, if you do this, you will bring down upon America an increase in the Divine Judgment of rain, hail, snow, wind, earthquakes, pestilence and famine that is already witnessed in the country. As you go about destroying other nations and cities, you will bring this kind of Divine Wrath on the American people and on American cities.

Please reconsider your plans.

May Allah (God) guide you to make the right decision for this nation and for the future of the world.

I Am Your Servant in the war against evil,

The Honorable Minister Louis Farrakhan

Servant to the Lost-Found Nation of Islam in the West

HMLF/sm[390]

---

[390] Louis Farrakhan, "2nd Letter of warning to President George Bush: October 30, 2002."
NOI.ORG. https://www.noi.org/letter-of-warning-to-president-george-bush-october-30-2002/

9.3 *Open Letter to the Abraham Foxman*

Summary:

The following letter was written in 2010 to Abraham Foxman, former National Director of the Anti-Defamation League (1987 to 2015). He is currently the Anti-Defamation League's National Director Emeritus. In this letter Minister Farrakhan presents to Abraham Foxman the book, "The Secret Relations between Blacks and Jews, Volume One" and "Volume 2" of the same title. Minister Farrakhan defends the position of the Nation of Islam and offers Mr. Foxman and the Jewish Community and opportunity to revisit the proposed dialogue that he has offered for many years. He also warns Foxman and the Jews who seek to interfere with the work of the Honorable Elijah Muhammad of what is to come for being aggressive towards blacks and the Nation of Islam. The relationship with Minister Farrakhan and the Jews resembles the drama with Jesus and the Jews in the New Testament. Throughout the New Testament the Jews sought to do harm to Jesus. They questioned him on his authority to demand of them obedience to God. Eventually, they agreed to kill Jesus, but wipe their hands of the matter as to remain in the eyes of the people as the benevolent, and humble chosen people of God. This letter represents the root of that confrontation in this modern time. These two books were sent to about a dozen Jewish Rabbis and leaders of the Jewish world.

Minister Louis Farrakhan
National Representative of the Honorable Elijah Muhammad and the
Nation of Islam

In the Name of Allah the
Beneficent the Merciful. I Bear
Witness that there is no God
but Allah and I Bear Witness
that Muhammad is his
Messenger

June 24, 2010

President Abraham Foxman
Anti-Defamation League
605 Third Avenue
New York, New York 10017

Dear Mr. Foxman,

Please accept these two books enclosed from our Historical Research
Department.

The charge of anti-Semitism has been
leveled against the Honorable Elijah
Muhammad, Malcolm X and the
Nation of Islam for many years. For
twenty-five of the thirty-three years of
my rebuilding of the Nation of Islam,
I and we, in the Nation of Islam have
suffered under the charge of "anti-
Semitism" because I have dared to be
critical of what I and many others feel
is Jewish behavior that has ill-affected

Abraham Foxman

Black people and others. Our Nation of Islam Historical Research Team
was motivated by these false charges to study the works of Jewish
scholars, historians, and Rabbis, being very careful to omit any words

written or spoken, no matter how truthful, by those who are considered "anti-Semitic."

We can now present to our people and the world a true, undeniable record of the relationship between Blacks and Jews from their own mouths and pens. These scholars, Rabbis and historians have given to us an undeniable record of Jewish anti-Black behavior, starting with the horror of the trans-Atlantic slave trade, plantation slavery, Jim Crow, sharecropping, the labor movement of the North and South, the unions and the misuse of our people that continues to this very moment.

As you have constantly labeled me and done everything within your power to hinder me and us from the civilizing work that Allah (God) has given to The Honorable Elijah Muhammad and myself to do, I ask you to find one act committed by me or those who follow me that has injured one Jewish person, stopped Jews from doing business, hindered their education, injured their families, sullied or desecrated their synagogues. You will not find one. So,  except for our willingness to tell the truth and our unwillingness to apologize to you for telling the truth, on what basis do you charge me and us as being "anti-Semitic"?

Armed with this knowledge from the pens of Jewish scholars, Rabbis, and historians, we could now charge you with the most vehement anti-Black behavior in the annals of our history in America and the world. We could charge you with being the most deceitful so-called friend, while your history with us shows you have been our worst enemy.

I do not write this with vitriol, hatred, bitterness, or a spirit of vengeance, because One greater than you and me has permitted this for His own wise purposes.

However, what is done is done. We cannot change the past. You and I, your children and mine, your people and mine are living in the present.

Your present reality is sitting on top of the world in power, with riches and influence, while the masses of my people here in America, in the Caribbean, Central and South America and elsewhere in the world are in the worst condition of any member of the human family.

I have pleaded with you over the years for a sensible, intelligent dialogue. You have rejected me, and some Rabbis have given me terms for friendship that any self-respecting person could never accept. So with this truth in our hands and yours, and soon in the hands of tens of thousands, I again ask you for a dialogue.

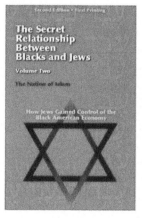

You are in a position to help me in the civilizing work that The Honorable Elijah Muhammad was given to do by Allah (God), whose burden and Mission –Allah and He – has made me to share. With this historical research in your hands, you may either gather your forces for an all-out struggle against me, the Nation of Islam, and the truth that I and we speak and write, or as an intelligent and civilized people, we can sit down and carve out a way forward that can obliterate the stain of the past and render us, Jews and Blacks-before Allah (God) and the world-in a new, honorable, and mutually respectful relationship.

This is an offer asking you and the gentiles whom you influence to help me in the repair of my people from the damage that has been done by your ancestors to mine. This is a wonderful way of the present generation of Jews to escape the Judgment of Allah (God) by aiding in the repair of His people.

However, should you choose to make our struggle to civilize our people more difficult, then I respectfully warn you, in the Name of Allah (God) and His Messiah, The Honorable Elijah Muhammad, that the more you fight and oppose me rather than help me to lift my people from their degraded state, Allah (God) and His Messiah will bring you and your people to disgrace and ruin and destroy your power and influence here and throughout the world.

I pray that you will make the wise and best choice.

Respectfully and Sincerely Submitted,

The Honorable Minister Louis Farrakhan
Servant to the Lost-Found
Nation of Islam in the West

Cc: Chairman Alan Solow, American Conference of Presidents of Major Jewish Organizations
President William Hess, American Zionist Movement
President Bob Elman, American Jewish Committee
President Dennis W. Glick, B'Nai B'Rith International
President Richard S. Gordon, American Jewish Congress
President Rabbi Moshe Kletenik, Rabbinical Council of America
President Rabbi Ellen Weinburg Dreyfus, Central Conference of American Rabbis
Executive Director Jerry Silverman, Jewish Federation of North America
President Stephen J. Savitsky, Union of Orthodox Jewish Congregations of America
Executive Director Martin Schwartz, Jewish Labor Committee
President Lee Rosenberg, American Israel Public Affairs Committee
President Wayne Firestone, Hillel: The Foundation for Jewish Campus Life
National Executive Director Herb Rosenbleeth, Jewish War Veterans of the United States of America
President Morton Klein, Zionist Organization of America
Executive Director Jeremy Ben-Ami, J Street[391]

---

[391] Louis Farrakhan, Farrakhan, Louis. "The Honorable Minister Louis Farrakhan's June 24, 2010 letter to the National Director of the Anti-Defamation League, Abraham Foxman." NOI.ORG. http://www.noi.org/statements/letter_06-24-2010.html

9.4 *Open Letter to the Muammar Gadhafi*

Summary:

Minister Farrakhan has provided warning and guidance from God to his friend Muammar Gadhafi. Below is the full transcript of that prophetic warning to the Libyan leader, but as a concerned friend and brother. Minister Farrakhan was aware of the plot to kill Muammar Gadhafi, but the revelation of this was told to him in his vision experience in a cryptic conversation with the Honorable Elijah Muhammad. As a result, in 1986 Minister Farrakhan set out to warn Muammar Gadhafi and the Libyan people. After U.S. failed assassination attempts on Gadhafi, Libya continued to be a thorn in the side of America, and the plot continued. The North Atlantic Treaty Organization (NATO) initiated airstrikes on Libya killing Gadhafi's youngest son and three of his grandchildren in Tripoli in 2011. This following letter opens with Minister Farrakhan sending condolences, and further providing guidance to the Libyan leader.

In the Name of Allah the Beneficent the Merciful. I Bear Witness that there is no God but Allah and I Bear Witness that Muhammad is his Messenger.

June 14, 2011

Brother Leader Muammar Gadhafi
Tripoli, Libya

Dear Brother Gadhafi,

May this letter find you, your family and the faithful people of the Libyan Arab Jamahiriya in the best of health and spirit in spite of the prevailing circumstances.

Please accept on behalf of myself, my family, the members of the Nation of Islam and all in America who you have helped, our deepest sympathy on the loss of life of your son and three grandchildren. It is written in the Holy Qur'an that "no soul dies but with the Permission of Allah". We may not know Allah's purpose in permitting what is happening in Libya, but again Allah says in the Holy Qur'an "whenever a misfortune befalls the Believer, He says, 'Allah is my Patron (Friend, Protector, Supporter) and to Him is my eventual return".

I am deeply deeply troubled over what I see happening to our Beloved Libya and our Brother Leader Muammar Gadhafi. We are drinking of the bitter cup of betrayal which is prophesied to come to us in the last days of this wicked world to separate from among us those whom Allah (God) will use in the building of His Kingdom and those who are marked for severe chastisement and utter destruction.

I observed those whom you trusted: Prime Minister Berlusconi of Italy, President Sarkozy of France, Prime Minister Cameron of United Kingdom, and President Obama of the United States of America, who have joined forces with the weak Arabs from the Arab League and others to join the enemies of

Muammar Gadhafi

Righteousness and Justice to destroy you and the Revolution that brought about the rise of Libya into her present strength and greatness.

These betrayals hurt deeply, but probably not as much as the betrayals from your inner circle. To hear that Russia and China supposed friends are now asking you to step down; and the President of Russia promising you their protection and a place for you to go, this to me is laughable. Anyone who will ask you to step down, step aside and leave the country because of what America, NATO and others are doing does not understand the resolve of a true Muslim. Allah warns us in the Holy

Qur'an "O you who believe, take not My enemy and your enemy for friends. Would you offer them love, while they deny the Truth that has come to you, driving out the Messenger and yourselves because you believe in Allah, your Lord? If you have come forth to strive in My way and to seek My pleasure, would you love them in secret? And I know what you conceal and what you manifest. And whoever of you does this, he indeed strays from the straight path." Allah and Allah alone, is your and my Protector. The Holy Qur'an teaches, "Only Allah is your friend and His Messenger and those who believe," We know that Allah and His Messenger are our true Friends, but we do not know who the Believers are until they have been tried and found to be true.

My dear Brother Leader, in the general orders that we were given by the Honorable Elijah Muhammad whose desire was to make us brave fighters, willing at any time to give our lives for Allah's sake and righteousness, it states in general order number five "do not quit your post until properly relieved." Allah put you on your post and neither NATO, the President of the United States or the Arab League or anybody else has the power or authority to tell you to quit your post. Elijah Muhammad told me "die on your post".

These next few words again from the Holy Qur'an are for the Believers. It is written in the Holy Qur'an, "surely I am going to try you with something of fear, hunger, loss of property, loss of life, and diminution of fruit, but give good news to those who are patient and steadfast under trial".

Again, Allah asks the question in the Holy Qur'an, "Do men think that they will be left alone on saying, we believe, and will not be tried? And indeed We tried those before them, so Allah will certainly know those who are true and He will know the liars".

In the life of Prophet Noah, he was under such great strain he asked Allah when will my help come and Allah answered your help is nigh. Your help Brother Leader is nigh. Be patient and be resolved that it is Allah, and Allah alone who will deliver you and me as he delivered those before us from the wicked evil intentions and harm from our enemies.

I know that what you are suffering will soon come to me and the Nation of Islam and I pray that the guidance that I give to you that Allah will make me strong enough to be that as Allah asked the Believers to be.

In closing, the last two surahs of the Holy Qur'an are called the chapters of refuge and my plea to you is to seek refuge in Allah and know if it pleases Allah, He will deliver you and with you the Libyan Jamahiriya.

My dearest of Brothers, know that no death can touch Muammar Gadhafi for it is written in the Holy Qur'an "And speak not of those who are slain in Allah's Way as dead. Nay, (they are) alive, but you perceive not". The great work that you have done will live regardless to what happens. The work you have started by Allah's Grace will be furthered by those who love you and those who know the value of what you have contributed to Libya, Africa and the World. Remember Brother Allah says He will never waste the work of a worker.

I will do all that I can to help, but Allah's Help is Sufficient.

Thank you for reading these words and I pray that in these words you will find comfort, solace, guidance and strength In the Words of Allah, the Lord of the Worlds.

Give my greeting to your beloved wife and family, and to the faithful ones whose faith is being greatly tested.

With much love I greet you again in Peace, Wa-Alakium Salaam.

I Am Your Brother and Servant

The Honorable Minister Louis Farrakhan
Servant to the Lost-Found
Nation of Islam in the West[392]

---

[392] Louis Farrakhan, "The Final Call." An Open Letter to Col. Muammar Gadhafi of Libya by Minister Louis Farrakhan. June 14, 2011.
<http://www.finalcall.com/artman/publish/Minister_Louis_Farrakhan_9/article_7917.shtml>.

This Page Intentionally Left Blank

Bibliography

6X, Theodore. "The Prelude to My Visions", Muhammad Speaks Newspaper, April 17, 1970, 15.

Abdullah Yusuf Ali. *The Meaning of the Holy Quran.* Betsville, MD: Amana Publications, 1989.

Agus, Jacob B. "The messianic ideal and the apocalyptic vision." *Judaism* 32, no. 2 (March 1, 1983): 205-214.

Ali, Maulana M. *The Religion of Islam.* Columbus, OH: Ahmadiyya Anjuman Isha'at Islam, 1990.

Anti-Defamation League. "ADL Slams Farrakhan For Blaming Jews For Financial Ruin Of Blacks.' ADL: Fighting Anti-Semitism, Bigotry and Extremism." NOI.ORG. http://www.noi.org/statements/letter_06-24-2010.html (accessed July 4, 2010).

Baigent, Michael, *The Jesus Papers: Exposing the Greatest Cover-Up in History*, New York, NY: Harper Collins, 2006.

Bartlett, David L. "John 13:21-30." *Interpretation* 43, no. 4 (October 1, 1989): 393-397.

Bernard, Raymond. *The Hollow Earth.* New York: Fieldcrest Publishing Co. Inc., 1996.

Brand, Chad, Charles Draper, and Archie England, eds. *Holman Illustrated Bible Dictionary.* Nashville, TN: Holman Bible Publishers, 2003.

Braylan, Marisa. "Report on Anti-Semitism," (June 2007): 234-35, http://www.adl.org/Anti_Semitism/as_argentina_report_2006.pdf (accessed July 14, 2010).

Brown, Raymond. *Introduction to the New Testament,* New York, NY: Bantam, Doubleday, Dell Publishing, 1 ed. 1997.

Bruce, Robert. *Astral Dynamics: A NEW Approach to Out-of-Body Experience.* Charlottesville, VA: Hampton Roads Publishing, 1999.

Bruyere, Rossalyn L. *Wheels of Light: Chakras, Auras, and the Healing Energy of the Body.* Edited by Jeanne Farrens. New York, NY: Simon &Schuster, 1994.

Cahill, P Joseph. "Hermeneutical implications of typology." *Catholic Biblical Quarterly* 44, no. 2 (April 1, 1982): 266-281.

Dale, Cyndi. *The Subtle Body: An Encyclopedia of your energy Anatomy,* Boulder, CO: Sounds True, 2009.

Daly, Corbett. "Clinton on Qaddafi: 'We Came, We Saw, He Died.'" CBS News, CBS Interactive, 20 Oct. 2011, www.cbsnews.com/news/clinton-on-qaddafi-we-came-we-saw-he-died/.

Derrett, J Duncan M. "The Iscariot, Mesîrâ, and the Redemption." *Journal for the Study of the New Testament* no. 8 (July 1, 1980): 2-23.

Ehrman, Bart D. *The Lost Gospels of Judas*, New York, NY: Oxford University Press Inc., 2006.

——.*Peter, Paul, and Mary Magdalene: The Followers of Jesus in History and Legend*, New York, NY: Oxford University Press Inc., 2006.

Farrakhan, Louis. "2nd Letter of warning to President George Bush: October 30, 2002." NOI.ORG. https://www.noi.org/letter-of-warning-to-president-george-bush-october-30-2002/

Farrakhan, Louis. "A Final Warning a Final Call." Press Conference, Watergate Hotel, Washington, DC, November 16, 2017. Accessed December 14, 2017. https://study.noi.org/documents,

Farrakhan, Louis. "A Saviour is Born for the Black Man and Woman of America." Keynote speech, Saviours Day from The Nation of Islam, Chicago, IL., February 22, 1981.

Farrakhan, Louis. "International Press Conference, J.W. Marriott Hotel, Washington, D.C." Official Nation of Islam Statements. http://www.noi.org/statements/.

Farrakhan, Louis. "Letter of warning to President George Bush: December 1, 2001." NOI.ORG. https://www.noi.org/letter-to-president-bush-12-01-2001/

Farrakhan, Louis. "The Announcement: A final warning to the U.S. Government", Chicago, IL: FCN Publishing, Co., 1989, 1991

Farrakhan, Louis. "The Final Call." An Open Letter to Col. Muammar Gadhafi of Libya by Minister Louis Farrakhan. June 14, 2011. <http://www.finalcall.com/artman/publish/Minister_Louis_Farrakhan_9/article_7917.shtml>.

Farrakhan, Louis. "The Honorable Minister Louis Farrakhan's June 24, 2010 letter to the National Director of the Anti-Defamation League, Abraham Foxman." NOI.ORG. http://www.noi.org/statements/letter_06-24-2010.html (accessed June 30, 2010).

Farrakhan, Louis. *Self Improvement the Basis for Community Development: Study Guide 17, Hypocrisy and Conspiracy Part 2.* Chicago, IL: Final Call Inc., n.d.

Farrakhan, Louis. "Union of the Black and Red" YouTube. Flash video file. http://youtu.be/M_mp9Q6_Ko4 (accessed July 19, 2014).

Farrakhan, Louis. "A Saviour is Born for the Black Man and Woman of America" Lecture, Saviours' Day from The Nation of Islam, Chicago, IL., February 22, 1981.

Fillmore, Charles. *Atom Smashing Powers of Mind.* Lee's Summit, MO: Unity School of Christianity, 1949.

Fritsch, Charles T. "Biblical typology." *Bibliotheca sacra* 104, no. 414 (April 1, 1947): 214-222.

Gibson, Claire. *The Hidden Life of Ancient Egypt: Decoding the Secrets of a Lost World.* New York, NY: Fall River Press, 2009.

Grace To You. "Caught Up to the Third Heaven." GTY.ORG. (accessed July 6, 2014). http://www.gty.org/resources/bible-qna/BQ011613/?term=2%20Corinthians%2012

Gundry, Stanley N. "Typology as a means of interpretation: past and present." *Journal of the Evangelical Theological Society* 12, no. 4 (September 1, 1969): 233-240.

Haddow, Angus. "Out-of-body and near-death experiences: their impact on religious beliefs. *Journal of Religion and Psychical Research* 14, no. 2 (April 1991): 75-85.

Haley, Alex, and Malcolm X. *The Autobiography of Malcolm X.* 1964. Reprint, New York, NY: Ballantine Books, 1992.

Halsall, Paul. "Christopher Columbus: Extracts from Journal", *The ORB: Online Reference Book for Medieval Studies.* 3/1996. http://www.fordham.edu/halsall/source/Columbus1.html

Harrison, Everett Falconer. "The Son of God among the sons of men." *Bibliotheca sacra* 105, no. 418 (April 1, 1948): 170-181.

Heindel, Max. *The Rosicrucian Mysteries: An Elementary Exposition of Their Secret Teachings.* Oceanside, CA: Rosicrucian Fellowship, 1916.

Holzinger, Brigitte "Lucid dreaming – dreams of clarity". *Contemporary Hypnosis*; Vol. 26 Issue 4 (December 2009): 216-224.

Hubatz, Men. *Secrets of Mayan Science/Religion*. Translated by Diana Gubiseh Ayala and James Jennings Dunlap II. Santa Fe, NM: Bear & Company, 1990.

Islam, True. *Master Fard Muhammad: Who Is He? Who Is He Not?* Atlanta, GA: A Team Publishing, 2008.

———. *The Book of God: An Encyclopedia of Proof that the Blackman is God*. Atlanta, GA: A-Team Publishing, 2007.

———. *The Truth of God: The Bible, The Quran and Point Number 12*. Atlanta, GA: All In All Publishing, 2007.

Lampe, W. H. "The Reasonableness of Typology" in *Essays on Typology*. Alec R. Allenson Inc., 1957.

Leadbeater, Charles Webster. *The Astral Plane: Its Scenery, Inhabitants and Phenomena*. 3rd ed. London: Theosophical Society, 1900.

Leagle, Inc. "FARRAKHAN v. REAGAN CIV. A. NO. 86-1783." Leagel.Com. http://www.leagle.com/decision/19871175669FSupp506_11072.xml/F ARRAKHAN%20v.%20REAGAN (Accessed July 4, 2014).

Long, Burke. O. "Reports of Visions among the Prophets" *Journal of Biblical Literature* 95, no. 3 (1976) 355.

MacArthur, John. "On Faith: Read the Gospels: Jesus Christ is not Politically Correct." *The Washington Post*, August 14, 2009

———. *The Murder of Jesus* Nashville, TN: Thomas Nelson Inc., 1984.

McFadden, Robert D. "Earthquake Shakes Parts of 5 Northeastern States." New York Times" 20 October 1985. http://www.nytimes.com/1985/10/20/nyregion/earthquake-shakes-parts-of-5-northeastern-states.html?pagewanted=all. (Accessed November 15, 2017).

McGiffert, Arthur C. "Mysticism in the Early Church." *The American Journal of Theology, Vol. 11, No. 3 (Jul., 1907), 407.*

Minero, Luis. *Demystifying the out-of-body Experience: A Practical Manual for Exploration and Personal Evolution.* Woodbury, MN: Llewellyn Publications, 2012.

Muhammad, Elijah. *Message to the Blackman in America.* Chicago, IL: Muhammad's Temple 2., 1965.

——— . *The Fall of America.* Chicago, IL: Muhammad's Temple 2., 1973.

——— . *The Mother Plane.* Cleveland, OH: Secretarius Memps Publications., 1995.

——— . *Theology of Time.* Atlanta, GA: MEMPS., 1997.

Muhammad, Jabril. *A Special Spokesman.* Phoenix, AZ: Phnx Sn & Co., 1984

——— . *Closing the Gap: Inner Views of the Heart, Mind and Soul of the Honorable Louis Farrakhan.* Chicago, IL: FCN Publishing, Co., 2006.

——— . *Is It possible That The Honorable Elijah Muhammad Is Physically Alive???.* Phoenix, AZ: New Books Publication., 2006.

——— "Farrakhan the Traveler: Escape From a Death Plot: The Departure of the Honorable Elijah Muhammad", FinalCall.Com, November 2, 2010. http://www.finalcall.com/artman/publish/Columns_4/article_7395.shtml

"Farrakhan the Traveler: Family And Unity In Bringing Hearts and Minds Together", FinalCall.Com, January 9, 2018. https://www.finalcall.com/artman/publish/Columns_4/article_103979.shtml

"Farrakhan the Traveler: More Than A Vision And A New Book For The Change Of Worlds", FinalCall.Com, October 4, 2016. http://www.finalcall.com/artman/publish/Columns_4/article_103327.s html

____"Farrakhan the Traveler: More than a vision—bearing witness to the Minister's profound experience", FinalCall.Com, March 9, 2016. http://www.finalcall.com/artman/publish/Columns_4/article_102953.s html

____"Farrakhan the Traveler: Prophecy is much more than a prediction", FinalCall.Com, August 20, 2014. http://www.finalcall.com/artman/publish/Columns_4/article_101697.s html

____ "Farrakhan the Traveler: The death plot against the Hon. Elijah Muhammad and his escape", FinalCall.Com, December 7, 2010. http://www.finalcall.com/artman/publish/Columns_4/article_7481.sht ml

____ "Farrakhan the Traveler: The Honorable Elijah Muhammad's escape from a death plot", FinalCall.Com, November 8, 2010. http://www.finalcall.com/artman/publish/Columns_4/article_7401.sht ml

____ "Farrakhan the Traveler: The Messenger, Minister Farrakhan and how Allah controls circumstances", FinalCall.Com, October 26, 2010. http://www.finalcall.com/artman/publish/Columns_4/article_7378.sht ml. "Farrakhan the Traveler: The True Meaning of Prophecy", FinalCall.Com, July 24, 2014. http://www.finalcall.com/artman/publish/Columns_4/article_101638.s html

____. This is the One: We need not look for another! 3rd ed. Phoenix, AZ: Jabril Muhammad, 1996.

Muhammad, Rashad Ilia, *UFO's and The Nation of Islam: The Source, Proof, and Reality of the Wheels*. Memphis, TN: Nation Brothers. 2013.

Muhammad, Tynnetta. *The Comer by Night*. Chicago, IL: Honorable Elijah Muhammad Educational Foundation, Inc., 1994.

Muhammad, Tynnetta. "Unveiling the Number 19: The Sign of Egypt— On the Heels of a Death Plot." *FinalCall.Com*, March 22, 2010. www.finalcall.com/artman/publish/Columns_4/article_6834.shtml

_____ ."Unveiling the Number 19: Bright Object Photographed Over the Dome of the Rock in Jerusalem—Sign of the Changeover of Worlds." *FinalCall.Com*, February 14, 2011. http://www.finalcall.com/artman/publish/Columns_4/article_7611.sht ml

_____ . "Unveiling the Number 19: City in the Sky, the New Jerusalem," *FinalCall.Com*, February 9, 2014. http://www.finalcall.com/artman/publish/Columns_4/article_101213.s html

_____ Unveiling the Number 19: Entering into the World of the Telepath, FinalCall.Com, June 14, 2014.

_____ "Unveiling the Number 19: Journey to Korea - Meeting with the Rev. and Mrs. Sun Myung Moon, FinalCall.Com, September 1, 2003.

_____ Unveiling the Number 19: Entering into the World of the Telepath, FinalCall.Com, June 14, 2014.

_____ "Unveiling the Number 19: Revisiting the Honorable Minister Louis Farrakhan's Vision-Like Experience On the Great Mother's Wheel and Its Connection to Us Today." FinalCall.Com, Sep 23, 2010. http://www.finalcall.com/artman/publish/Columns_4/article_7303.sht ml

——Unveiling the Number 19: Talking Crystals, Radio in the Head—Attuning to the Telepathic Voice Within, FinalCall.Com, June 26, 2013

——."Unveiling the Number 19: Tracing King Tut's Genealogy and the 18th Dynastic Age to Their Black Descendants Living in America Today," *FinalCall.Com*, June 21, 2006. http://www.finalcall.com/artman/publish/Columns_4/Tracing_King_Tut_s_Genealogy_by_Mother_Tynnetta_Mu_2710.shtml

——."Unveiling the Number 19: The Meaning of the Crystal Skull and the Expansion of Spiritual Consciousness," *FinalCall.Com*, May 14, 2007. http://www.finalcall.com/artman/publish/Columns_4/My_Living_Testimony_by_Mother_Tynetta_Muhammad_3469.shtml

——."Unveiling the Number 19: The Power of Prayer: Reflections on Minister Farrakhan's Stages of Recovery." *FinalCall.Com*, February 9, 2007. http://www.finalcall.com/artman/publish/Columns_4/The_Power_of_Prayer_Reflections_on_Minister_Farrak_3246.shtml

——."Unveiling the Number 19: Understanding the Evolution of Time and Its Manifestation of Light In Our Physical Universe." *FinalCall.Com*, June 10, 2014. http://www.finalcall.com/artman/publish/Columns_4/article_101512.shtml

——."Unveiling the Number 19: The Story of Ta Ha: A Struggle between the Forces of Darkness and Light." *FinalCall.Com*, November 8, 2005. http://www.finalcall.com/artman/publish/Columns_4/The_Story_of_TA_HA_by_Mother_Tynnetta_Muhammad_2266.shtml

Muhammad, W. F. *The Supreme Wisdom.* Chicago, IL: Final Call Inc., 1995.

Paffenroth, Kim. *Judas: Images of the lost disciple* Louisville, KT: Westminster John Knox Press, 2001.

Panchadasi, Swami. *The Human Aura: Astral Colors and Thought Forms*, Yogi Publication Society, 1940.

Pentecost, Dwight. J. *Things to Come: A Study in Biblical Eschatology.* Grand Rapids, MI: Zondervan Publishing House, 1965.

Powell, Arthur E. *The Astral Body and other Astral Phenomena.* London, EN: The Theosophical Publishing House, 1929.

Rassoull, Abass. *The Theology of Time, by The Honorable Elijah Muhammad, Messenger of Allah.* (Hampton, VA: U.B. & U.S. Communications Systems, 1992)

Roehrs, Walter R. "The typological use of the Old Testament in the New Testament." *Concordia Journal* 10, no. 6 (November 1984): 213

Sharamon, Shalila, and Bodo J. Baginski. *The Chakra Handbook.* Wilmot, WI: Lotus Light Publications, 1988.

Shaw, Ian, and Paul Nicholson. *The Dictionary of Ancient Egypt.* 2nd ed. New York, NY: Harry N. Abrams, Inc., 2003.

Sprutson, Nelson. "Pyramidal neurons: dendritic structure and synaptic integration." *Nature Reviews Neuroscience* 9 (March 2008): 206-21. http://groups.nbp.northwestern.edu/spruston/Publications/pdfs/Sprusto n_NRN_2008.pdf.

Sutherland, Mary. "In Search of Shambhala." Living in the Light... Believe in the Magic. http://www.livinginthelightms.com/shambhala-read.html

The History Channel. "History of UFO's" History.Com. http://www.history.com/topics/history-of-ufos (accessed July 2, 2014).

Thrall, Margaret E., Trevor J. Burke, and J. K. Elliott. Paul and the Corinthians: studies on a community in conflict: essays in honour of Margaret Thrall. Leiden: Brill, 2003.

van Dyke-Platt, Nancy, and Hall, Richard H. "Betrayal and healing: the aftermath of Judas' kiss." *Journal of Pastoral Care and Counseling* 59, no. 4 (December 1, 2005): 361-64.

This Page Intentionally Left Blank

Glossary

This Glossary is important to understanding terms that are mentioned in this book. These terms have different meanings, in different schools of thought. It is recommended that you reference the Glossary and do further research to understand these terms and rules and how they apply differently. The following is how they are to be understood in this book.

Astral Body – The spiritual body of man sometimes called the [A]etheric body or Soul. The non-physical counterpart of the physical body that has the ability to separate and travel on the Astral Plane.

Akasha Record – In Hindu philosophy, thoughts stored in [A]ether as the collective memory of all, past and present.

Astral Projection – The traveling of the astral body as it is projected from the physical body during sleep or a suspended conscious state.

Anti-Type – Person, place, institution or incident that mirrors or fulfills a historical person, place, institution or occurrence.

Chakra (pronounced Sha-kra or Cha-kra) – Sanskrit word meaning turning or spinning. Also called Chakram. These are body centers that are said to conduct the flow of vital energy throughout the body. There are several major charkas, but there are at least 12 to 18 major chakras that have been noted.

Close Encounter - An experience in which a person eyewitnesses an unidentified flying object.
Context Principle – The manner in which different scriptures are viewed that carry a similar theme.

Double Reference – The principle by which two events or people that are divinely connected in type, refer to one another in meaning, purpose and fulfillment.

Dreams – Impressions of images, thoughts and ideas that manifest into activities acted out by a person during sleep.

Deuteronomist - One of the believed sources of a portion of the Hebrew canon; Pentateuch (first five books of the Bible). The source for recognizing a component of the Pentateuch as the writing of the *Deuteronomist.*

Elohist - One of the believed sources that comprise the original elements of the Pentateuch (first five books of the Bible). The source for recognizing a component of the Pentateuch as the writing of the *Elohist.*

Ether (Aether) – Often termed the *fifth element,* it is subtle material that interpenetrates matter and is known to be finer than light. Different from the organic compounds "Ether". In its Greek (αιθήρ) root it means to burn, kindle or shine.

Ethereal – Referring to and related to the substance Ether.

Etheric Body – Often called the *double* of the physical body. The subtle body or aura of the physical body; vital body that provides the physical body with *vital life force* to maintain it.

Eschatology – The study of the last days. The end of times, or the final days; the Messianic days of fulfillment.

Hermeneutic – Derived from the Greek word representing the god Hermes, meaning to interpret. Hermeneutics refers to the theory of interpretation of a religious text.

Judas Iscariot - According to the New Testament, one of the twelve original apostles of Jesus Christ. He is notoriously known as the "betrayer" of Jesus, and represents in Christian tradition the disillusioned disciple.

Kundalini – Sanskrit word meaning "coiled". The hidden force residing at the base of the spine known as the energy of Self. Kundalini is also considered the *Serpent Fire*, representing the purest form of desire energy.

Law of Recurrence – The repeated occurrence of an event in scripture, but related to the fulfillment of prophecy.

Lucid Dreaming – Process by which the person dreaming is aware that they are dreaming and have control of the dream experience.

Messiah – Anointed (*Mašíah*) as *Khristós* (Χριστός) Greek transliteration Μεσσίας, Hebrew: *Mashiah;* Latin: *Messias* meaning "Anointed One".

Markan Priority – A theory that implies that the Gospel of Mark was the first and most authentic of the synoptic gospels. This theory claims that the other gospels borrow its text from Mark.

Numerical Principle – The idea of applying the meaning of numbers to the scriptures and God's plan.

Out-of Body Experience (OBE) – An experience where a person witnesses himself or herself floating or moving outside of their body. This is also called Astral Projection and is sometimes associated with and Lucid Dreaming.

Occult – In the contemporary sense; one who studies that which is hidden, esoteric or spiritual.

Pericope (pronounced /pəˈrɪkəpi/) – A set of verses that form a theme or collective message and idea, particularly in scripture.

Principle of Agreement – Meaning that the scriptures agree with one another in divine unity for the purpose s of fulfilling God's purposes.

Prophecy – A message that foretells of a future event spoken through some form of divine intervention.

Revelation – Revealing or disclosing divine knowledge, wisdom, and understanding through means of communication with God or his angelic beings.

Soul – The essence of a person, often referred to as the conscious, mind, or heart. A manifestation of the *Life Force* that exist in all living things. Soul is often identified as being related to the Spirit.

Spirit – A force that is directed or influenced by the conscious of a person; produced by thinking; often referred to as a feeling or intuitive thought. Spirit is often identified as being related to the Soul.

Synoptic Gospels – The scriptures of Matthew, Mark and Luke, and their scriptural similarities and parallels. Synoptic meaning, *seen together*.

Theophany – The appearance of God in human form; The Self-Creation of God.

Theology – The study of deities or the study of God.

Trance – A state of consciousness or awareness that often occurs when the person is asleep.

Transitional Dependency – The transitioning of functions, roles, and identities in relation to types and anti-types and their dependency on each other in the fulfillment of scripture.

Three-fold Principle – The revelation of scripture as it applies to the past, present and the future.

Type – In theology; referring to a person, place or institution that pre-figures a future person, place or event. This term is often meant to show the relationship between Old Testament and New Testament figures.

Typology – The study of types, but theologically.

Yahwist - One of the believed sources of a portion of the Hebrew canon; Pentateuch (first five books of the Bible). The basis for recognizing a component of the Pentateuch as the writing of the *Yawhist.*

Index

A

Aaron....46, 58, 113, 188, 197
Accession 71, 193
Acts....71, 96, 188, 193, 194, 207, 208, 209, 214, 215, 216, 227
Adam... 49, 130, 132, 224
Akhenaton 75, 76, 78
Allah....15, 18, 19, 22, 27, 29, 30, 34, 43, 44, 45, 46, 55, 64, 65, 67, 70, 82, 84, 93, 113, 116, 126, 128, 129, 131, 132, 133, 135, 139, 140, 141, 143, 144, 145, 148, 149, 152, 155, 179, 182, 183, 186, 187, 197, 205, 208, 214, 219, 227, 228, 230, 232, 268
Allegory 40, 41, 42
America....15, 17, 24, 27, 34, 36, 47, 54, 55, 56, 59, 60, 61, 66, 67, 76, 79, 83, 88, 110, 111, 116, 126, 131, 132, 138, 140, 141, 144, 145, 146, 148, 149, 189, 205, 206, 209, 232, 261, 264, 267
Annas 229, 230
Announcement....93, 110, 112, 139, 194
Anti-type....27, 36, 38, 43, 48, 50

Apocalypse.................. 19
Apostle58, 95, 127, 187, 213, 229
Apparition 149, 170
Arabic....140, 142, 183, 212
Argatha....................... 82
Astral....125, 162, 164, 165, 166, 167, 169, 170, 172, 173, 174, 175, 176, 178, 180, 183, 186, 187, 190, 271
Astral body....165, 169, 173, 174, 176, 178, 186
Astral Projection....167, 271
Atlantis....................... 82
Atoms................ 157, 161
Atum 165, 166

B

Ba 165, 166, 167, 168
Belief....15, 16, 45, 152, 154, 214, 223
Believers....203, 207, 214, 219, 223, 225
Betrayal....94, 135, 202, 204, 207, 209, 212, 216, 217, 220, 223, 227, 229
Bible....15, 16, 18, 19, 22, 24, 27, 28, 34, 35, 36, 37, 39, 40, 41, 42, 44, 45, 47, 51, 53, 55, 58, 60, 61, 62, 63, 65, 70, 71,

95, 96, 127, 132, 134, 138,
141, 144, 145, 146, 151, 160,
162, 170, 179, 185, 190, 192,
193, 202, 204, 208, 209, 211,
212, 213, 219, 227, 233, 259,
263

Biblical typology........*See*
Typology, type

Black...24, 64, 70, 110, 126,
131, 144, 149, 209, 222

Blackman....15, 17, 19, 27, 34,
35, 60, 61, 65, 66, 95, 145,
148, 151, 152, 154, 155, 212,
263, 264

Buddhists....... 81, 82, 164

C

Caiaphas206, 207, 213, 215,
229, 230

Caucasian 16, 116

Chakras 173, 174, 271

Chinese............... 81, 165

Christ...11, 25, 37, 38, 42, 49,
57, 62, 63, 76, 111, 126, 127,
128, 130, 132, 144, 150, 183,
185, 188, 189, 193, 205, 207,
213, 215, 220, 230, 232, 233,
263

Christian...37, 39, 151, 204,
209, 217, 219

Christianity...37, 39, 41, 160,
164, 179, 215, 229, 262

Christians...37, 146, 210, 217,
230

Close Encounters .. 53, 73

Clouds...59, 60, 62, 63, 137,
184, 193

Columbus...30, 79, 80, 139,
259, 262

Communication...58, 73, 76,
77, 87, 88, 126, 127, 140,
141, 150, 187, 274

Companions...61, 80, 134, 218,
220, 221, 222

Comprehension...153, 154, 186

conspiracy202, 203, 206, 208,
216, 226

Controversy......... 53, 140

Corinthians........ 132, 183

Crucifixion 4, 202

D

Daniel.... 61, 62, 137, 188

David...31, 47, 208, 217, 259

Death...17, 24, 25, 47, 64, 109,
128, 129, 130, 131, 132, 142,
146, 150, 163, 164, 165, 166,
167, 179, 180, 186, 187, 202,
203, 208, 212, 213, 262

Departure...25, 57, 64, 150

Devil...24, 58, 127, 138, 152,
179, 209, 214

Disciples...30, 70, 71, 141, 188,
191, 202, 204, 217, 218, 219,

220, 221, 222, 223, 225, 227, 228, 231

Divine...17, 26, 29, 30, 42, 50, 81, 87, 141, 154, 166, 203, 205

Dogon.......................... 78

Double Reference...34,   205, 272

Dreams...19, 58, 139, 140, 141, 142, 150, 169, 188, 231, 262

E

Earthquake...112, 135, 186

Egypt...16, 35, 57, 75, 76, 140, 164, 165, 166, 183, 196, 262, 266, 268

Egyptians...60, 81, 163, 164, 166

Electricity.......... 158, 161

Electromagnetic 158

Elijah Muhammad11, 15, 16, 17, 18, 20, 23, 24, 25, 26, 27, 31, 32, 34, 35, 38, 41, 42, 43, 44, 46, 47, 48, 50, 53, 54, 55, 57, 58, 59, 61, 63, 64, 65, 66, 67, 68, 69, 70, 74, 75, 76, 77, 79, 80, 83, 84, 88, 93, 94, 96, 109, 110, 111, 112, 113, 114, 116, 126, 127, 128, 131, 132, 133, 134, 135, 138, 139, 140, 141, 142, 143, 144, 145, 146, 148, 149, 150, 151, 152, 153,

154, 155, 157, 160, 161, 162, 176, 183, 186, 187, 188, 189, 196, 197, 202, 204, 205, 206, 208, 212, 213, 214, 219, 226, 230, 264, 266, 268

Elisha.......................... 67

Enemies...28, 58, 65, 128, 130, 131, 132, 135, 187, 203, 205, 206, 207, 213, 215, 231

Enemy...131, 132, 203, 205, 213, 219, 229

Energy...157, 160, 161, 163, 166, 173, 260, 271, 273

Eschatological..17, 38, 49

Ethereal...59, 149, 163, 166

Exalted...57, 61, 76, 126, 127, 129, 143, 205, 208, 209, 213, 230

Exodus..... 46, 59, 67, 196

Explosives 65

Extraterrestrial....... 75, 76

F

Fard Muhammad...15, 20, 42, 46, 50, 54, 55, 58, 64, 74, 79, 81, 82, 127, 131, 139, 140, 141, 142, 143, 144, 148, 149, 154, 183, 186, 187, 220, 230, 263

Farrakhan...3, 4, 15, 17, 19, 20, 21, 23, 24, 25, 26, 27, 29, 30, 32, 34, 38, 39, 41, 42, 44, 45,

46, 47, 48, 50, 53, 57, 59, 61, 64, 65, 66, 67, 68, 75, 77, 78, 79, 80, 81, 88, 93, 94, 96, 110, 112, 113, 115, 116, 125, 126, 127, 131, 132, 133, 134, 135, 138, 139, 140, 141, 142, 143, 144, 148, 151, 154, 158, 172, 175, 176, 179, 182, 183, 186, 187, 188, 189, 193, 194, 195, 196, 197, 204, 205, 206, 207, 212, 213, 214, 215, 216, 218, 219, 220, 221, 222, 223, 224, 226, 229, 230, 231, 232, 233, 259, 261, 264, 267

Flying saucers *See* UFO, Wheel

Foolish............... 129, 222

Force...81, 155, 157, 158, 160, 161, 163, 165, 166, 216, 228, 272, 273

Fulfillment...15, 22, 23, 24, 25, 26, 28, 35, 41, 42, 43, 44, 45, 47, 48, 49, 51, 67, 147, 272, 273, 275

G

Gabriel............. 29, 61, 86

Galilee....... 194, 208, 231

Gentiles187, 188, 202, 207, 208, 215, 224

Geologist..................... 84

Gethsemane....... 217, 218

Ghost.................. 62, 149

God15, 16, 17, 18, 19, 20, 22, 23, 25, 26, 27, 28, 29, 30, 31, 35, 36, 37, 41, 42, 44, 45, 46, 47, 49, 50, 53, 55, 57, 58, 59, 60, 61, 63, 64, 66, 67, 69, 70, 71, 75, 76, 80, 81, 82, 113, 116, 126, 127, 128, 129, 130, 131, 132, 133, 134, 135, 137, 138, 139, 141, 142, 143, 145, 146, 150, 151, 152, 153, 154, 155, 158, 160, 161, 162, 163, 166, 170, 179, 182, 183, 184, 185, 188, 189, 193, 195, 203, 204, 205, 206, 207, 208, 209, 212, 213, 214, 215, 216, 219, 220, 221, 224, 226, 227, 230, 231, 232, 262, 263, 273, 274

Gospels...190, 202, 204, 209, 210, 211, 215, 223, 226, 227, 229, 230, 260, 263, 274

H

Habakkuk 61

Healing...81, 209, 220, 269

Heaven...17, 28, 61, 62, 63, 67, 69, 70, 96, 137, 143, 166, 183, 184, 185, 188, 193, 194, 205, 208, 227

Hebrews 47, 64

Hermeneutics 34

Herod......... 207, 208, 231

Hindus 81

History...15, 16, 18, 21, 23, 28, 35, 38, 50, 57, 70, 73, 75, 76, 78, 79, 86, 126, 128, 132, 139, 183, 204, 210, 220, 226, 268

Holy Quran...15, 16, 22, 28, 30, 32, 34, 35, 39, 41, 42, 43, 44, 45, 51, 55, 58, 60, 125, 126, 127, 128, 129, 133, 134, 138, 140, 141, 144, 166, 178, 179, 182, 183, 186, 187, 195, 196, 197, 208, 209, 212, 213, 214, 220, 228, 259

Hypocrisy 94, 140

Hypocrites.. 213, 219, 231

I

Independence 110

Infinite... 81, 93, 128, 151, 158, 174

Intergalactic................. 87

Interpretation...16, 34, 36, 37, 38, 39, 40, 42, 43, 45, 51, 262, 272

Islam...16, 19, 20, 24, 25, 26, 27, 29, 30, 31, 32, 53, 54, 69, 70, 73, 79, 80, 82, 96, 110, 112, 131, 132, 139, 148, 151, 154, 155, 161, 164, 179, 187, 205, 215, 219, 222, 223, 233, 259, 261, 263

J

Jerusalem...32, 57, 60, 137, 142, 157, 182, 193, 194, 202, 209, 216, 227, 266

Jesus...16, 30, 35, 42, 47, 48, 50, 53, 57, 62, 63, 64, 67, 70, 71, 76, 88, 96, 127, 128, 129, 130, 133, 141, 144, 145, 159, 160, 188, 190, 191, 192, 193, 194, 195, 196, 202, 203, 204, 205, 206, 207, 208, 209, 211, 212, 213, 214, 215, 217, 218, 219, 220, 221, 222, 223, 224, 225, 226, 227, 228, 229, 230, 231, 259, 260, 263

Jews...16, 37, 187, 188, 205, 209, 212, 213, 215, 216, 220, 221, 229, 230, 232, 233, 259

John...40, 65, 69, 71, 86, 162, 191, 194, 195, 203, 207, 208, 213, 214, 215, 217, 221, 223, 224, 227, 228, 229, 230, 231, 232, 259, 263, 268

Judas...202, 203, 204, 205, 206, 207, 210, 217, 218, 219, 220, 221, 222, 223, 224, 225, 226, 227, 228, 229, 232, 260, 268, 269

Judgment...24, 67, 129, 217

K

Ka..................... 165, 166

Khat... 164, 165, 166, 168
Kingdom…17, 41, 130, 132, 137, 227, 229
Kingdom…28, 146, 202, 226
Knowledge…16, 17, 18, 20, 34, 43, 53, 63, 70, 77, 78, 80, 83, 93, 128, 129, 132, 150, 152, 153, 154, 195, 197, 223, 228, 274

L

Lamb…49, 144, 145, 146, 186
Law of Recurrence…23, 273
Libya 113, 115, 116
Lucid Dreaming…167,169, 273, *See* Lucid Dreams
Lucid Dreams............ 167
Luke…63, 71, 191, 195, 211, 212, 213, 227, 229, 230, 231, 274
Lumeria 82

M

Magnetic . 51, 80, 85, 158
Mahdi 46, 147, 230
Mark…62, 63, 65, 71, 191, 195, 203, 210, 211, 212, 217, 221, 222, 223, 224, 225, 227, 230, 274
Markan Priority…210, 273
Mary…70, 86, 129, 208, 220, 229, 260, 268

Master W. F. Muhammad, .*See* Fard Muhammad
Material…28, 39, 87, 151, 153, 155, 157, 161, 162, 174, 175, 272
Matter…22, 25, 48, 51, 86, 87, 109, 129, 147, 155, 162, 165, 172, 173, 174, 226, 228, 231, 272
Matthew…62, 70, 71, 191, 194, 196, 202, 211, 212, 217, 218, 219, 226, 227, 229, 230, 231, 274
Melchizedek 47
Messenger…19, 23, 29, 30, 61, 93, 129, 179, 208
Messenger…17, 26, 27, 28, 132, 145, 146, 149, 206, 208, 214, 268
Messiah…22, 28, 46, 47, 62, 71, 129, 149, 192, 205, 208, 220, 273
Messianic Secret 47
Mexico…57, 83, 110, 111, 112, 116, 125, 175
Mind…17, 19, 20, 21, 30, 34, 43, 45, 79, 83, 84, 88, 111, 112, 113, 130, 132, 134, 140, 141, 155, 158, 160, 162, 170, 173, 174, 188, 203, 213, 220, 224

Moses...37, 46, 47, 58, 59, 62, 67, 113, 134, 138, 144, 145, 188, 191, 192, 196, 197

Mother Wheel *See* Wheel

Mount Everest............. 82

Mountain...66, 111, 134, 137, 175, 191, 192, 193, 194, 195, 196

Mountains . 16, 55, 65, 85

Muslims..69, 70, 155, 230

Mystery...., 150, 151, 152, 153, 154, 155

N

Neurons............. 158, 268

New Book 81

New Testament27, 36, 37, 40, 41, 44, 69, 71, 141, 144, 189, 190, 203, 204, 211, 212, 213, 214, 260, 264, 268, 275

Night journey 70

O

Occultist 174

Old Testament22, 27, 36, 37, 41, 44, 51, 65, 268, 275

Osiris......... 163, 164, 166

Out-of Body Experience172, 273

Out-of-body...125, 132, 164, 167, 169, 172, 175, 176, 177, 178, 180, 264

P

Particles............. 157, 158

Passover 207, 227

Paul71, 75, 79, 96, 141, 164, 170, 183, 184, 185, 187, 188, 205, 215, 216, 219, 229, 233, 260, 262, 268

Perfection 126, 162

Pericope............. 222, 224

Peter95, 96, 170, 187, 188, 191, 193, 194, 195, 205, 207, 209, 228, 229, 260

Phantom 149

Pharisees ... 207, 213, 216

Pilate...204, 207, 208, 212, 213, 217, 230, 231

Planet...18, 19, 53, 55, 65, 73, 74, 76, 79, 81, 83, 84, 111, 189

Principle of Multiplicity...48

Projection Catalepsy...178

Prophecy...11, 15, 16, 17, 19, 22, 23, 24, 25, 26, 27, 28, 34, 36, 37, 40, 42, 43, 45, 47, 48, 50, 51, 65, 138, 145, 147, 187, 196, 202, 226, 273

Prophecy . 15, 23, 43, 274

Prophet...16, 19, 22, 25, 28, 30, 45, 46, 58, 62, 64, 70, 130, 138, 139, 141, 144, 179, 226

Prophet Muhammad24, 30, 32, 70, 182, 183, 195

Q

Quetzalcoatl 82, 111

R

Reference...19, 20, 38, 45, 46, 48, 61, 62, 63, 67, 82, 128, 130, 139, 165, 169, 179, 183, 185, 187, 191, 195, 204, 208, 209, 220, 223, 230, 271

Revelation...15, 20, 29, 64, 69, 70, 71, 142, 143, 144, 145, 146, 186, 274

Romans 207, 229

S

Sadducee 213, 231

Sahu........................... 166

Sanhedrin...62, 206, 207, 215, 216, 231

Satan...17, 19, 42, 205, 206, 207, 213, 219, 227, 228, 232, 233

Scholars...22, 24, 36, 38, 47, 50, 65, 70, 96, 129, 145, 185, 188, 208, 211, 212, 220

Science...39, 59, 77, 79, 140

Scientists...18, 19, 24, 27, 35, 69, 78, 80, 87, 145

Scripture...15, 16, 23, 28, 34, 35, 36, 37, 38, 40, 41, 42, 45, 46, 47, 50, 138, 139, 144, 183, 187, 190, 194, 204, 209, 211, 215, 273, 274, 275

Scriptures...15, 19, 20, 23, 26, 28, 34, 36, 37, 40, 41, 42, 44, 45, 50, 51, 53, 65, 134, 144, 209, 211, 213, 223, 273, 274

Secret...17, 74, 82, 96, 135, 152, 206, 212, 213, 214, 227

Self- bilocation.......... 177

Shabazz 16, 76

Shamballah.................. 82

Son of Man...62, 63, 154, 202, 205, 207, 224, 226, 227, 230

Soul...32, 111, 161, 162, 165, 166, 167, 169, 172, 177, 178, 179, 183, 184, 195

Spirit...42, 43, 68, 111, 137, 138, 149, 150, 151, 152, 153, 154, 155, 160, 161, 162, 163, 165, 166, 173, 177, 178, 179, 185, 187, 205, 213, 216, 227, 228

Spirit...16, 29, 30, 69, 137, 153, 157, 160, 161, 163, 166, 193, 195, 208, 227

Suffering...22, 28, 44, 193, 204, 227

Sufism 169

Supreme...18, 20, 45, 79, 82, 83, 128, 131, 147, 154, 155, 206, 267

Synoptic...190, 191, 211, 230, 274

T

Telepathy.............. 87, 88

Tepotzlan... 111, 175, 195

Theologians...25, 36, 65, 70, 151, 202

Theological 40, 212

Theology...16, 22, 24, 31, 35, 88, 126, 127, 138, 140, 145, 146, 147, 150, 155, 161, 183, 186, 264, 268, 274

Theophany................... 50

Thessalonians...... 64, 232

Thought...22, 36, 77, 83, 84, 85, 87, 127, 131, 155, 160, 162, 163, 179, 206, 217, 218, 224, 228, 271

Tibet 76, 82

Trance 170, 275

Transfiguration...30, 190, 191, 192

Transitional Dependency..... 48, 49, 275

Transported...30, 31, 32, 111, 182

Truth...15, 16, 24, 41, 42, 43, 49, 54, 58, 85, 93, 94, 109, 116, 127, 131, 139, 153, 161, 204, 205, 212, 216, 222, 226, 228, 233

Twenty-four elders...70, 145, 147

Typology...34, 35, 36, 37, 38, 40, 41, 43, 44, 51, 262, 263, 275

U

UFO53, 73, 74, 75, 111, 194, 268, *See* Wheel

Ufologist 56, 80

Universe...64, 70, 87, 151, 162, 185

Unseen...58, 127, 163, 175, 214

V

Veil................ 29, 30, 139

Vision...19, 21, 23, 26, 29, 30, 32, 39, 50, 53, 57, 58, 61, 62, 64, 65, 66, 67, 71, 78, 94, 96, 111, 112, 113, 116, 125, 126, 127, 131, 134, 137, 138, 139, 140, 141, 142, 143, 148, 149, 151, 154, 172, 175, 176, 182, 183, 185, 187, 188, 189, 193, 194, 195, 213, 219, 259

Vision experience...21, 26, 32, 50, 53, 57, 61, 64, 66, 78, 94, 96, 125, 127, 131, 134, 138, 139, 140, 142, 143, 151, 172, 176, 182, 186, 187, 189, 193, 195, 213, 219

W

Wheel...21, 23, 25, 29, 32, 50, 53, 54, 55, 57, 58, 59, 61, 63, 64, 65, 66, 67, 74, 77, 80, 81, 88, 94, 110, 111, 112, 113, 126, 127, 133, 134, 139, 140, 141, 143, 176, 186, 189, 190, 193, 194, 197, 233

White race...18, 63, 132, 145

Y

Yacub .. 16, 132, 151, 152

Yoga.......................... 169